*Understanding Human Action*

SUNY Series in Philosophy
Robert C. Neville, Editor

# Understanding Human Action

## SOCIAL EXPLANATION AND THE
## VISION OF SOCIAL SCIENCE

MICHAEL A. SIMON

*State University of New York Press*
*ALBANY*

*For Jason and Jennifer*

Published by
State University of New York Press, Albany

© 1982 State University of New York

For information, address State University of New York Press,
State University Plaza, Albany, N.Y., 12246

*Library of Congress Cataloging in Publication Data*

Simon, Michael A.
Understanding human action.
(SUNY series—in philosophy)
Includes index.
1. Social psychology.   2. Human behavior.
3. Social sciences—Methodology.   4. Science—Methodology.
I. Title.   II. Series.
HM251.S622      302      81-5280
ISBN 0-87395-498-X      AACR2
ISBN 0-87395-499-8 (pbk.)

# *Contents*

# Preface

For anyone who is curious enough to wonder why things are the way they are and not some other way, science is a source of enormous fascination. One is pleased to find out why the sky is blue, why offspring resemble their progenitors, and why there are tides and seasons of the year, not because such information is useful, but because it is interesting. What makes a scientific answer acceptable has nothing to do with extrinsic considerations. Like mathematics, science has its own ways of establishing truths. The pursuit of theoretical knowledge has a logic and methodology that render it distinct from any practical activity.

In principle, there is no restriction on the range of possible objects of theoretical knowledge. They can be items that have no connection at all with matters of practical concern, or they may be things that make a great deal of difference in human life. A theoretical attitude can be adopted not only with respect to the movements of the heavens and the vegetation of the forest, but also with respect to the workings of the human body and the conditions of human social life. Why not pursue theoretical knowledge of things that really matter to people—what they do, how they live, their aims, their biases and prejudices, their interpersonal relations?

The purpose of this inquiry is to explore the limitations of a theoretical or scientific approach to such phenomena. The question is whether a naturalistic science is capable of making sense of human actions and social life, or whether the kind of understanding they require is precluded by the conditions that make theoretical knowledge possible. We need to ask whether it is possible to understand human beings as free rational agents and at the same time to understand their behavior as determined in accordance with causal law. Is the understanding and prediction of intentional actions a matter of fitting them to discovered regularities, or is it a matter of figuring out the way people reason? Are the facts of human social life understandable as law-governed occurrences, or are such phenomena not the sort of things that can be caught with a scientific net? Can there be a science that will explain why we do as we do?

This book is an attempt to see what it is about human social life that makes a social science based on the model of natural science impossible. It also can be seen as a philosophical response to the failure of social science to contribute much understanding of the universe of human affairs. Crime, war, terrorism, urban strife, and interpersonal conflicts of all kinds still cry out for interpretation and explanation. At one time I believed, naively, that the way to set things right was to work toward a comprehensive and detailed theory that would enable us to understand why people and institutions behave as they do. Though I no longer have confidence in such a vision, I do see that there are better and worse ways of conceiving the human condition, that there is useful information to be gathered, and that there are ideas and plans that are worth pursuing. The fact that no social science has been able to provide a suitable theoretical backing for social practice does not mean that politics and social activism are pointless or futile. It is futile only to try to erect a body of scientific theory that will offer a systematic and predictive account of the way people and societies perform.

Many people have played important roles in helping to bring this project to completion, though it is difficult to say how much of what is here presented any of them would be willing to endorse. Of numerous friends and colleagues among philosophers and social scientists to whom I owe a debt of gratitude, two deserve special mention for their wise commentary: John Troyer and Peter Winch. Thanks go also to Marie Becker, Carol Leary, and Martha Smith for their unfailing assistance in preparing the typescript. I am grateful to the University of Connecticut and its Research Foundation for sabbatical-year funding during the early stages of writing, and to Robert Neville for his advice and encouragement on behalf of the State University of New York Press. Finally, to Shannon, and to Jason and Jennifer, I wish to express appreciation for contributions that I cannot begin to list. There is very little I could have done were it not for the support and sustenance of those with whom I have lived and worked.

Of the eleven chapters of this work, two either have been or will be published in somewhat different form in other places. An essay based on an earlier version of Chapter 1 is scheduled to appear in a forthcoming volume of *Philosophy and Phenomenological Research*. Another essay, bearing the title "Biology, Sociobiology, and the Understanding of Human Social Behavior," has been published in Ashley Montagu, ed., *Sociobiology Examined* (New York: Oxford University Press, 1980) and contains the substance of Chapter 6. Another much shorter version of that essay entitled "Sociobiology: The Aesop's Fables of Science" appeared in the February, 1978 issue of *The Sciences*. I am pleased to acknowledge the editors' and publishers' willingness to allow these redundancies.

March, 1981
Rockville Centre, New York

# Introduction

Fish gotta swim,
Birds gotta fly,
I've gotta love
One man 'til I die;
Can't help
Lovin' that man o' mine.

—Oscar Hammerstein, *Showboat*

A human being, the song suggests, is sometimes unable to do other than he or she does. Human behavior in such cases is like the behavior of animals: it is necessitated; it cannot be helped. Such behavior is understandable as part of nature and is approachable by the methods of natural science. But how general is the feature that Hammerstein's lyric calls attention to? How much of human behavior can be conceived in this light? Humans are not like birds and fish, and their behavior is not like that of these modest creatures—or is it?

Two powerful traditions lie behind attempts to understand human action. One of these holds that the human being is not a proper object for science, the other that it is. The first insists that human actions are radically different from any other kind of happening, that the human being is unique in virtue of its freedom, its capacity for choice, and its ability to exert active power; the second denies that human action need be regarded as *sui generis* and consequently stresses the possibility of studying humans as organisms and their behavior as causally

1

determined. The actions of human beings may be viewed either as events that free agents *make* happen, or as occurrences that *merely* happen and that have the characteristic of involving human organisms.

Deciding whether a social science or science of human action is possible depends on understanding both what action is and what science is. There are accordingly two aspects to the investigation that follows: an inquiry into the nature of social phenomena and the challenge they present to science, and a consideration of what understanding of human social being and its compounds must be like. Together these constitute an approach to the question of whether a social science adequate to explain why people do what they do is possible. The central problem to be addressed is that of whether actions and social phenomena call for a science that is significantly different from natural science.

The principal argument of the book can be stated very simply: the social studies have essentially to do with human actions; actions are free in the sense that they are not subject to explanation and prediction on the basis of strict causal laws; what empirical science is capable of investigating successfully cannot be free in that sense; hence the social studies cannot be empirical sciences. The strategy I have chosen to follow is to begin with an investigation of human action and its connections with the idea of the social, and to conclude with an examination of the nature of understanding and of the quality of the output of social research. In between is a consideration of the problems of approaching action and other social phenomena through the various kinds of social inquiry.

The arrangement of chapters is intended to carry out this program. The first three chapters are concerned with the nature of social science's subject matter. Chapter 1 argues that the idea that lies at the core of all social explanation is the concept of human action, which must be viewed as a logical primitive, as irreducible to other kinds of event concepts. In Chapter 2 it is argued that action is a concept whose roots are essentially social, and that the meanings of actions depend on a system of social relations, the most important of which involve the ascription of responsibility. Chapter 3 deals with the question of what the proper units of social phenomena are, and seeks to determine whether, and in what sense, the social sciences can be said to be about anything other than individual human beings.

Chapters 4 to 7 consider the topic of social explanation and examine a number of approaches to understanding why people behave as they do.

2

The explanatory role of reasons for acting is discussed in Chapter 4, where the question of whether rational explanation is a form of causal explanation is considered. Causation itself is the topic of Chapter 7, where it is argued that explanations of actions are not causal in the Humean sense: they depend for their validity not upon general laws but upon practical reasoning, which rests on an entirely different explanatory paradigm. Further ramifications of rational explanation are considered in Chapter 5, which also takes a brief look at functional and structural explanation. Chapter 6 examines the biological approach to understanding human social behavior.

The last four chapters are concerned with the nature of social science's output. Why social science has apparently achieved so little with respect to law and theory is considered in Chapter 8. Objectivity in social research is the topic of Chapter 9, where the question is asked to what extent and in what sense the various types of social explanation can be considered objective. Chapter 10 represents an effort to characterize the kind of understanding that social inquiry yields and to hold it up against prevailing ideas of what a science is supposed to achieve. The basic thrust of Chapters 1 to 10 is to show why no one should be surprised to find that the project of naturalistic social science seems to have gone awry. In Chapter 11 it is suggested that the advocates and practitioners of that kind of social science are mistaken as to the real nature of their enterprise, that what social science yields is something other than objective scientific knowledge of human social activities. The social studies, it is argued, are better seen as a set of humanistic disciplines. As ways of making sense of human social life, they are more like literature or philosophy than they are like natural-scientific inquiry.

As I am presenting it, the program of working toward an adequate understanding of human behavior requires that there be such things as free actions, whose explanation and prediction in accordance with deterministic causal law is necessarily precluded. The issue is a crucial one: what would be the point of showing that naturalistic social science cannot deal with free actions if there were no such thing as free actions? Only if human behavior can be shown to resist naturalistic treatment are we justified in insisting on the need to resort to nonnaturalistic, or humanistic alternatives.

There is no way of ruling out the possibility that human behavior could, under some description, be found to be subsumable under strict scientific laws and hence subject in principle to a complete predictive account, just as there is no way of ruling out the possibility that, for any given putatively occult phenomenon, there is a deterministic scientific explanation to be discovered that will bring the phenomenon in question under the umbrella of natural science. If such a deterministic conception of human behavior were to be adopted, freedom—along with the idea that human beings are responsible agents—would come to be seen as an illusion. Indeed, to a believer in strict psychological determinism like B. F. Skinner, who maintains that there is no such thing as human freedom or dignity in any ultimate sense, the idea that there are no free actions may not seem significantly different from the idea that there are no witches, or that there are no such phenomena as witchcraft.[1] All we need to do to make the denial of the existence of witches or any occult phenomenon seem reasonable is to be able to argue that the feats that are supposed to be attributable to nonnatural entities or forces are more properly explained in ways that do not involve such intervention. Why should we ascribe occurrences to witches or free agents if we can treat these happenings equally well as results of the ordinary workings of the natural causal order?

Obviously there can be no such cognitive discipline as the study of witchcraft if there are no such things as witches. The same holds true for the study of free action: whatever the appropriate science of that domain is, it will not be a science of action if there are no free actions. Deciding whether or not there are free actions, however, is not so simple as deciding whether or not there are witches. For all we have to do to discredit the idea that there are witches is to show that all of the phenomena that witches are supposed to be responsible for are accountable for in an entirely naturalistic way. The concept of a witch would merely have to be shown to be eliminable from all of those contexts in which it might be thought to play an explanatory role. But what would it be like to discover that there are no free actions? Could we ever show that people are not really responsible for their actions, that there is no fundamental distinction between choosing and being chosen, no spontaneous displays of affection, no uncoerced laughter or offers of assistance? To abandon the idea that human beings act freely would require us to deny that people ever deserve praise or blame. We would have to cease to identify humans as *persons,* as moral agents.

The reason it is easier to resist the idea that there are witches or demonic processes than it is to discard the idea that there are free actions is that we already have a conceptual scheme that enables us to deal

4

adequately with events in the universe without making implicit or explicit reference to such things as witches or demons. That is not the case for free actions It is doubtful that it is possible to have any sort of conception of ourselves and our human associates without acknowledging some idea of freedom and responsibility. Human social interactions, as we conceive them, are based on relations between free individuals. Human institutions, be they economic, educational, religious, or legal, all presuppose people's capacity to control their own behavior. Social life without free agents would not be human.

We could no more discover that humans are not free agents than we could discover that words have no meaning. What makes a sound a word for us is that it has a meaning; what makes a creature a person is that it is a performer of free actions. Humans are creatures whose behavior is constituted as free action, just as money is paper that is constituted as currency. It may be true that we could construe the behavior we recognize as human action in some other way, but the fact is that we do not. We neither discover that the human world as we conceive it is the way we have conceived it, nor do we decide to conceive it that way rather than some other way. That world is the world we live in, and it is the world that social science is asked to describe and explain.

An assessment of social inquiry as a mode of scientific investigation requires, of course, that we already have an idea of what science is. The philosophy of science that may be found lurking in the background of the present work is the one that has dominated much of twentieth-century thought about science: positivism, or logical empiricism. Three main ideas are associated with this approach: the sciences comprise a unity, at least to the extent that a single method is appropriate for all areas of scientific inquiry; the exact physical sciences provide the model or standard against which all other attempts to do science are to be measured; and science employs a characteristic type of explanation, according to which explaining a phenomenon amounts to showing how it fits under causal laws.

Recent philosophy of science—and this includes work done over a period of more than twenty years—has mounted a number of attacks on the logical-empiricist model.[2] While it has long been acknowledged that theories are underdetermined by facts, so that no theory is uniquely applicable to a given domain, the wider implications of this point have not been explored until relatively recently. Theory change has now come to be seen as a revolutionary process, in which nonrational

5

considerations such as values, traditions, and general metaphysical assumptions play an important part in determining theory acceptance. Statements of facts themselves are recognized to presuppose concepts whose meaning is laden, at least in part, by concepts belonging to the theories that employ them. Explanations, so far as they explain anything, are found to presuppose conceptual frameworks that are not revealed by any strictly formal account of what constitutes a scientific explanation. Whatever else these challenges have succeeded in doing, they have shown that science is not a monolithic pursuit and that it does not always display the sort of unitary structures that defenders of the formal model have supposed it does. There is more to understanding how science explains than seeing how the explanations of natural phenomena conform to an abstract formulation.

Whatever the inadequacies of logical empiricism as a theory of science, however, it is still not inappropriate to view the enterprise of a putatively naturalistic social science against this background. Logical empiricism is, after all, the philosophy of science that social scientists have tended to espouse, especially those who believe that the social sciences should emulate the natural sciences. Law, prediction, testability, and objectivity are precisely the goals that naturalistic social science seeks to achieve, and these are what the natural sciences are taken to exemplify. If social science can be shown not to be capable of meeting the standards that its practitioners think natural science sets, that gives at least some reason for suspecting that, whatever science is, social science is something else.

Even if there is no set of formal characteristics that constitutes a given activity as science, even if there exists no unitary model to which all natural science can be found to conform, it does not follow that the efforts and achievements of social science have to be assimilable to those of natural science, or that its program is "scientific" in the same sense that, say, physics or physiology is. To say that many things can be considered science is not to imply that all rational procedures deserve to be considered science. The point of this project, moreover, is not to hold social science up against any particular scientific paradigm; rather it is to see what happens when we approach human social phenomena as an object of inquiry and take the idea of a social science seriously. The results of this examination should give some indication of what, if anything, there is about the understanding of that subject matter that makes it different from understanding in the natural sciences, however the latter is conceived.

6

# 1. The Primacy of Action

Consider a marketplace: human beings are standing, sitting, strolling, and sweeping; goods are being bought, sold, and transported; there are people hawking, haggling, conversing, and scolding children. What we perceive is a system of objects whose behavior we describe in the vocabulary of intentional human actions. Yet we can also describe the scene using a vocabulary having a very different character: there are a number of discrete, multicolored objects, some moving about, others stationary; objects appear in a variety of changing and seemingly irregular configurations; many of the individual figures themselves are observed to undergo changes of shape; several objects are heard to emit sequences of sounds, intermittent and varying in pitch.

Of the two accounts, the first is obviously richer and more informative. Identifying behavior as action and utterances as speech allows us to make sense of what we see in a way that (mere?) physical description does not. The question is, how shall we understand these phenomena that we pick out as actions? Can there be a science of human action, and if so, what will it be like? Does human behavior lend itself to the kind of description and explanation that is typical of the natural sciences?

This chapter is concerned with the concept that lies at the core of all social phenomena, the concept of human action or agency. Action, I shall argue, must be conceived as a logical primitive, as a concept that is irreducible to any other concepts that do not themselves presuppose the notion of action or agency. I shall also try to show that there is no proper study of human social behavior that does not so regard action, that there is no eliminative account of action or agency that does not abstract from

7

those features of social phenomena that give them their peculiarly human character.

What sort of phenomena are actions? From a naturalistic perspective, they may be regarded as a species of bodily movements. Not all bodily movements are actions, of course; we would not count involuntary movements such as tics and sneezes as actions, nor would we include internal processes such as acid secretion and blood circulation. The movements we call actions must be limited to voluntary behavior, or at least behavior that is sometimes voluntary. Actions are not things that happen to people; they are things that people do.

Let us suppose that, although not every bodily movement is an action, every action is nevertheless a bodily movement. If there were a science of action, it would have to pick out this class of movements and describe them. Any science will need to identify and classify phenomena before it can provide a systematic ordering of them. A difficulty arises, however, with respect to how one specifies these movements: a given action type may be associated with bodily movements of quite disparate types. An action such as combing one's hair or paying a bill can be performed in any of a number of different ways, using different sequences of bodily movements. There is more than one way to skin a cat, but a proper bodily-movement description must pick out all the possible cat-skinning specifications if the equivalence of action description and bodily-movement description is to be sustained. Since action descriptions ordinarily pick out rather loosely defined classes of bodily movements, it will be impossible to know on the basis of an action description alone what bodily movements are supposed to occur, or even what all the possible movements are that will satisfy the description. If actions are a species of bodily movements, bodily-movement descriptions cannot be restricted to specific lists of arm and leg motions.

The fact that a given action description does not entail any *particular* movement description does not rule out the possibility that *some* bodily-movement description *or other* is implied whenever any action description is employed. Stating that a person has closed a door does not reveal what moves he has made, but it does imply that he has made some moves.* We are entitled to conclude that, if a systematic account of

---

*Throughout this book, terms such as "he" and "his" should be understood as abbreviations for "he or she," "his or her," and so on.

actions is possible, actions will have to be specified using a vocabulary that is not so rudimentary as what we would use for "mere" (i.e., ordinary) bodily movements. Even if actions are no more than bodily movements, the observation language of a science of action need not be translatable into the more fundamental vocabulary of bodily movements.

It is worth noting that this feature of action description, the fact that it warrants its own terminology, is by no means unique to that domain but is a feature of scientific description in general. The biologist does not identify what he seeks to explain simply as a change in color, shape, or position; he describes it rather as a change in neuromuscular structure or in the chemical composition of the blood, or as an instance of an organism going to sleep or becoming rigid. Nor does the meteorologist have to describe what he sees as clouds and columns of mercury and movements of pointers; the things he deals with are more likely to be described as storm centers and cold fronts. Even in chemistry and in the several areas of physics, wherein one "observes" such phenomena as crystallization or absorption or superconductivity, concepts enjoy descriptive autonomy, in the sense that translatability into a "more basic" terminology is neither demanded nor assumed.

It is therefore not an objection to the identification of actions with bodily movements that one cannot plausibly substitute movement descriptions for action descriptions. Another possible objection arises when one notices that a particular bodily movement may, in different surroundings, count as an instance of two or more quite different actions. The hand movement that in one context is an act of hailing a taxicab could in another set of circumstances be an act of volunteering to answer a question. Removing one's eyeglasses in one situation may be getting ready to fight, whereas in another it could be making a bid in an auction. The objection is the converse of the previous one: it points out that not only is there no unique movement that corresponds to a given action description, but there need be no unique action that corresponds to a particular movement.

What makes a bodily movement an action of a given type is often not revealed in the description of the movement alone. All that this shows, however, is that a movement has to be properly connected in order for it to count as an instance of a particular type of action. Movements become actions only when they are executed in appropriate contexts. Pulling down a lever counts as casting a vote only when certain conditions are fulfilled: the lever must be part of a voting machine, there must be an election actually being held, and the machine must be hooked into the electoral process in such a way as to give its operation a definite connection with the outcome. The fact that turning a key in a lock may either turn on a light or open a door does not contravene the thesis that actions are a species of bodily movements, any more than the fact that the spontaneous snapping of a cable may amount either to the collapse of a bridge support or to the cutting off of a town's electricity supply falsifies the claim that both of these events are cases of a mechanical breakdown. Action descriptions, it should be noted, are typically relational—but then, so are most movement descriptions.

The distinction between an action and a bodily movement cannot, therefore, be made on the basis of the impossibility of obtaining translations between action descriptions and movement descriptions. If there is a distinction to be made, it must depend on something that an action is and a movement is not. It is a distinction that resides in the fact that an action involves somebody *doing* something, whereas a bodily movement connotes merely a *happening*. To say that there is a difference between an action and a bodily movement is to say that there is a difference between Jack closing his fist and Jack's fist closing. Whether or not every action entails some bodily movement or other, it is clear that the converse does not hold, even in the case of a movement that carries the same description as one that *is* an action. Not every movement of my arm or leg is an action that I perform. My actions comprise only those movements that I *make* happen.

Therefore actions cannot be *simply* bodily movements. How shall we delimit the sphere of actions? One suggestion might be to suppose that only persons and other creatures that can move their bodily parts intentionally can properly be said to perform actions. To adopt such a suggestion, however, would amount to legislating the usage of a term whose range of ordinary application is in fact much broader. It would make it incorrect, for example, or at least suspect, to speak of the action of the wind on the sand or that of a dye on a piece of fabric, or of the action of a padlock or heart valve. A more general definition of action appears to be needed, one that allows for a category of inanimate action. One such definition has been offered by D. G. Brown: action is the producing of effects in other things.[1] By this definition, actions are distinguished from movements in that they presuppose agents; they are movements that are attributable to things that produced them.

If action can be adequately characterized in such a general and nonanthropocentric manner, then a science of human action would amount to a systematic means of accounting for those effects that happen to be produced by humans. Persons, however, produce their effects in ways that are quite different from the ways inanimate objects do.[2] When a person performs an action he does what he does at will. He sets something in motion, and it is *he* who sets it in motion. When the sun melts a piece of ice, on the other hand, or an injection slows a patient's heartbeat, the change that is effected is one that is understood as a causal consequence of something else that happens. It is not simply the sun that melts the ice, but the event of the sun shining on it. But when I move my finger in the act of pushing a button, the "I" that performs the action is not similarly understandable as an incomplete specification of an event. This point is revealed by the fact that we do not ordinarily say that one causes one's finger to move; rather we say that one moves it. A human agent, unlike a nonconscious one, stands outside the causal processes whereby its actions are mediated.[3]

Actions thus have a very special status as a kind of event: that is the upshot of our discussion of attempts to assimilate them to bodily movements. The disposition to participate in such events, furthermore, can be taken as the thing that distinguishes humans from other creatures. To be human, as Marx saw, is to be a potential agent, a doer and a maker. How then shall we make out the distinction between human events that are actions and human events that are not, between events such as pulling off one's gloves and digesting one's lunch? An appropriate reply, I believe, is suggested by Aristotle when he says of the voluntary that it is "that of which the moving principle is in the agent himself."[4] Voluntary acts are distinguished from compulsory acts, he says, by the fact that in the case of the latter, "the moving principle is outside, the person compelled contributed nothing."[5] Actions are events that are *originated* by a human agent: "Man is a moving principle or begetter of his actions."[6]

Since it is unclear just how and in what sense agents are supposed to initiate or contribute to the movements that comprise their actions, the suggestion is unfortunately a rather crude one. Nevertheless, it does succeed in capturing an important part of what we mean when we describe something that occurs as an act that someone performed: that what we do when we act freely we do on our own, of our own accord. Saying of action that it "originates" with the person who performs it also conveys the implication that it is an occurrence that might not have occurred, even if everything else had been the same. Or, as Aristotle put it, "the things of which the moving principle is in a man himself are in his power to do or not to do."[7] Of course, we do not *know* that the event that we have designated as an action could have been forborne even if all of the antecedent conditions had been the same. The point is rather a conceptual one: when we identify an event as a free action, we *presume* that the agent could have done otherwise, that he did not *have* to do as he did.

Conceiving of action in this Aristotelian manner requires us to see actions as coming into existence in a way that is radically and irreducibly different from the way other kinds of events do. The account also has important implications with respect to the way actions are explained, and hence with respect to the nature of a possible social science. For according to the "standard" view of scientific explanation, as it is supposed to operate in the natural sciences, explanation consists of showing how a phenomenon that is to be explained may be subsumed under a covering law.[8] To explain why something happened is to indicate what caused it, what antecedent event or circumstance made its occurrence inevitable, or at least highly probable. But if actions are necessarily initiated by agents, then explanations of actions must be expected to reveal not what made them happen, but what made their agents undertake to perform them. Actions will have to be looked at as the products of what agents bring to the situations in which they act—their reasons and motives—rather than as results of regular sequences of occurrences.[9]

In order to defend the idea that human action should be conceived as a logical primitive, I shall try to show that the leading alternative modes of conceiving it either fail to capture what is distinctive about human action and what is important with respect to its explanation, or else are themselves reducible to the view being put forward. I shall be concerned to reply both to accounts that seek to deny special or irreducible status to action as a subject for inquiry, and to attempts to analyze human action in terms of other putatively fundamental motions. Action, I want to argue, is itself sufficiently distinctive to be the mark of what is distinctively human.

Probably the most persistent, and for many the most persuasive, alternative to the sort of position I am proposing is the form of materialism known as behaviorism. Understood as a philosophical thesis and not merely as a methodological directive, behaviorism holds that whatever humans do is capable of being analyzed in terms of overt behavior and dispositions to behavior. Behavioral science is supposed not to need to pay attention to the distinction between human actions and bodily events that are not actions. The behaviorist cannot deny, of course, that there is a difference between what a person does and the physical changes his body undergoes—for example, between his act of biting down hard and the event of his jaw snapping shut. The position the behaviorist must take is either that the distinction is an irrelevant one, or else that it is capable of being characterized and elucidated in terms that do not presuppose the very difference that is to be illuminated. What he must reject is the view that action is irreducibly different from other sorts of events, and that its explication requires that it be set outside the framework of natural events.

I have said that what precludes assimilating actions to bodily movements is the special character of human agency. The behaviorist who denies that the distinction between these two classes of events is a meaningful one will insist that his program does not require separating out and marking off for special treatment those items of human behavior that we have identified as voluntary actions. He may argue that the distinction is not a tenable one from the point of view of behavioral science, because there are in fact no clear dividing lines by which we can separate what people do consciously and deliberately from what they do unconsciously and unwittingly or from what they do unintentionally or automatically. He may also note that behavior includes a range of bodily responses that are not actions at all, such as blushing, bleeding, and shivering. So long as the event can readily be identified at the level of overt behavior, it might be maintained, there is no need to pay serious attention to the distinction between actions and other kinds of behavior and bodily changes.

The lack of a clear line of demarcation between actions and nonactions cannot be used to show that there is no distinction to be made, however. It certainly does not damage the claim that there is a difference between red and orange to point out that there is no natural way of separating shades of red from shades of orange. If there are reasons for wanting to study actions apart from other human events, such a program does not automatically become groundless upon discovering that actions apparently grade into nonactions, any more than biology must be supposed to lack a proper domain once it is pointed out that organisms can be seen to grade into actual or possible artifacts.

The behaviorist who finds it acceptable to ignore the peculiar facts of agency does so because he believes nothing turns on it. He is, after all, concerned only with how people behave and what makes them behave as they do. He may very well acknowledge that the events we call actions are brought about by different sorts of events and circumstances from those that produce (mere) bodily movements. The difference between actions and nonactions will be presumed to depend entirely on a difference in causal histories. A shaking of the head that signifies a negative reply will simply have different causal antecedents from one that occurs as the result of a tic. So far as behaviorism embraces the causal analysis of all kinds of behavior, and actions can be construed as events having certain kinds of causes, the behaviorist does not have to set up a special class of events that pick out actions specifically.

According to the behaviorist thesis, all behavior can be represented as a function of prior behavior and external events. The program can be seen to run into trouble with regard to actions, however, once it is noticed that it is not external events and circumstances that explain a person's actions but rather his beliefs about them. Someone may lock his doors not because there have been thefts recently but because he *believes* that there have been, or that locking the doors may in fact prevent a theft. A particular set of circumstances may trigger off different kinds of behavior, depending on the beliefs and desires of the individuals acting. The behaviorist, however, is constrained to provide an account that avoids mention of such unobservables. The behaviorist program assumes not merely that behavioral patterns and dispositions determine the knowledge conditions for the correct ascription of beliefs and desires, but also that there is no need to appeal to intervening variables or mediating occurrences, whether these are supposed to be mental events or internal physical ones. If there are such things as beliefs and intentions, and their presence, at least in some cases, is what makes a piece of behavior an action, then no behavioristic account will be able to show that actions do not deserve to be regarded differently from other kinds of events.

If the behaviorist does not want simply to ignore the distinction between actions and movements, he may try to resist the view that action deserves separate explanatory treatment by insisting that actions are not irreducible. Action statements are translatable, it may be claimed, into statements in which the notion of agency has been eliminated. We should then be able to replace a statement such as "Harry pulled his hat down over his ears" with an event description in which there is no ascription of agency except in the sense that inanimate things such as chemicals are said to be agents. If what Harry did can be reduced or assimilated to something that happened, then actions should be treatable as entirely on a par with other events in the world.

One way that has been suggested of assimilating human agency to ordinary causal processes involves the notion of agent causation. According to this idea, *Harry* is the cause of his hat being pulled over his ears. Just as the sun may be the cause of ice melting and digitalis may be the cause of an increase in rate of heartbeat, so a person is the cause of whatever he does, the actions he performs. Agents, it is supposed, may themselves be caused to act by prior events, allowing us to conceive what the agent does as part of a causal chain, the elucidation of which may be taken to fall within the purview of behavioral science. What I do, the changes I bring about in the world, are caused by me, and I may be caused to do these things by other things that happen to me. This is not the only interpretation of agent causation that has been offered, but I believe it is the only one that seeks to reconcile agency with behaviorism.

Appeal to agent causation will not help the behaviorist, however, unless he can show that that kind of causation is reducible to event causation and that the events involved are identifiable solely on a behavioral level. That seems not to be the case, so far as Harry's pulling down his hat is concerned. Harry is not a cause in the sense that the sun or digitalis is, for in the latter two cases definite events are in fact designated: the shining of the sun and the taking of digitalis. In Harry's case there is no event, at least of a behavioral sort, other than the event of Harry pulling down his hat. Agent causation, unless it involves some sort of nonbehavioral process, introduces an entirely different notion of causation from that presupposed in any behavioral account. So far as the causal explanation of behavior is concerned, agents are not causes but substitutes for causes.

It may be concluded, then, that the notion of human agency cannot be eliminated by analysis on the behavioral level. If there is a theory of action that is capable of representing actions as a species of bodily movements, it will have to consider events below the level of the whole organism. Such a move has been made by a different sort of materialist, one who argues that the way to resist the idea that agency is irreducible is to regard human actions as causal consequences of certain kinds of internal bodily processes.[10] Actions can be understood as a species of bodily movements, on this view, only if the latter are allowed to include those neural events that can be identified with the mental events that are the concomitants of actions. Thus, to say that a person P performed action A is taken as equivalent to saying that events in P's brain caused a bodily movement or series of movements that constituted the performance of A. Actions are interpreted as bodily movements that result from certain sorts of brain processes. The difference between bodily events that are actions and ones that are not is preserved, on this account, by identifying actions with just those bodily movements that are mediated by the brain states that are associated with the agent's intentions in performing the actions he does.

In order for an account of this sort to be plausible, it must be capable of showing that the concept of agency or agent causation is eliminable: the facts that it is supposed to explain must be analyzable in terms of ordinary event causation. A method that would achieve this result would enable us to *subtract* the movement from the action and to obtain as remainder only elements that are linked to the movement in the same way that physiological events are linked. An action would have to be regarded as a compound event consisting of the event whose occurrence is what happens as a result of someone's performing the action and whatever remains after that event hs been subtracted. (Cf. Wittgenstein: "What is left over if I subtract the fact that my arm goes up from the fact that I raise my arm?")[11] If what is left over is another event, then actions will have been analyzed in terms of event causation. And if all of the constituent events are physical or physiological events, then actions must be identical with a subclass of bodily processes.

There are at least two problems with this suggestion. The first is that it is not clear that it even makes sense to speak of subtracting movements from actions.[12] The fact that an action involves some physical movement does not imply that that movement is a separable part or element of the action. Every act of visual perception requires the reflection of light by

16

an external object, but the reflecting of light by that object is not a part of the perceptual act. Nor are inscriptions, which are presupposed by reading, elements of the act of reading that can properly be subtracted from it. Movements certainly do not *have* to be related to actions as parts to wholes, and if they are not, then subtraction must be construed as merely a metaphor for what occurs in a certain kind of thought-experiment.

The second difficulty associated with attempting to analyze actions as compounds of physical events is that, even if subtraction is conceptually possible, it may be a mistake to assume that what is left over is an event. If an action is an event that includes an overt bodily movement that is its culmination, what is obtained upon removing that bodily event may be an unrepresentable conceptual fragment, like a voice without sound. Only if we insist that what makes a bodily movement happen *must* be another event do we need to believe that what is left over after the movement has been subtracted from an action is an event.

There is another argument that may help us see why the materialist's analysis of actions into bodily processes does not enable him to dispense with agency. Suppose it is possible to subtract movements from actions, and that what is left over are events that are causally linked to the movements. Consider, for example, Arthur Danto's suggestion that "m does b" can be resolved into two events, m does-b and b, where the former involves an *intentionalistic* sense of doing, according to which "m does-b" could be true without b occurring; one could be said to do something without that thing actually happening, just as one can (intentionalistically) see a dagger without there in fact being a dagger that one sees.[13] The problem that besets an analysis of this kind is that it leaves us with an anterior event that still involves someone doing something. Agency is not eliminated; it is merely detached from the successful outcome of the action. If we try to analyze this event still further, we will still generate an event in which an agent (or proto-agent) occurs. Continuing the analysis leads to an infinite regress. So the idea of agency is not capable of being eliminated through any procedure of analyzing actions into constituent parts.

Many of the arguments that have been adduced for denying the materialist thesis that actions are reducible to physical events also apply to dualistic attempts to account for the facts of human agency. Like the materialist, the psychophysical dualist wants to show that actions can be

17

resolved into components that are causally connected. Actions differ from bodily movements, according to the dualist, in that they include mental states or processes such as volitions and intentions: the difference between my leg swinging and my swinging my leg is that in the latter case the bodily happening is driven by a mental concomitant, which is what gives it its character as an action. What I do when I perform an action is what happens to my body as the result of my willing that my body should so move.[14]

To regard volitions as essential ingredients of action is to view actions as bodily events with mental causal antecedents. Actions are represented as events that occur at the interface of the mental and the physical; volitions are the way the soul or self gets things to happen in the physical world. Volitions are reckoned as caused by prior mental or physical events or, conceivably, by nothing at all. A volition, in any case, is what is supposed to be left after subtracting the bodily movement from an action.

The attempt to account for agency by analyzing it in terms of volitions and bodily movements is no less problematic than the attempt to reduce agency to brain processes and bodily movements. For how is this volition that is supposed to be obtained by subtracting the bodily movement from an action related to the person whose volition it is? If volitions are the causal antecedents of actions and are what make bodily movements voluntary, then either they are actions themselves, in which case nothing is explained, or else they are things that happen to people such that their occurrence is sufficient to trigger off behavior that we identify as actions. But, as Ryle has argued, absurdities result from both suppositions.[15] Volitions cannot be actions, for that would involve an infinite regress, since every volition would itself need to be caused by an action. But if volitions are events that are not actions, then it is hard to see how we can plausibly call the bodily movements that result from them voluntary.

The idea that every voluntary act is accomplished by a volition or act of willing is attended by other problems as well. There is a question as to what grounds we have for supposing that there are such occurrences. We are, after all, rarely if ever aware of a separate experience of willing as distinct from acting, even though we do know which pieces of our behavior are voluntary. Ultimately, the only basis we have for ascribing volitions or acts of will is the performance of the movements that they are supposed to cause.

Then there is the problem of how volitions are supposed to be connected with actions. The concept of willing seems to imply that it is logically impossible for someone to will something without doing that thing unless he is specifically thwarted or dissuaded subsequent to the act of willing. To say that a person willed to move his fingers but they failed to move makes no sense in the absence of explicit or implicit reference to circumstances that could be cited to explain the nonoccurrence of what was willed. Willing *must* lead to acting, or at least to an attempt at acting, if it is willing that occurs. If the occurrence of a volition is not logically distinct from the occurrence of the movement it precedes, it cannot be the cause of movement.[16]

If, on the other hand, volitions are logically independent of the voluntary acts with which they are associated, then they cannot serve as part of the analysis of action. For if volitions can occur as discrete events, then there could be cases of bodily movements preceded by volitions that would not deserve to be counted as actions. If a pistol in my hand fires as the result of a sudden seizure, the firing of the gun would not be a voluntary action, even if it were preceded by my thinking that I wanted to shoot. In order for a mental occurrence to make a bodily movement a voluntary action, it must be connected with the movement in a more intimate fashion. A mental occurrence that gets me to *do* something must get *me* to do it; it must work through *my* agency. If actions are movements produced by volitions, the volitions cannot be separable from the actions. In other words, if actions presuppose volitions, they cannot be *analyzed* in terms of them. A volitional account cannot reduce agency.

An agent is someone who is able to bring about states of affairs; he is able to change the world. I want to say that an action is an event of which it can be said categorically that the agent *could have done otherwise*. A person can be said to have acted when and only when it can also be said that he could have acted differently, not merely under different circumstances, but that he could have acted differently right there and then.[17] To ascribe agency to a person is to say of him that there is something X that he has brought about such that he could also have brought about not-X; where he could have failed to bring about X only if certain conditions were present, the bringing about of X was not an action.

Whether or not there are such happenings as actions (in this sense) depends on whether persons may properly be conceived as executors of events for which there are alternate possibilities. When we say that someone has performed a free action, we are saying that he did not *have* to do as he did, that he could have refrained from doing it. But what about the situation in which a person does something, not knowing that, were he to attempt to do anything else, he would be prevented and forced to do just that thing?[18] In such a case, it might be argued, a person could be said to act freely despite the fact that it is false that he could do otherwise.

One way of responding to this objection would be to deny that the behavior in question deserves to be counted as free action. To give this reply would imply that agents and others who claim to recognize a piece of behavior as an action may very well not be in a position to know whether it is an action or not. It would imply that actions are not always identifiable as such on the level at which we conceive them as actions. Knowing whether an event is an action, on this interpretation, could depend on knowing that is not available to those present.

But there is no reason why there has to be an incompatibility between acting freely and unknowingly acting in circumstances that would have precluded any alternative. The phrase "could not have done otherwise," so far as it is analytical of the concept of a free action, does not have to be interpreted as having a reach beyond what the agent is in a position to know. A person who jumps from a diving board does so freely even if he would, at that very instant, have been blown off by a sudden gust of wind had he not jumped, just so long as he does not know that he could not have prevented himself from going off the board. Furthermore, the fact that a person would have been knocked off the diving board had he not jumped does not show that it is false that he could have done otherwise. Falling off a board is not the same as jumping off, so we can still maintain that if he performed the act of jumping he *could* have done otherwise—namely, not jumped off. In fact, any story we tell about what will happen if a person does not act in a certain way presupposes the possibility of his not acting in that way, and thus that he *can* do otherwise.

The case of overdetermination does not show that an action can be both free and unavoidable; it rather points up the fact that, for a piece of behavior to be identifiable as an action, it need only be *conceived* as free. Recognizing one's own actions as free is quite obviously connected with acknowledging the possibility of choice. The same is true for the actions of others: identifying the behavior of another person as action, as opposed to bodily response, requires that we assume that the person could have refrained from carrying it out. The conceptual necessity that attaches to the connection between action and alternate possibilities can thus be represented as follows: behavior that one takes to be action cannot at the same time from that point of view be conceived as constrained in such a way as to make no other behavior possible.

The peculiar logical status of action statements can be seen by considering the role they play in explanations of things that happen in the world. Chains of explanation, like chains of movers, can in principle go on forever. When we seek an explanation of why a bridge collapsed, we may be given an account in terms of the structural features and forces that led to its collapse. If we pursue the matter further and ask how the bridge came to be built in the way it was, we may find that the explanation is made to rest on someone's action (or inaction). In many cases, that is where the explanation ends; attributions of agency often serve as terminators of explanatory series. By identifying an event as the result of someone's action, as something he had the power to do or not to do, we are designating that event as a starter-event in a causal series. The agent is what gets the causal process going.

It is true that we can continue the search for explanation by asking what caused the agent to act as he did. To do so, however, either means reverting to a behaviorist conception of action and hence abandoning the idea of human agency, or else it involves a shift to a different mode of explanation, one that focuses on the agent's reasons for acting as he has. When a free action is cited as the thing that sets a causal sequence in motion, the action itself is not conceived as a causal intermediary. Since a person who acts for a reason is free to act or not act for that reason, having a reason for acting is not a necessitating cause. Reasons can explain without having to show that the thing that happened had to happen.

In arguing that there is no way of analyzing human action that satisfactorily eliminates the notion of agency, I am not saying that the human organism is an entity that fails to behave in accordance with the laws governing the behavior of matter in other animate and inanimate bodies. Neither am I saying that it is impossible to look upon humans as complex systems whose behavior can be treated merely as the effects of

21

interactions between external stimuli and internal configurations. We do not *have* to characterize as agents those entities that ordinarily get classified as human beings. The question is not whether a science of human beings qua objects or qua organisms is possible, but rather whether a science of that kind is capable of telling us what we want to know about people and society.

No account of human behavior that ignores or tries to reduce action and its related concepts can capture those features or aspects of behavior that will be counted as distinctively human. So far as social science is concerned, the question is not whether we *can* dispense with talk about actions—talk, I have argued, that commits us to treating action as a category that is not reducible to other concepts of scientific description—but whether we can do so and still have an account of behavior that is adequate to persons. Action descriptions are employed because they are useful; they provide means of organizing our experience with respect to those things we call persons. An approach to human behavior that treats as unimportant the difference between behavior that is action and behavior that is not action assumes a different standard of cognitive usefulness from the standard that is implicit in an approach that takes action as fundamental.

The kinds of features that are missing from a reductionist or materialist account of action are precisely those that are important from the point of view of anyone who coexists in the society of human subjects whose behavior is being studied. The notion of action is bound up with a whole cluster of concepts that are constitutive of the human condition—ideas of freedom, morality, and responsibility. Actions, as distinguished from movements, play a special role in human societies, and it often matters a great deal whether an event that occurs is someone's action or not. The distinction between what a person does and what merely happens is at the core of all ethical and legal systems, and is relevant for every society that employs any sort of concept of individual or collective responsibility. Whoever tries to fashion a natural science of human behavior, a science that seeks to treat actions as on all fours with other kinds of observable events, allows no place for such concepts.

It is a contingent fact that the world allows for the possible use of action concepts, that there exist creatures that can be characterized as agents. It is another contingent fact that these concepts are in fact deployed. That they are deployed reveals something about the nature of human existence, given that the notion of agency is tied to a whole network of concepts that are constitutive of persons' being-in-the-world—concepts that include those of ethics, law, politics, religion, and human relationships in general. Part of being human is being a responsible agent and recognizing other responsible agents. Action concepts have sustained their place in language because of the continued relevance of moral and legal ideas to human life and the dependency of such ideas upon them. Action is not a strictly behavioral notion, nor is it behavior alone that prompts us to use the language of action. The study of action is *essentially* anthropocentric: in order for action terminology to be employed, the subjects of actions—agents, in other words—must already be identified, if not as persons directly, at least as things that are to be conceived on the model of persons. The distinction between what happens and what is done by agents is one that both presupposes and conditions a human social life that treats it as a distinction that matters.

If the concept of action is both primitive and indissolubly linked to that of a person, and persons are essentially doers, then a science of human beings will have to be intrinsically anthropocentric and hence separate from a science of nature. Human events cannot be construed merely as happenings or occurrences, for that is precluded by our interest in their rationale, their morality and legality, and their social significance in general. The content of a human science must be what people do—how they live, what they make, what they do to each other, for each other, and with each other. That humans are agents as well as patients is what makes them unique as a subject for science, and it is also what makes the idea of a human science different from the start.

# 2. The Social Nature of Action

I have been arguing that the notion of human action is central to any social science adequate to the task of providing an understanding of why people and societies behave as they do, and that this notion must be construed in a way that makes it irreducible to other kinds of event concepts. In this chapter I wish to argue that action is a concept whose roots are essentially social. What is distinctive about the behavior we identify as human action, I shall maintain, is that it is *meaningful;* actions have subjective and intersubjective meanings that must be grasped before anyone can begin to understand why they occurred. The meaning of an action, furthermore, is not necessarily given by the agent's intentions alone, but also depends on a system of social relations that determine the conditions of ascription of responsibility. A science of action will therefore have to be a science of social meanings.

An idea that has been prominent in much of the recent literature in the philosophy of action is that of a basic action.[1] Basic actions are those actions, such as raising one's arms or closing one's fist, that are not performed through doing something else. They are the actions by means of which one performs actions that are nonbasic. A philosophy of action that is based on this notion will treat voluntary movements as fundamental, as units that may be converted by contextual factors into gestures and given a social meaning. Actions are not significant in themselves, on this view, but are rendered significant by the apparatus of interpretation that is brought to them.[2]

The conception of human action that I want to defend contrasts sharply with this view. I shall argue that the so-called basic actions are themselves derivative from and conceptually dependent upon other kinds of actions, and that actions have a character that is essentially rather

24

contingently determined by what people do in or by performing them.[3] The meaning of an action, I want to say, is not something that is clapped onto an event that is already understandable as itself a kind of action. The paradigm of human action is not basic action but social action, action whose identity depends upon social meaning.

The point that Danto noticed and based his "discovery" of basic actions on is that actions are typically *mediated*: we do what we do by doing other things *through* which the first things are done. But in order for us to enter the chain of mediated actions, there must be some *basic* actions the performing of which does not depend upon doing anything else. There *have* to be basic actions if there are any actions at all.

Basic actions do not exist in isolation, however. Actions occur in contexts, the recognition of which is crucial for their being identified as the actions they are. The circumstances of the occurrence of a bodily movement are what afford us the basis for presuming that it is an action and not, for example, a twitch. Basic actions are performed *only* when we do other things: we do not merely pull and push things, we do so in order to open or close a door, clear a pathway, or operate a machine. Even the most aimless of activities, such as swinging one's arms or wiggling one's ears, are ordinarily performed and identified in terms other than those that might be used in characterizing basic actions. One cannot just perform a basic action, even to make a philosophical point, for to do so would be to perform, or try to perform, the nonbasic action of making a philosophical point.

The concept of a basic action is a result of one kind of analysis of human action. It is analysis that may be useful for someone wishing to understand how human actions occur, how beliefs, intentions, and human physiology come together in the form of human agency. There is a quite different question, however, for which the analysis involving basic actions is of doubtful value: how is the recognition of human action possible? Given that the events we identify as actions are usually not basic actions but rather have a much richer content, we cannot use the fact that there are basic actions, which we discover only by analyzing other actions, to show how we are able to identify actions in general. If basic actions are identifiable only as a result of our being able to pick out actions that are nonbasic, then we cannot expect the concept of a basic action to help us understand how we are able to acquire and deploy action concepts.

25

The identification of actions requires the perception of bodily movements as purposive or meaningful. Behavior, in order to be picked out as action, must be recognized as intentional. A human agent is something that is credited with having intentions in accordance with which it behaves, and these intentions are what must be taken cognizance of in interpreting behavior as action of one kind or another. When an action is identified, the description that reveals the agent's intention is not the description of a basic action. Knowing that a piece of behavior is an action does not depend on being able to identify basic actions. We would not be aware that there is a distinction to be made between basic actions and bodily movements if we did not know that we can do things that, it happens, are analyzable into basic actions.

If there are actions that are basic actions and that deserve to be treated as logically prior to the actions that one specifically intends to perform, then we should expect the concept of a basic action to be applicable to animals as well as to people. It is difficult to see how this concept can be employed at all with respect to nonhuman animals, however, for there is no straightforward way of distinguishing those bodily movements *through* which an allegedly mediated action is performed from those movements that merely make the action possible. The notion of a basic action is of no use, for example, in describing how a bird uses its wings in flight. We may be able to discover the movements a goldfish makes in swimming up to the surface, but we will not know which of these are basic actions and which are mediated actions. We know what a bear does in catching a fish, but we have no basis for designating any of the particular moves he makes in swooping down with a swinging paw as actions in themselves. Without a means of assigning intentions, or of identifying certain occurrences as voluntary actions of specific types, it is not possible to apply the concept of action at all, or to draw meaningful distinctions among basic actions, mediated actions, and the consequences of actions.

The fact that the meaning of an action is ordinarily associated with the agent's intentions might be thought to imply that the essential characteristic of action is purposiveness. Indeed, every successful action, be it the tying of a shoelace, the licking of a stamp, or the spanking of a child, does involve the achievement of some end or goal. And even unsuccessful attempts to perform actions, so far as they include actions that are successfully executed, involve the achievement of ends of a proximate nature.

26

One consequence of treating purposiveness as the defining trait of action is that it allows us to assimilate human action to the purposive behavior of animals. Since animals chase flies, bury bones, and climb trees, they as well as people can be said to perform actions, if behaving purposively is what constitutes action. Such a conception provides a simple model for interpreting human action, whereby acts such as picking berries and warding off blows are taken as fundamental, and acts involving social practices and personal interaction are treated as complex variations. Only the particular ends and circumstances of human action have to be viewed as different from those of animal action.

But if basic action is not an adequate place to ground the attempt to understand the nature of human action as meaningful behavior, purposiveness is no better. It is true that actions are purposive, but so are bodily processes and growth. Anything whose behavior or the behavior of whose parts is organized around or oriented toward the attainment of a specific goal or end-state is purposive, but not all such phenomena are actions, at least in the sense that the voluntary behavior of humans is action. Human actions, though not always implying choice—they may be performed on the spur of the moment, as Aristotle points out[4]—nevertheless are worthy of choice at the time they are done. Actions, we have acknowledged, are those things that are in the agent's power to do or not do. Hence goal-directed processes that do not exhibit this feature should not be considered actions. At most, they are derivative cases of action, like reflex behavior. The purposive behavior of a snail drawing into its shell, or a bird returning to its nest, does not have to be construed as intentional action.

I want to argue that the home of action concepts is to be found in the domain of social phenomena, that they are concepts whose primary application is to behavior whose meaning depends on a system of social interactions. My thesis is that social relations as we know them are not possible without a concept of action which they presuppose, and that this concept has no essential role in language other than to serve this mediating function. Like money, the concept of action has no value without the occurrence of a set of transactions that it mediates.

The link between actions and the social is provided by the notion of responsibility. Human social relations require that people be able to deal with one another as responsible agents. Social life consists of situations in which people do things to and for each other. One of the things that is peculiarly human—and, I would insist, the principal thing—about the

27

interactions of human beings is that people may be held responsible or accountable for things that happen that affect other people. To be responsible is to have the power or capability of determining whether or not something occurs. But to have such a power is to be an agent, to be capable of performing free actions. Hence social life (as we know it) presupposes action of a peculiarly human sort.

The preceding argument does not show that social life is the only source of action concepts. What it shows is that, if social life in humans depends on the possibility of deploying notions such as praise and blame, there have to be concepts of free action. But if human action is something that is fundamentally social in nature, then it is possible only in social contexts. What we need to do, if we are to prove that human action is a social concept, is to specify a sense in which actions do presuppose a system of social interactions.

Since actions are in general what people are held responsible for, and responsibility presupposes a set of social sanctions, a possible way of connecting actions with the social is through the suggestion that actions comprise precisely those events for which a person can be held morally responsible. That equation cannot be sustained, however. There are surely actions that have no moral content at all, if only because they affect no one other than the agent. And there are other actions, such as ones performed under extreme duress, for which it would be inappropriate to say that the agent is morally responsible. Furthermore, a person may be held responsible not only for what he does, but also for certain things that happen that he did not himself enact. One can be responsible for occurrences—the destruction of a neighbor's garden by one's dog, for example—that one may not have participated in in any way.

The link between action and responsibility and thus with the social is not one of direct entailment, but is rather to be found at a foundational level. Action descriptions are what enable us to assign credit and blame, and the need to ascribe responsibility is what forces us to make distinctions between actions and movements, between deliberate and purposive behavior, and between the things we do and the things that happen to us. The conduct of social life is the point of there being action concepts; it provides the contexts that allow such concepts to gain a foothold.

The foundations of human-action concepts, I have argued, are found among the conditions of human social interaction. Understanding such interaction requires grasping the notion of responsibility. Not every action is subject to praise or blame, of course, though every action could, given the proper circumstances, be something for which one could be held accountable. To identify an item of behavior as a free action, as distinct from a purposive bodily movement, is to conceive it on the model of cases in which praise and blame are appropriate. There are indeed actions that do not presuppose social relations, but what makes them actions is that they are imputable to agents who *make* them happen, who are responsible for their occurrence. And if what is required for such imputations is a language that permits the assignment of credit and responsibility, then it must be such features of human social interaction that provide the basis for even the most asocial of human-action descriptions.

If action concepts have their roots in human social relations, then it is incorrect to regard human social action as a special kind of action. There is no point in trying to analyze social action in terms of nonsocial action if the concept of action already presupposes a domain of human social interaction. Indeed, we would do better to say that nonsocial action is a special case of social action. It is not as though we already have an independent characterization of action that we can use as a basis for analyzing social action, the way that we can analyze the performance of a musical ensemble in terms of the behavior of solo musicians. Explicating nonsocial action is more like explicating a one-person game in terms of the two-person variety.

It is worth noticing that this way of conceiving action implies a broader conception of sociology than is frequently held, even among sociologists. For if action is itself ultimately a social category, then sociology must be concerned with *all* action, not just with what Weber calls social action, viz. action that "takes account of the behavior of others and is thereby oriented by its course."[5] Anything that a person does, as long as it is something he *does*, can have sociological interest, because it is something he might otherwise not be permitted to do or might, under different social conditions, choose not to do. The mere fact that a particular kind of nonsocial action is not viewed as a form of deviance, or as a so-called "victimless" crime, may not be without sociological significance. A sociology that restricts itself to social action as Weber defines it may be too narrow to yield an account of every kind of action that deserves to be considered.

Social science is concerned with what people do and why they do it. But that is not all that social science is concerned with, for it must also deal with phenomena that are results of human action that were intended by no one. It is not by the design of any individual that there are economic recessions, demographic shifts, or bank failures, and yet these are definitely social phenomena that come about through the actions of individuals. Social life is a fabric woven not only of intentional actions but also of what Karl Popper has called "the indirect, the unintended and often unwanted by-products" of intentional actions.[6] The significance of actions, their social meaning, must include all of their consequences, both intended and unintended.

There are thus two places to look for social significance with regard to a given action or set of actions. One of these, stressed by Weber, is in the intentional meaning of the action as it is conceived by the agent; the other, noticed by Popper, is in its unintended consequences. It would be tempting to suppose that all social meaning is comprehensible in terms of this twofold division. I want to resist this suggestion, however, and to argue that there is a third possibility, that the meaning of an action is often identifiable neither with what the agent intended nor with effects that no one can be said to have produced by his own actions. Actions have meanings, I shall maintain, that go beyond the agent's subjective intentions but are not encompassed by the notion of unintended consequences.

The approach to human action taken here is one that denies that it is either instructive or useful to regard the distinctively human or social character of actions as the result of a conversion or enrichment of basic actions by means of contextual factors. Actions are *already* human and social if they are actions at all. That is, they are social in virtue of the roots of the concept of action. But actions are also social in virtue of the meanings they have. Their meanings are what identify them; they are already filled with the meanings that are expressed in the descriptions that are used to pick them out.

I have characterized actions as meaningful pieces of behavior. The question is, how are actions meaningful, what makes a piece of behavior full of meaning? A way to approach this question is by considering action descriptions. A single item of behavior or sequence of movements may be described in any of several ways, only some of which can be said to capture the meaning of the act performed. The problem is that of determining which of the ways of specifying a given occurrence properly express the meaning of an action.

According to one widely held view, the meaning of any action can only be found in the mind of the person performing it. Actions, on this interpretation, consist only of things the agent specifically intends to do. The agent is supposed to be in a privileged position with respect to identifying the goals he is pursuing and the practices he is following; he is the final arbiter as to what his gestures mean. Thus it will be said that only the agent can be counted on to know what he is doing when, during a chess match, he taps a certain piece causing it to fall over—whether he is resigning from the game or merely testing the piece's stability.

If actions are ascribable to agents only so far as intentions are, then no one can correctly be said to have performed a given action if he did not know he was performing it or did not intend to perform it. Arthur Danto, a defender of this interpretation of action, insists on "limited liability" in action: a person's responsibility is limited to what he knowingly brings about. Danto rejects the suggestion that "we do everything which can be truly said of what we do" in favor of a view that allows for reference to our representations: Oedipus, he avers, can be said to have performed the action of making love to the Queen but not of making love to his mother, because he did not in fact represent that lady *as* his mother. When Atrius ate what was served him, he was not performing the action of eating his children because he did not *know* that it was his children he was eating. One cannot be said to *do,* on Danto's view, what one does not intend to do.[7]

Against this view, I want to argue that actions have meanings that go beyond the agent's subjective intentions, that the concept of action needs to be construed more broadly than is done by an account that restricts a person's actions to acts that an agent believes himself to be performing. The reason I believe that a broader concept of action is required is that there are actions, excluded by the narrower concept, that persons can properly be credited with performing even though they may not have been aware that these were their actions. We need to acknowledge that there are actions that are correctly characterizable under descriptions that agents may not accept. The fact that a politician may not *believe* that the acceptance of favors to which he responds by enacting policies favorable to the donor is a case of bribery does not by itself prove that that is not a proper way to describe his actions. A person who is rightly convicted of a crime but who still sincerely believes he has done nothing wrong is likely to have as a characterization of his actions something quite different from the one that the jury correctly assigns to them. It is not a requirement either of our legal system or of our everyday concept of committing an act that the agent must assent to the description under which an act that he has performed is socially recognized.

Action, as we have already seen, has an important link to responsibility. One of the reasons for insisting on a broader conception of action than is demanded by the criterion of self-ascribability is that it allows action descriptions to reflect this connection. A person *is* sometimes liable for occurrences that he did not perceive himself as enacting; not all of these deserve to be excluded from the class of actions. There are acts with unintended and unforeseen consequences for which one is nevertheless responsible; why not say that the proper way to characterize actions in such cases is in terms of the consequences, the enacting of which *is* what is done? We are, after all, inclined to say of a cook who serves his guests mushrooms that he mistakenly takes to be harmless thereby causing their deaths, that he does actually poison them, especially when his mistake is the result of carelessness, laziness, or a frivolous propensity to experiment. It is because we hold a person responsible that we are willing to say not just that what happened occurred as a result of what he did, but that he did it.

When a person is properly ascribed responsibility for something that happens, it must be the case either that it is something he did or that it is something whose occurrence is the result of something he did or failed to do and that he was capable of doing or not doing. When a farmer is held responsible for his cattle having contracted hoof-and-mouth disease, for example, the presumption is that he could have taken steps to prevent that from occurring. If there is no action that he could have performed or forborne that would have made a difference in what eventuated, then there can be no moral responsibility.

The connection between responsibility and action may also be seen by considering the way in which ascriptions of responsibility are explained or justified. Justifiably holding someone responsible for something he did not himself do can be made intelligible only by assigning a connection between the occurrence and that person's role as an agent. Thus if we want to explain why a certain military officer should have been held responsible for acts committed by members of his unit, we must claim that it was exercise or nonexercise of authority that either contributed to or made possible what occurred. Where no connection can be established, the ascription of responsibility is unexplainable and unjustifiable. Explanations of why someone is responsible always terminate in statements about what that person did or did not do.

If a person is morally responsible for something E that happens, he must be an agent and his agency must be connectable with E. There must, furthermore, be more than an accidental connection between what he did or failed to do and what happened. A way of expressing this connection is by using action locutions, such as "made E happen" or "allowed E to happen," or, more simply, by using action verbs that replace these more indirect expressions. Thus we say of an aircraft-company employee who is responsible for a crash because he has intentionally falsified a report certifying that a known safety hazard has been corrected, that he is guilty of endangering the lives of airline passengers. The occurrence for which a person may be held responsible may not be the action he intended; it may instead be an action that he performed but did not intend.

Intentions are necessary for actions only in the sense that every action requires some intention or other. It is not necessary that a person intend to do everything that he in fact does. What is necessary is that a person is responsible for any action that is correctly ascribed to him. It is obvious that we are responsible (though not always blamable) for the foreseen consequences of our actions, but we are not ordinarily responsible for their unintended and unforeseeable consequences. When we do credit or blame someone for bringing about something that he neither foresaw nor intended, we are also willing to accept a description that mentions that result. In a case like this, we assume that the agent *ought* to have known what he was bringing about, or that he could reasonably have been *expected* to anticipate the results of his actions; such is the situation with respect to instances of negligent or reckless behavior. Another kind of example is provided by the journalist who engages in sharp and repeated criticism of a politician: he *is* responsible for angering his target, and regardless of what he *thought* he was doing, that is what he did. Another case is that of the elected official who orders a drastic cutback of welfare expenditures: not only can we say that he is responsible for the hardship that his action brings to the least well-off members of his constituency, but also that bringing such hardship is what he is doing, regardless of whether he is aware of doing so.

I am suggesting that action and liability should be understood as having the same limits. There are actions we can correctly be said to perform that we do not specifically intend to do, and there are occurrences for which we are responsible that we do not intend to enact; but there is never responsibility without the possibility of action, nor is there action, in the sense being discussed, without the possible imputation of responsibility. Actions are kinds of occurrences for which agents bear responsibility, and the ascription of responsibility makes sense only in the context of action.

We can expect these aspects of actions to be reflected in the analysis of action sentences—sentences that characterize human actions. Because actions are events and not substances, they are denoted not by nouns or by verbs, but by sentences. Every action involves both an agent and a movement or forbearance, and every sentence that describes an action indicates the predication of one or the other. Action sentences express a certain meaning and reveal certain relationships between individuals and their environments.

Several types of analysis of action sentences have been proposed. One of these begins with the suggestion that to perform an action is to exemplify a property.[8] On this account, actions are not things or entities, but rather are attributable to certain entities, namely persons: to say that person P performs act A is merely to suppose that A is predicated of P, as traits are predicated of organisms.

This sort of analysis is far too simple for our purposes, however. Performing an action is not a property of a single thing in the way that sneezing is, for example. Except for basic actions, which I have argued represent a special, abstract case, actions essentially have to do with something outside the agent. They are inconceivable unless they are conceived as in the world. Performing an action involves the agent in doing (or not doing) something in relation to his surroundings.

A more promising analysis of action is one that treats it as a relation between a person and an event that is made to happen by his doing it. Action verbs may be construed not as one-place predicates but as two-place relations between persons and events in the world. For an action to occur, it must be the case that something happens (or fails to happen) in the world and that someone has done (or not done, i.e., forborne) it.

If doing or acting is a relation, however, it cannot be any sort of extensional relation, because the terms that are supposed to be related are not entirely independent. In the logic of relations, if "aRb" expresses a relation between a and b (for example, "is taller than" or "is politically to the left of"), the truth or falsity of the statement that expresses the relation should be independent of how a and b are designated: if Edwin Booth was the brother of John Wilkes Booth, then the greatest American Shakespearean actor of the nineteenth century was the brother of Lincoln's assassin, if in fact Edwin Booth was the greatest American Shakespearean actor of the nineteenth century and John Wilkes Booth was Lincoln's assassin. On the other hand, it is extremely doubtful whether the truth of action statements is automatically preserved when specifications of the alternative event are substituted. It is a moot point whether Oedipus committed patricide, even though the man he killed was in fact his father.[9]

The policy of "limited liability" referred to above amounts to treating action verbs as creating what Quine has called "referentially opaque" contexts, wherein substitution of terms having the same referent cannot be counted on to preserve truth.[10] The important implication of this interpretation of action statements, so far as the analysis of their logical form is concerned, is that performing an action cannot be a simple (extensional) relation between a person and something that happens, since it allows the truth of an action statement to depend on how the event the person is supposed to make happen is described. A statement, "X brings it about that p," is true, on this view, only if "p" is expressed in the same terms in which it is represented by X. Acting is thus treated as a relation between a person and the world, but because the relation must be mediated by that person's representations, the terms of the relation are not conceived as logically independent in the sense of being independently characterizable. The agent and the part or aspect of the world in which he effects change must be additionally related through his representations, if he can be said to have performed the action at all.

More formally, the analysis of "x does (or brings it about that) y" may be expressed as "xBy." According to a strict interpretation of "doing" as an extensional relation, "xBy" is true under any specification of y at all. On the other hand, if "xBy" is interpreted in Danto's way, wherein action contexts are treated as referentially opaque, "xBy" is true only if y is represented in the way it is represented by x. Thus rendered, the relation is not an extensional one because it depends on the way the agent conceives the event he makes happen.

35

Treating action verbs as creating referentially opaque contexts does indeed reflect a feature of such verbs that distinguishes them from verbs used to specify bodily movements or inanimate changes. Killing a certain frog is not the same action as killing the prince when the killer does not know that the frog is in fact the prince; nor is injecting vaccine that someone else has clandestinely and maliciously replaced with a lethal solution the same action as administering a fatal injection. We do need to block the inference from "xBy" and "y is logically equivalent to z" to "xBz."

This feature of action sentences is preserved by analysis that interprets "x does y" as "x acts y-ly."[11] Acting y-ly will not be the same as acting z-ly, on this rendering, unless x *takes* them to be the same.

There are problems with this analysis, however. For one thing, it gives the mistaken impression that actions are fundamentally nonrelational, that they bear no essential connection with anything outside the agent. More importantly, it ignores the intentional aspect of performing an action. Furthermore, it appears to license the suggestion that animals, trees, and machines—things that we presume are not capable of deliberating and choosing—can perform full-fledged actions, unless we are to assume that the use of the unanalyzed verb "acts" precludes such a possibility. If, as I have argued, the use of action concepts with respect to the behavior of animals and other nonhumans is derivative from or parasitic on the use of such concepts in the domain of human social life, this point should be reflected in the analysis.

An analysis of action sentences that comes closer to capturing the features of action that I have been stressing is one that parses "x does y" as "x makes-true 'y' and 'y' means z."[12] In this formula 'y' is a sentence, and "'y' means z" asserts that 'y' is true if and only if z, a certain event or state of affairs, obtains. In tying action to language in this way, the analysis helps us to explain why action should be conceived as a fundamentally human trait and also preserves the opacity of action descriptions. A person performing an action thus makes-true a particular sentence but not every sentence to which it is logically equivalent. That is, it is not possible to infer from "x makes-true 'y'" and "'y' means z" that "x makes-true 'y.'" The inference is a valid one only if some additional premise is supplied, such as "x knows that 'y' and 'y' are logically equivalent."

The analysis that has been presented accurately reflects the policy of limited liability in ascribing actions. It can also be seen to fit the broader conception of action that I have been defending. The policy of limited liability, I have argued, is too restrictive. Since we are responsible not only for the known consequences of our acts but also for those effects that we ought to have known were likely to ensue, it is sometimes proper to credit one with actions whose descriptions mention effects that one did not in fact anticipate. A person can be said to perform and be responsible for acts that he did not know but should have known he was performing. This feature of action ascription, this widening of a person's liability for some of the things that happen as the result of his intentional actions, may be incorporated in the analysis at hand: we specify that the additional premise neded to license the inference from "x does y" to "x does y," is "x knows or ought to know that 'y' implies 'y.'"

Since the correctness of a given characterization of a person's action depends not only on what he knows but also on what he ought to know, the agent is not always the final judge as to just what actions he is to be credited with performing. Actions are public in a way that thoughts are not. In accepting Weber's definition of action as "all human behavior when and in so far as the acting individual attaches a subjective meaning to it,"[13] we must not make the mistake of identifying the meaning of an action with its subjective meaning. As Weber himself recognized, the fact that an action must be subjectively or intersubjectively meaningful need not be taken to imply that its meaning has to be what the agent thinks it is. Behavior, in order to be counted as action, need only have a subjectively understandable orientation.

If it is true, as I have been arguing, that the way a social science must deal with behavior is not as bodily movements or basic action but as behavior endowed with meanings, then it is these meanings that such a science will have to confront. Because agents are not the ultimate authority with respect to the meanings of their actions, social science has the chance to play an important role in the effort to understand human actions. For if people are not always aware of the nature of their own actions, then someone else—an outside observer—is sometimes in a better position to provide a characterization. Social inquiry is able to pursue meanings without having to rely exclusively on agents' testimony for the interpretation of actions.

There are at least three ways in which we may find it useful to give an account of an action in which we employ a characterization not available to the agent. One of these involves the use of vocabulary that the agent himself would not use or possibly even recognize. A person dealing through the stock exchange may "sell short," without having learned that concept; a person may engage in a pattern of contact and withdrawal in his relationship with another person, without being prepared to so characterize his behavior; and a leader may effect a centralization and bureaucratization of administrative functions, without being able to recognize any such representation of his behavior. Though there are obviously constraints on what sorts of activities can be imputed to an agent by an outside observer, these need not limit action descriptions to what the agent himself would say in his own behalf.

A second class of actions for which a proper characterization may come from someone other than the agent is made up of actions that the agent may be totally unaware he is performing, under any description. These are actions the agent may never admit to, even after becoming familiar with the terminology in which they are described. They include items of unnoticed behavior, such as curling one's feet around the rungs of one's chair, replacing the cap on one's pen, or failing to secure the latch of a door upon closing it. Though inadvertent, these occurrences nonetheless deserve to be counted as actions, at least to the extent that they may be subject to voluntary control. These seemingly innocent movements that only someone other than the agent is likely to notice and identify as meaningful acts are just the sort of things that psychoanalytic theory tries to interpret.

Another type of case of performing an action unknowingly involves the exercise of unconscious preferences. One may choose for one's associates, for example, only persons having certain distinguishing but not necessarily consciously noted physical characteristics. The result of such actions, given a sufficient number of instances, may be widespread patterns of discrimination. If those who perform such actions are blamable, what makes them so is their failure to recognize their behavior *as* discriminatory and to prevent them from occurring. An act does not have to involve conscious discriminatory intent in order to be properly characterized as discriminatory.

There is a third way in which actions may be found meaningful by investigators whose perspectives differ from that of the agent. Recognition of an act's meaning or significance may in some cases be possible only by someone who is historically, intellectually, or emotionally removed from it. The significance of an action is not simply what it leads to; it also depends on the context in which it occurs. If this context can be identified only within a historical, psychological, or sociological perspective, this perspective will contribute features not ordinarily accessible to the agent. A patient is unlikely to be aware of the psychological meaning of sending a particular gift to his analyst. People are not ordinarily alert to the sociological significance of the jobs they hold or the hobbies they pursue. Interpretive identification of actions is often required to reveal not only the consequences of actions but also their contextual meaning or significance.

It was probably Hegel who first pointed out that historical agents need not be supposed to have grasped the significance of their actions: history is made by people who may truly be said to have not known what they were doing. It is indeed most unlikely that the significance of a historic act such as the firing of a shot or the signing of a document, particularly in the cases where these acts are especially significant, will be perceived by the person performing it. An act comes to be seen as a revolutionary act only when it is placed in a context in terms of which it may be accorded that significance. We often fail to comprehend the meaning of our behavior—which is to say that we often do not know the nature of the acts we perform—because we frequently lack the perspective and contextual information that is required to make sense of what we do.

An important reason for insisting that actions may be correctly characterizable under descriptions that the agent may not acknowledge is that doing so allows social explanation to reveal the moral content of human activity. Whether something that happens is represented as someone's action, and not merely as a consequence of someone's action, can make a difference with respect to how an occurrence is regarded. To call something a consequence of action stops short of ascribing responsibility to anyone for what has happened. But if it is important—as I believe it must be—for social science to reveal the role human agency plays in determining the conditions of social life—whether humans are spectators or perpetrators, as it were—then it must not fail to indicate where the ascription of responsibility is appropriate. We are entitled to expect an account of human affairs to tell us whether something that has occurred—be it a pregnancy or the collapse of an industry—is the work of responsible agents or whether it is merely "just one of those things." The language of action, because of its ties to responsibility, provides a means of making this distinction.

39

In Chapter 1, I argued that actions are best conceived as primary, as fundamental with respect to the human sciences. In this chapter I have tried to show that actions so understood have intrinsic meanings that are what individuate them. Because actions have subjective or intentional meaning, and because action descriptions are not analyzable into components in the way physical event descriptions are, the identification of actions presents problems of a sort not encountered in the physical sciences. These problems become especially acute when one tries to understand the nature of social explanation, a topic that will be discussed in several subsequent chapters beginning with Chapter 4. Before undertaking that investigation, however, we need to look further at the question of what the subject matter of social science comprises. That will be the subject of Chapter 3.

# 3. What Social Science Is About

Everything that a social science seeks to illuminate is either an action or a result of action. The domain of social phenomena contains only things that people do and things that come into existence as a consequence of things that they do. Thus a legislature is a social phenomenon, as is an incest taboo, an irrigation ditch, and a monarchy. So also is the physical deterioration of a city, provided it is conceived as something that would not have come about had people acted differently. What is not a social phenomenon is any sort of occurrence whose incidence is independent of human action.

Yet the social sciences themselves typically have very little to say about actions directly. Sociology, anthropology, and economics rarely if ever deal with individual actions as such; they rather tend to study human societies by attending to goods, groups, and institutions. What people do gets counted less than what they have: bathtubs, television sets, vehicles, tons of steel, and money. An understanding of human society that is based on such findings is one that concentrates not on individuals but on families, bureaucracies, political parties, and the economy. One talks not so much about people as about phenomena such as population growth, stratification, the division of labor, industrialization, and international relations and war. Institutions are treated as though they have lives of their own, and societies are represented as complex wholes whose elements consist of things other than individuals.

There is a view of social explanation that sees the human sciences as concerned only with what people do and what happens to them. The fundamental units of social reality, it is maintained, are individual human beings. Social science is supposed to make social life intelligible

41

by making actions and patterns of actions intelligible. Explanations of social phenomena are expected to rest on accounts of what individual people do and why they do it. If social reality is constituted only by individual people whose behavior can be understood solely in terms of their dispositions, capacities, and understanding of their situation, then, it is argued, all social phenomena are capable of being represented in terms of these individuals.

The position just sketched is generally known as methodological individualism, a doctrine whose fundamental tenet is that all purported explanations of social phenomena, if they are to count as genuine or as rock-bottom explanations, must be couched solely in terms of facts about individuals.[1] Although it is supposed to be only a methodological thesis, it is usually supported by a corresponding ontological claim, that all there are in society, ultimately, are individual people. The position it is meant to contrast with is holism, which recognizes the existence of suprapersonal entities such as states, institutions, social systems, and the *Weltgeist*. The methodological individualist typically believes that the reason explanations need to be framed in terms of individuals is that there are no social entities over and above human beings that could provide the basis for any sort of social explanation.

If methodological individualism is construed as proscribing explanations that make reference to or otherwise presuppose features of social groups or institutions, it is problematic at best. We certainly *do* explain actions in terms of the context of institutions and practices, and merely to describe most actions involves at least a prima-facie commitment to preexisting social structures, roles, and relations. One can emigrate only because there are nations and one can go to work only because there are working establishments. Understanding human social behavior demands the use of what Mandelbaum has called "societal facts," facts that concern the forms of organization present in a society.[2] These are facts without which we would be unable to explain such behavior as that of a bank customer handing a withdrawal slip to a teller, or that of the occupants of a courtroom rising upon the entrance of a black-robed judge.

What makes the existence of such facts damaging to methodological individualism, Mandelbaum argues, is that they are not reducible to individual facts such as those of psychology, because they involve concepts that cannot be defined in terms of concepts that concern only the thoughts and actions of individuals. Statements about the behavior of bank depositors and courtroom participants are not translatable into statements that make no societal references and are devoid of concepts of status or role.[3] It makes no difference, furthermore, whether our inability to carry out these translations is a theoretical or merely a practical limitation. It does not matter whether the reason that sociological concepts cannot be translated into psychological concepts without remainder is that the former are irreducible in principle, or that the translations would be indefinitely long and would require knowledge we do not have. So long as we have to *use* the societal concepts to explain an individual's behavior when he enters a bank or courtroom, no analysis of the behavior that reduces it to psychological or other individualist terms will be relevant to explaining what is going on. If the meaning of an action is irreducibly social, then no attempt to replace the description of the act with one that bears no social meaning can explain the action that has taken place.

In fact, most of the defenders of methodological individualism have allowed the individual's relations with others and his beliefs about the social situation to figure into explanations of social phenomena. Popper's view is that "institutions (and traditions) must be analyzed in individualistic terms—that is to say, in terms of the relations of individuals acting *in certain situations,* and of the *unintended consequences* of their actions."[4] These situations and consequences, Popper makes clear, are often social in character. It is further conceded, by Watkins, that individuals referred to need not be any individuals in particular: "An explanation may be in terms of *typical* dispositions of more or less anonymous individuals."[5] These anonymous individuals are presumably identified by their role in social contexts.

Construed in such a broad fashion, methodological individualism has very little content, and is in fact fully compatible with Mandelbaum's conclusion that irreducibly societal facts are essential for understanding the actions of humans as members of society. It is not clear that anything is gained over speaking about institutional wholes directly by having the sentences in an explanation mention individuals' institutional roles, since such sentences will in any case either entail or presuppose propositions about social phenomena other than individuals.[6] Once it is acknowledged that individual social actions can be characterized only in terms of their institutional settings, it scarcely matters whether social phenomena are described in terms of the behavior of groups and collectives or in terms of the actions of appropriately situated individuals. And since the individuals whose actions are invoked are not expected to be identified in any way other than as persons who happen to occupy a role or be present in a situation, the force of so-called methodological individualism amounts to no more than a reminder that society and social structures are composed of and created by humans.

The methodological individualist's insistence that explanations of social phenomena are never ultimate or rock-bottom when they are couched in terms of the features of institutions or collectives represents not so much a thesis about explanatory adequacy as a claim about ultimacy. Methodological individualism is surely true if all it requires is that every explanation of a social occurrence, whether the phenomenon is a rise in the interest rate, the success of a religious reform movement, or the contraction of a national economy, can be explained in terms that refer only to the behavior of appropriately situated individuals. A more interesting methodological question is not whether such an "ultimate" explanation is possible, but whether such a reduction is either necessary or illuminating for the purposes of explanation, whether explanations that exhibit social phenomena as dependent on individuals are always *better* than explanations that stop at features of some system. It is easy to concede that every social event is ultimately comprised of individuals doing things, but it is quite another matter to insist that all facts about society must be explained solely in terms of facts about individuals.

One way to see that individualist explanations are not always better is to notice that when we extend an account so that it mentions agents' dispositions, doing so does not always enhance its explanatory value. In the first place, statements that express the behavior of typical individuals in terms of the logic of their social situations, as we have seen, are effectively interchangeable with statements about groups of institutional wholes: to appeal to a so-called individualist explanation may simply be to turn a holistic one inside out, as it were. Second, the dispositions we are likely to discover or ascribe to individuals behaving in a social context are often of no use in explaining why a certain social process has occurred as it has. This point has been made by Gellner, who uses as an example the fact that certain tribes have and are able to maintain over time a particular type of family organization called a segmentary patrilinear structure. It is no explanation to say that the tribesmen have

44

dispositions whose effect is to maintain that system. Any disposition that is specific enough to account for a particular cultural phenomenon will itself be a causal or logical consequence of the phenomenon it is supposed to explain.[r]

If, on the other hand, there is a plausible explanation for a particular social practice or cultural happening that can be given in terms of a general disposition, we will still need to explain why one manifestation of it rather than another has occurred. Differences between cultures, or between the political processes of different nations, are not explainable in terms of fundamental psychological traits; particular traditions and circumstances need to be cited. To the extent that this is true, an explanation that focuses on individual psychological elements and relegates the particular features to the status of background conditions will not be as good as one that accords prominence to societal facts. The maxims that methodological individualism offers do not always yield the most satisfying explanations.

Stripped of its ontological cutting edge, methodological individualism turns out to be a very dull instrument. In fact, the writings of methodological individualists such as Popper, Hayek, and Watkins reveal a strong animus toward theories that countenance nonhuman social entities. What these people object to is the idea that social wholes constitute a set of objects that are given to us as things to be studied and are governed by laws that are irreducibly sociological. However, the ax they are grinding is not so much an ontological as an ideological one; they are concerned to resist the idea that institutions and societies represent independent forces, that they have or should be accorded the power to run roughshod over the lives of individuals who might stand in their way. The enemy that methodological individualism is to be used against is any form of collectivist totalitarianism that can be perceived as a threat to laissez-faire liberalism and the idea that individuals can control and alter their environment, if they want to and if they possess the appropriate information. Methodological individualism is supposed to reaffirm the importance of the individual.

My concern here is not with the ideological issue, however, but rather with the question of what sort of entities one should be committed to if one is to have an adequate understanding of why people do what they do. Even if we grant that individual human beings are the most important things there are in the social domain, we need to consider how they are related to their institutional settings, and whether the behavior of putative suprahuman social entities is in some sense reducible to that of individuals. We have seen that the characterization of social action demands recognition of social facts; what is not yet clear is what this recognition commits us to with respect to the nature of social wholes. On the one hand, it seems reasonable to deny that there exist such things as collectives that move independently and thereby determine what happens to individuals within a society; on the other hand, it seems wrong to deny that institutions have lives of their own, in a sense, and that the way they develop does not affect the lives of individuals. Banks maintain policies that span the careers of several generations of employees, and markets fluctuate in ways that may not reflect the ideas or intentions of any of the participating individuals whose behavior produces the fluctuations. The fact that institutions and other social productions never move or vary without concomitant behavior on the part of human individuals does not imply that they are nothing but human instruments.

Institutions have a kind of autonomy, even on the terms of an individualist view such as Popper's. They are rarely if ever consciously designed at all, he points out, and even those that are have consequences that no one ever anticipated. Furthermore, these consequences include effects on people whose beliefs, desires, and expectations have been shaped and conditioned by their society's institutions. What Popper denies is that these institutions have aims and intentions: institutions have lives of their own, but they do not have minds of their own. The capacity of institutions to exert independent influence over the lives of individuals, Popper argues, consists entirely in their tendency to produce unintended and unforseen consequences.[8]

Popper's view of institutions is entirely consistent with and may even be entailed by his insistence that social phenomena can be explicated in terms of individual action and the logic of the situation. The power that he accords to social wholes, however, is enough to destroy much of the force of his own methodological individualism. For if institutions have effects on persons that neither their designers nor their practitioners could have anticipated, then they are indeed significant things to be reckoned with and there will be occasions in which it will be appropriate to treat institutions and not individuals on the independent variables in explanatory accounts. When we notice that serving in the Army can have a significant effect on a person, we are acknowledging that this effect is determined by the character of the military institution, not that of its operatives. Army discipline can have far-reaching consequences, and when these include effects that no one intended, the power of the institution is all the more impressive. A robot whose behavior is not fully predictable is a good deal more interesting (as well as more dangerous) than one that merely carries out the wishes of its creator. The fact that something has been created and sustained by humans does not prevent it from having ontological or explanatory significance, especially if its mentors cannot always know what to expect of it. The threat to individual liberty that holism poses according to the methodological individualist is not reduced by the latter's ability to represent the behavior of social wholes as unintended results of individual actions.

There is a reply that the methodological individualist can make at this point. He could argue that it is not social entities that determine what people do but rather their experiences in certain social situations; instead of saying that the army did certain things to someone or exerted an effect on him, we could say that his army experiences affected what he became and what he did. What institutions can be said to do to people can always be paraphrased in terms of events involving individuals in institutional settings. People's actions are influenced not by what supraindividual social entities do but by what people experience in the social situations in which they participate.

The reply is without force. So long as the experiences that individuals undergo and the actions they perform are identified in terms of social situations and these can only be rendered in terms of irreducible societal facts, nothing is gained by providing individualistic translations of these occurrences. Something that is made intelligible only by appealing to the forms of social organization involves the same commitment to the existence of social entities as does an account that directly refers to these social entities themselves. If social entities are eliminable as subjects only to reappear as entities referred to in predicates, it can only be pedantic to insist that they are susceptible to paraphrase in this fashion.

Sociologists who do not shrink from embracing social wholes often see fit to represent them as emergents, as having properties that arise from the behavior of individuals acting and interacting but that are not deducible from the biological or psychological characteristics of the individuals themselves. The notion of emergence has its most familiar associations with chemistry and biology; historically, it was first used in

47

the attempt to establish that the properties of living systems are not reducible to—and hence are not fully explicable in terms of—the physicochemical properties of matter. Applied to social science, the doctrine is supposed to amount to a recognition of the possibility for a social whole to have properties that can neither be predicated of individuals nor predicted on the basis of their independent behavior.

Many of the most ordinary facts of the universe are represented by emergence. The sound of two (or more) hands clapping, the texture of a woven fabric, the taste of a soup—all of these can be considered "emergents" in the sense that they may not have been anticipated on the basis of familiarity with the elements alone. There is nothing exceptionable about these claims, nor is there about the properties of chemical compounds, despite the fact that these properties may not have been predictable from a knowledge of the properties of the constituents taken separately. Since unpredictability of this sort is merely a manifestation of the commonplace that constellations of things behave differently from the way the individual things behave in isolation, all that has to be done to eliminate the unpredictability is to include some of the relational or combining properties of these properties along with their simple (nonrelational) properties. Emergence *must* occur, if the objects of any science are to be reckoned as aggregates of the objects of any other science.

Applied to social phenomena, the doctrine of emergence similarly amounts to very little. It is obvious that there are a number of properties that groups and institutions may be endowed with that cannot be attributed to individuals. In many cases the reason for this nonattributability is that the properties are collectively but not distributively attributable. A society may disintegrate, the stock market may crash, and a bureaucracy may expand, without being composed of disintegrating, crashing, and expanding persons. So long as the characteristics of the group or whole are understandable as connected in some plausible way with the behavior of the constituent individuals, there is nothing more mysterious involved than there is in the fact that a long, strong rope can be composed of short, weak fibers. If the slow-moving character of a legislative body made up of fast-talking, dynamic individuals is an instance of emergence, then emergence cannot be a deeply puzzling phenomenon.

Another kind of emergence that may seem more problematic is what has been called existential emergence, in which a new entity is supposed to arise whose properties are not explainable in terms of the properties of individuals. An example of this is Durkheim's "group mind," which is identified as the repository of collective sentiments and modes of representation that would never have arisen apart from group life and cannot be identified with any individual's actions, thoughts, or feelings.[9] What is problematic about such a case is not how there can arise such properties but whether the emergent itself need be assumed to exist. It is important to note that the emergent properties that allegedly occur are typically ones that *could* attach to individuals, whether or not they actually do. In the case where the "emergent" feature is one that is exhibited by one or more members of the collective, what we have is determination of individual dispositions by a social situation. Where there are no individuals who embody the collective feature, the case is similar to one already discussed, wherein the property is collectively but nondistributively attributable, the difference here being that we can talk about the group *as if* there were individuals who possessed the property. The point is that no such hypostatization as group mind is necessary to explain the features that are observed. There is no need to posit an existential emergent if it is possible, as I have suggested, to handle its putative properties as features of an aggregate of human individuals.

If social wholes exist, then there are things other than humans that comprise a subject matter for social science. That there are such things is what the nominalist or individualist denies. Thus Hayek considers it a mistake to treat social wholes such as a nation or an economic system or a society as definite objects on the grounds that they "are no more than constructions," mere "mental models."[10] Similarly, Popper stresses that the objects of social science are theoretical constructions that "are the result of constructing certain *models*...in order to explain certain experiences."[11] Like Hayek, he believes it would be an error to take such a theoretical model for a concrete thing, an error he associates with a tendency "to feel that we see it, either within or behind the changing observable means, as a kind of permanent ghost or essence."[12] It is precisely such entities that the emergentist is willing to countenance.

Popper and Hayek can be seen to go wrong in at least two ways in their attempt to deny ontological status to social wholes. One of these is traceable to a dubious conception of the status of theoretical entities in scientific knowledge. The questionable assumption that both make is

49

that what is constructed cannot be real. Models that we constitute are regarded as fictions that are devised for the sake of ordering concrete elements as we perceive them. Yet neither philosopher is willing to extend this view to its instrumentalist conclusion: Hayek, in asserting that "the wholes about which we speak exist only if, and to the extent to which, the theory is correct,"[13] is acknowledging that theories can be true and that when they are, they are about real existents. Popper, for his part, certifies that social wholes are theoretical in precisely the same sense that our models of atoms and molecules are: they represent the content of hypotheses that we imaginatively frame in order to explain certain experiences.[14] But the fact that theories and hypotheses are always provisional, that they "must be submitted to the method of selection by elimination,"[15] does not imply that they are never true or that they never refer to real unobservables. If a social theory that contains reference to social wholes were as well confirmed as are the theories of structural organic chemistry or biochemical genetics, there would be little reason, even on Popper's or Hayek's grounds, to deny that these social wholes exist.

The second way in which methodological individualists tend to go wrong about the status of "collectives" is in treating social institutions as theoretical models or hypothetical constructs at all. According to Popper, a nation or an army or the Supreme Court is merely something we hypothesize as a means of interpreting the behavior of concrete individuals. But as Winch has pointed out, it is simply not true that the concepts of these institutions are introduced to account for individual behavior, for they are themselves constitutive of the behavior in question.[16] We do not posit judicial institutions to explain what goes on in a courtroom; the behavior itself already presupposes the participants' awareness of these institutions. Citizens of a country at war must conceive of themselves as citizens of a country at war if that is what they are. In order for a person's actions to be correctly identifiable as a soldier's act of desertion or going on a scouting mission, that person must be a soldier and have acknowledged himself as one; there must already exist institutions that he recognizes and that define his role. The concepts of these institutions belong not only to the explanation but to the behavior as well. They are *internal* to it.

Institutions, therefore, must really exist as entities in the social domain. Individuals are no less dependent on institutions than institutions are on individuals. A social institution is neither a theoretical fiction nor something that can simply be identified with people or buildings, if only for the reason that institutions usually outlive any particular set of persons or things. A corporation is not the same as any specific set of individuals, nor can a language be identified with any particular group of speakers. Institutions, moreover, have observable features, such as the fireworks displays that are characteristic of certain holidays or the rituals that are associated with established religions. Because institutions are things that are constructed in actuality and not merely in theory, they constitute a set of objects that the student of society can observe and learn about.

On the other hand, what Popper and the methodological individualists say about institutions does have a degree of plausibility when applied to other social wholes. As far as social scientists have appealed to such notions as the Invisible Hand or the *Weltgeist* or the Group Mind as means of explaining whole patterns of individual social behavior they may very well be employing constructs that are in principle dispensable. Furthermore, Popper is quite right in suggesting that we need not believe in the independent existence of a construct in order for it to have explanatory use, at least on an informal level. It is surely possible to invoke the Invisible Hand (as that which causes production to decrease in response to diminished demand, for example) or the Collective Unconscious (as that which carries the accumulated normative principles from prior generations and distributes them among the members of a culture, thereby influencing their behavior) without being committed to the existence of these things or thinking that the business of social science is to chart their movements. There are at least some models that ought not to be taken literally, even if there are others that should be: just because one is not prepared to concede the existence of entities of a kind like Mother Nature, the Invisible Hand, or the Spirit of Capitalism, one need not eschew the use of such notions.

If there are any entities in the social domain whose status is that of theoretical constructs, they must have been postulated to explain facts that have been identified independently of the theory adduced. To suppose that such entities are real is to be committed to the view that what we observe are the manifestations of structures whose existence we can only infer; that is what we would be required to concede if we can be said to believe in the existence of an evil demon, a submicroscopic germ, or an unconscious desire. On a societal level, such a possible entity might be the *Geist* or the Group Mind. The case for admitting the existence of any of these things will be determined by the adequacy of the theory that posits it in accounting for the facts of human social life. The ontology that we accept for the social world can only be what we are justified in assuming to exist on the basis of what we see.

There is nothing objectionable in principle to positing theoretical entities, if they provide explanatory leverage not otherwise obtainable. Certainly chemistry and physics have achieved successes that would have been impossible without recourse to unobservables. The position I would defend with respect to the social sciences is that it is, in principle, an open question whether one ought to be committed to the existence of supraindividual entities in order to make social phenomena intelligible. Whether or not there are theoretically indispensable explanatory constructs in the social domain, whether there are unobservables analogous to atoms and molecules that social theory can plausibly claim to have discovered, will have to be determined on the basis of pragmatic considerations. If we take our ontological commitments to be determined by what we need to acknowledge in order to make sense of the phenomena we observe, we can say that social science must accept all and only those posits that our best explanations cannot do without.

The necessity beyond which entities ought not be multiplied in trying to determine what there is in the social universe is the necessity that refers to what an empirically adequate account of social phenomena requires. What Ockham's razor slices away are putative entities that do no work that cannot just as easily be assigned to things that already exist within the system. It is obviously gratuitous to invoke the existence of a Life Force to "explain" people's tendency, other things being equal, to avoid situations in which fatal injuries are likely to be incurred, or that of a Goddess of Transit as a means of accounting for the propensities of nations to build highways and dig subways. It is equally true that economists can get along quite well without the notion of the Invisible Hand, and that social historians can talk about change without adverting to the movements of the *Geist*. Whatever happens can be readily paraphrased in terms of what is done by individuals, groups of individuals, and institutions. Anything that can be gotten rid of without trace by means of paraphrase is not something that we need to count as a real existent.

More problematic as candidates for inclusion in a social ontology are the putative collective entities that some social theorists seem to have embraced, such as group minds and impersonal social and economic forces. For if a social group can be said to possess a tendency or attitude that can be ascribed to no one within the group, must there not be a nonhuman entity to which these properties can be ascribed? Not necessarily; we do not need to posit a group mind to explain the behavior of a group. A group is not itself a theoretical entity, even though it has features that are not distributively attributable to its members. The notion of a group mind may provide a way of talking about the behavior of group members that takes into account the fact that individuals behave in different ways when they are in groups, but it is not something we need to treat as an independent entity.

Because there has been much casual mention of the ineluctable course of history or the irresistible forces of the market, some people have come to believe that holists—those who talk in terms of such wholes—maintain that the individuals whose actions these processes embrace are coerced into behaving in ways contrary to what they intend. According to the approach to the question of supraindividual social entities being taken here, social forces, though sometimes useful as explanatory devices, do not need to be reckoned as real entities. They are not the independent variables of social life; people are not in fact dragged along by impersonal social forces against their will. The fact that a person's modesty may have forced him to decline an offer does not imply that he refused it involuntarily. Similarly, we need not suppose that what our training or upbringing forces us to do involves the overpowering of our will; rather we should say that these things, so far as we speak of them at all, work *through* our actions. The same may be said for the grand posits of a social theory.

History is not like geological transformation, wherein changes are imposed on the creatures of the world by things that are not creatures themselves. Social interaction is never other than between people, whether it involves people qua individuals or qua occupiers of institutional roles. What happens to people in the social sphere is done to them by people, not by impersonal forces. On the other hand, the independent variables that need to be identified in order to understand human social life are often not individuals, but institutions, for these are what constitute the actions of individuals acting in a social setting. Recognizing institutions as real allows one to say that it is the ruling of a court (or a judge whose action owes its meaning to the institution of the court) that triggers off a set of reactions by parents of schoolchildren, and that it is the ending of the military draft (done by officers of the government) that accounts for a decrease in enrollment in colleges and universities. Yet it is always individuals who are responsible for what institutions do; that is the kernel of truth in the methodological individualists' claim that institutions are not to be credited with aims, interests, and intentions beyond those of the individuals acting in their behalf. Nations, and not individuals, are what wage wars and conquer territories, save insofar as the individuals act in the name of their nations, but individuals are what can be held responsible if anything can. The reason it makes sense to ascribe responsibility to individuals for the effects produced by institutions is that there is no piece of institutional behavior that cannot be represented as the action of some (appropriately situated) individual or other; that is a consequence of the broad conception of action that I have been defending. If individuals are to be blamed for the destruction caused by an army or for the exploitation arising within an economic system, or to be praised for the success of a corporate merger or an environmental-protection program, it must be individuals who are to be credited with acting.

Institutions typically develop in ways that are neither foreseen nor intended by anyone. There are also patterns of institutional change that are even farther removed from the consciousness of individuals whose actions these changes reflect. Social changes may have an order that is not at all apparent to the individuals who participate in them and whose lives they affect. It is often useful and tempting to view such second-order processes as though they are the work of an unseen hand or transcendent force, but because we can resist doing so, we need not be committed to believing that there is some invisible agent or prime mover that makes them happen. There is no need to posit something to orchestrate the structural changes in human societies, just as there is no need (if the neo-Darwinian theory is correct) to posit a Creator to orchestrate biological evolution. If processes that no one designed and changes that no one planned can be understood as arising from the cumulative effects of circumstances on institutions, it is unnecessary to invoke any sort of theoretical entity as the driving force of history.

Human individuals, so far as their identity depends on their institutional roles, are noncontingently related to the societies to which they belong. Because behavior that is specifically human has significance only when it presupposes institutions and social practices, individuals are integral parts of their societies. The thesis that individuals are ultimate is therefore also a thesis about institutions, since individual human actions are unintelligible when conceived in solely individualist terms. An individual is a human person only in a setting of social institutions; it is only by virtue of having made such things as institutions that the species has become human. That humankind is everywhere social implies that human institutions as well as human beings are constitutive of social reality. A world without institutions, envisioned by Hobbes, is not a world in which human life is "solitary, poor, nasty, brutish, and short": it is a world in which there is no human life.

# 4. Reasons and Social Inquiry

Once we have identified what there is in the world of social phenomena, we may begin to ask why things are the way they are. The job of a social science is not merely to present the data but to explain it. A science should tell us what goes on in a certain domain, why certain configurations of properties and relations occur and not others, and how the events that take place come to be the ones that happen. A social science, if one is possible, would render the phenomena of human social life intelligible: its achievement would be the fulfillment of the promise of a systematic understanding of why people do as they do.

What the human sciences study are actions, practices, and institutions. The explanation of a phenomenon is something that serves to illuminate it, typically by citing some other event or circumstance. For social phenomena, as for phenomena in general, many kinds of information need to be gathered, depending on the nature of the thing to be explicated. If, for example, we want to know why Bertrand Russell acted in support of Britain's participation in the Second but not the First World War, we should like to know his reasons; whereas if we seek to understand why a particular tribe permits matrilateral but not patrilateral first-cousin marriages, or why the women in certain societies wear their hair longer than men do, we would not expect to gain much by looking for reasons, at least not of the sort that might be learned through interviews. Different sorts of evidence are required for the explanation of different sorts of phenomena; what we look for to explain a change in the rate of inflation or unemployment seems to bear little similarity to what we consider in trying to explain homosexual behavior or criminal recidivism.

The kinds of explanations that are sought in any inquiry are determined not only by the nature of the phenomena but also by the concerns of those who provide them or are expected to accept them. One is often confronted with competing claims as to how a given phenomenon is to be investigated. There tends to be controversy over where to look for explanations—for example, whether the causes of phenomena such as student rebellion, popular endorsement of an authoritarian regime, suicide, or depopulation of cities are to be found by considering the psychological traits of the persons or groups involved or by examining the societies in which they live. The approach taken may depend to a large extent on the interests of the investigators and on the uses to be made of the information that is yielded. If the floor of an overcrowded mountain lodge collapses, or a fire inside a space capsule still on the launching pad kills all the occupants, it is the decision as to what is to be considered most important that will determine what an investigator concentrates on, whether to focus on the structural and mechanical aspects of the matter or the circumstances that led to the presence of people in these potentially dangerous situations. Similarly, a decision whether to seek psychological or sociological data to try to explain a student's disaffection with the goals he was expected to pursue may depend on one's relative preferences for dealing with individuals or with social structures.

Human affairs are not unique, of course, in failing to reveal a single factor or chain of circumstances the identification of which is sufficient to show why a particular state of affairs has obtained or an event has occurred. Any event or situation, whether it is the crashing of an airplane, the spanking of a child, or the collapse of a government, can be located at the intersection of a number of streams of event sequences and within an environment of conditions, circumstances, and background regularities that constitute its context. To offer an account of why X happened or why Y is the case is to pick out something that one expects will satisfy the curiosity of the inquirer. The art of scientific investigation, in the natural sciences no less than in history and the social sciences, is that of selecting for inclusion in a putative explanation whatever is best able to make the thing being investigated intelligible.

In the human domain there is an added dimension that gives a still greater range of possibilities to explanations of what goes on there. Actions are accounted for in terms of not only the events that precede them and the circumstances that surround them but also the reasons for doing them. When a person performs an act that we wish to have explained such as committing a crime or liquidating a business, we may want to know the events and conditions that comprise the antecedents of the action, or we may seek the reasons or motives the agent had for doing as he did. Similarly, the existence of laws governing property ownership or of practices involving religious or economic institutions may be explained either in terms of what led to their adoption or in terms of the goals and intentions of those who created them. The social world has a teleological character that is reflected in the character of some of its explanations.

Knowing the ends or purposes of people's behavior comprises a large part of knowing what they are doing. We typically assume that what is done is done for a reason, that is, in order that some state of affairs may be either brought about or prevented. To understand what someone is doing often depends on knowing why he is doing it. We cannot even identify most actions without at least implicitly indicating the reason or purpose of the behavior that is being considered. One does not merely push a button; one pushes it for a reason, a reason that may be revealed in describing the action as one of turning off a machine or ringing a doorbell.

If the concept of explanation is taken in its broadest sense, then anything that serves to make clear an initially puzzling piece of behavior can be said to explain it. This will include giving the reason for an action merely by redescribing it. The reason someone turns a screw on a carburetor, for example, is revealed by redescribing the act as one of increasing the idling speed, and the reason for doing that is expressed by redescribing the act as one of eliminating stalling at traffic lights. Redescription amounts to providing an alternative specification of an action in a way that picks out features that are internal to its conception that were not mentioned in the original specification. Reasons thus treated are logically inseparable from the actions they are associated with. Where there is a different reason, there is a different action: digging a hole for burial purposes is a different action from digging a hole that is to be used as a barbecue pit.

In fact, a major concern of certain branches of social science, such as anthropology, is simply trying to understand behavior well enough to redescribe it. Much of social inquiry involves the attempt to discover the meaning or significance of actions. When we see a person pressing buttons or enclosing himself in a small booth, what we expect to receive in response to asking why he is doing these things is a broader characterization than the one we had initially used to pick out the behavior. The sort of answer that satisfies us is typically one that tells us merely *what* he is doing in terms of a wider context of goals and practices. Redescription is used by psychologists, sociologists, and anthropologists when they try to say in a more significant way what an individual or group is doing. There are many ways of talking about the behavior of a political leader who is responding to challenges to his competence or integrity, or that of a fiercely competitive entrepreneur in an emerging industrial society; these represent different efforts to capture significance through description and redescription.

So far as redescription serves to make social behavior more intelligible, it does so not by pointing to elements or aspects that were previously ignored but by ascribing a sense to the behavior and providing it with a meaning-context. Such redescription "fills out" the description of what has happened. One who is unfamiliar with a description that merely quotes utterances and mentions only bodily parts and external objects will not understand what is being done, say, in a courtroom scene or marriage ceremony. Redescription does not explain a piece of puzzling behavior in the sense of indicating what caused it, but merely makes its meaning clear. And because the meaning of an action, unlike its consequences, is not something that is logically separable from it, proper redescription is crucial to adequate characterization of the basic phenomena of any science that can be expected to help us understand actions.

It is true that redescription occurs in the natural sciences as well, but there it plays a logically and epistemologically different role. A dark area on a microscopic slide may need to be redescribed as a cell nucleus, and a line on a piece of photographic film may have to be redescribed as a sodium D-line; there is, furthermore, a sense in which the trained observer can be said to have recognized the "meaning" of what was present. In cases like these, however, redescription is intended to reveal something about the causal origin or causal dispositions of the thing being examined. Phenomena are thus represented as effects, as contingently linked to other events and states of affairs. To assign meaning to a piece of behavior by identifying it as an action of some sort, on the other hand, is not supposed to indicate what brought it about;

rather it is to say what the agent was actually doing. What gives a series of marks on a crystallographer's X-ray photograph their "meaning" is a set of causal facts; what gives a sequence of bodily movements their meaning as action to an observer of human behavior is that this *is* their meaning, knowledge of which is based not on observation of causal regularities but rather on familiarity with the institutions and social practices that define the act performed.

It has been remarked that observation reports, even in the natural sciences, count for very little when they are couched in the most basic or least theoretical terms; the freer an account is from interpreting the less informative it is.[1] A description of a physicochemical process in terms of colors and shapes, like that of a piece of behavior in terms of movements of limbs, tells very little about what is actually going on. There is an important difference, however, in the ways that the natural and the human sciences render phenomena meaningful through full-blown or interpretive description. In the case of the former, we may say that descriptions assign *causal* meaning to the phenomena observed, whereas in the case of the latter, at least with respect to action descriptions, what is ascribed is *semantic* meaning. The distinction is revealed in the difference between the meaning of an array of skin blemishes suddenly appearing in the face of a child and the meaning of a white flag raised in battle. Surrendering is not a *consequence* of hoisting a white flag; it is what one is *doing* in so behaving. So far as human actions are concerned, the claim is that these have meanings in the way that utterances do and occurrences in the insensate domain do not. Redescription in the human sciences serves not so much to clarify what may have been causally puzzling as to reveal or enlarge on the semantic content of what was previously incompletely specified. Such redescription amounts to elaboration of what is internal to the action event, as opposed to representing its connections with events and circumstances that are external to it.

If redescription were all there is to explaining human actions, there would not be much point in speaking of a possible science of action. Not all reason-explanation is redescription, however, and there are many cases for which it is very doubtful whether reasons can always be packed into action descriptions. A person can perform a given action for any of several reasons, and different people can perform the action for different reasons. Furthermore, one can have good or bad reasons for performing an action. The only way we can accommodate facts such as these is to suppose that reasons are identifiable separately from the actions they are called upon to explain. An important part of social inquiry may have to be the search for reasons for actions that have already been identified.

Recognition of the fact that reasons are distinguishable from the (rational) actions they explain has given rise to the suggestion that we interpret reasons as causes and reason-explanation as a species of ordinary causal explanation.[2] Behind this suggestion is a certain analysis of doing something for a reason: to do something for a reason implies having some sort of "pro attitude" (such as a desire or want) toward actions of a certain kind and a belief that one's action is of that kind. Assigning a reason for an action, therefore, consists in finding wants or desires that the agent has that, given certain of his beliefs, are what cause him to perform the action in question.

Beliefs and desires *rationalize* the actions they explain, as Davidson has put it: they place the action in a favorable light, provide an account of the reasons the agent had in acting, and allow us to reconstruct the intention with which he acted.[3] However, as Richard Norman has pointed out, there are important constraints on what can count as a reason.[4] Not just any want or desire can provide a reason for acting, and not all wants are explanatory, because some wants are irrational or unintelligible. Thus Anscombe asks us to consider the example of someone who says that he wants a saucer of mud, but denies that he wants it *for* anything, or that it has any aspect for which it is desirable.[5] Such a want cannot be a reason for anyone's action, because it is not a reasonable want. Likewise, a woman who says that it was her desire to be surrounded by dead bodies that made her kill all the members of her family has not given a reason for her action. Wants and desires, in order to be explanatory, must *already* be reasonable.

The point that I want to make is not merely that there are wants that will not serve as reasons for performing actions, but that reasons cannot simply be characterized in terms of wants and beliefs alone. If wants have to be reasonable or rational in order to be explanatory of actions, then reasons must be logically prior to wants. Rationalization of actions requires something more: conformity to a set of rational norms.[6] Every assignment of reasons for actions contains an implicit appeal to public standards of rationality, and these are what makes the wants that are cited as reasons intelligible and hence explanatory.

61

The idea that reasons must be tied to norms has led some people to think that the connection between reasons and action should be construed as much looser than a causal analysis implies.[7] For if providing a reason is understood as showing a connection between the action and a norm, then a reason does not need to be seen as something that impels a person to act. Reasons explain, not by showing that the thing done had to happen, but by representing the action as appropriate under the circumstances. Having reasons for acting is not always sufficient to get one to act, even when one has no reasons for acting. Unlike wants, which do entail action provided there are no conflicting wants or circumstances, reasons may be supposed to lack the force to bring anything.

Yet wants sometimes are reasons, and they are what get people to act. The reason someone turns off the motor of his car while waiting at a railroad crossing, for example, may be that he wants to save gasoline. It is true that only reasonable wants can explain actions, but these reasonable wants are often what impel one to action. Giving someone a reason—an offer one can't refuse—may be precisely the thing that causes him to act. Providing reasons *must* have force under certain circumstances if rational argument can be construed as anything other than a mere pastime. Explanations of actions in terms of reasons, so far as reasons are what get people to act, turn out to be a form of causal explanation after all.

So reasons may be cited to explain actions in a variety of ways. In some instances, giving reasons is done merely by redescribing the action. In other cases, explaining a person's actions in terms of his reasons consists in showing how his behavior is appropriate in the context in which it occurs. A third way in which reasons explain is as causal conditions of actions. If reasons are causes, and rationalization is a species of causal explanation, as Davidson has suggested, then the explanation of human action may be of a piece with explanation in the natural sciences.

According to the "standard" or covering-law view of scientific explanation (mentioned in Chapter 1), explanation consists of a set of statements (the *explanans*) that include one or more universal laws that together with a statement of antecedent conditions, allow the deduction of the description of the event to be explained (the *explanandum*). Ordinarily the explanation of an event takes the form of citing some prior event that can be linked with the explanandum by means of a causal law. Thus the discoloration of a piece of fabric may be explained by exposure to sunlight, which, given the law-governed nature of the effects of solar radiation on certain chemicals, caused the colors to fade. If reasons explain actions in the way that antecedent occurrences explain events in nature and in artifacts, it must be possible to assimilate reason-explanations to the same formal model.

The principal issue in the matter of whether reason-explanations arc like causal explanations in natural science is whether such explanations employ general laws. It is clear that reasons for acting must have generality or universality; if something is intelligible as a reason for one person performing a given action in a certain situation, it must also count as a reason for anyone in a similar situation. Some sort of general principle is therefore presupposed in every rational explanation, but it does not follow that it has to be a general law. Dray has argued that the principle involved is a *principle of action,* the form of which is "When in a situation of type C1...Cn the thing to do is x."[8] What the phrase "the thing to do" signifies is a normative element. Thus, according to Dray, reason-explanations differ from explanations in natural science in that they rely on principles that do not describe, but appraise.

Hempel, on the other hand, has argued that this element of appraisal can be eliminated from rational explanations by replacing evaluative principles by descriptive generalizations.[9] A rational explanation is interpreted as employing not a principle that tells us what is the thing to do in situation C, but rather a statement of how a rational agent will act in situations of that kind. Such a statement, he maintains, together with the assumption that the agent is rational, will enable us to deduce the occurrence of the action to be explained. We thus appear to be able to explain why A did x by showing his action to be a reflection of an empirical regularity.

Hempel's empirical generalizations are supposed to indicate what rational agents will do in certain kinds of situations. These are not simply propositions that express empirical regularities; they are rather statements of connections that must already be acknowledged as rational. To take one of Dray's examples (drawn from Trevelyan), one may ask: What sort of descriptive generalization could Hempel cite in explaining that, because of early-eighteenth-century smog conditions in London, William, England's weak-lunged king, lived at Hampton Court as much as he could? Presumably, one would use some such generalization as "Rational persons with respiratory ailments avoid sources of irritation whenever possible." But since what makes an action rational, according to Hempel, is that "it offers optimal prospects of achieving its objectives,"[10] the principle on which the explanation relies cannot be simply an empirical generalization. That people always act in such a way as to maximize expected utility is an empirical generalization, probably false; that rational people do so is a necessary truth, given a certain concept of rationality. To explain the king's living at Hampton Court by appealing to a statement of what rational persons do, therefore, is not to subsume his behavior under a descriptive generalization but rather to show that it has instantiated a particular concept of rationality.

It might be objected at this point that the principle that people act to maximize their expected utility, even though it is not free from exceptions, does nevertheless explain a large number of actions. It expresses an empirical regularity that every attempt at rational explanation must call upon. Whenever we explain a piece of actual behavior by displaying its rationale, it may be argued, we have to assume an empirical principle such as this one; to show an act to be rational, we need to show that it fits under a generalization about what people in fact do.

It is true that this concept of rationality does have empirical content, and that any attempt to show that behavior is rational presupposes this content. But it is important to notice that the general law that is invoked here is so general as to be capable of explaining any rational action whatever. What is lacking is an explanation of why one action rather than another was performed. If there are any covering laws that can be used to show how reasons explain actions, they will have to be statements that connect specific reasons with particular kinds of actions. The problem is that there appear to be no such laws. Not everybody responds in the same way to a given threat or encouragement. We simply do not know of any general laws under which we can subsume reasons and the actions they explain.

Davidson has offered a way out of this difficulty by arguing that giving a causal explanation does not require being able to state a law, but requires only that some law be presupposed that connects the causally related events under some description.[11] Thus to believe that a person's death was caused by a blow to the head of a certain severity requires not that one know a law connecting blows on the head with death, but only that one believe that there are lawlike connections between phenomena such as have been observed. Therefore, according to this view, in order for reasons to explain actions causally, it is not necessary to know of any laws connecting reasons and actions; all we need is to believe that there is a law statable in some theory—chemical or neurological, perhaps—under which the events that have been picked out can be subsumed. We do not need to know any covering law in order to know that two events are causally linked.

I believe that Davidson's proposal works for our understanding of causal connections between such events as the shattering of a window and its being struck by a rock, or a boxer falling down and his receiving a punch, but that its applicability to reasons and actions is doubtful. In cases of the former type, we do depend on our belief in the existence of a lawlike connection between events of that sort to support the idea that one occurrence was in fact caused by the other, whereas in cases involving reasons and actions we need to have no such belief in a lawlike connection. Suppose we are told that the reason a teacher threw a small boy out of a classroom is that the boy was belching loudly and repeatedly. We do not have to believe in the existence of any laws governing these occurrences in order to accredit the reason given as an explanation for the teacher's action. We accept the explanation because we recognize the action as appropriate under the circumstances. The appeal that such an explanation makes is not to laws but to norms of rational action. The knowledge that is operative in assessing reasons is concerned not with which phenomena are causally linked but with what is reasonable. We need to make a judgment or appraisal, as Dray has put it, that what was done was the thing (or an appropriate thing) to have done for the reason given.[12]

It is therefore not a belief in the existence of descriptive generalizations that allows us to recognize reasons as causes of actions but rather the acknowledgment of explanatory norms. Whether empirical regularities exist or not, normative principles are what do the work in enabling us to accept or reject putative reason-explanations. What makes a reason unsatisfactory may be the strangeness of a desire—consider the case of someone offering as the reason why he shaved his head that he wanted to alter the consistency of yak dung—or it may be the implausibility of a belief concerning the connections between one's actions and one's goals. An explanation has to make sense, not just to the agent, but to anyone who is to grasp his reasons for acting. The reasons stated must be good or sufficient reasons if they are to explain.

The idea that rational explanations must be anchored in social norms may be illustrated by a few examples. One of these involves the explanation of sunbathing: we want to know why some people in some societies seek to acquire a suntan. If we ask individual sunbathers for their reasons, we shall probably be told only that people like the suntanned look, that it makes them more attractive. For a social investigator to stop at such an "explanation" would obviously be unsatisfactory. It is certainly not an objective, culture-independent fact that people do look better after they have acquired suntans. To say that people pursue suntans because they *believe* they will thereby make themselves more attractive, on the other hand, is true but not very informative—although it does rule out other possible reasons, such as health. The explanation is more valuable for what it presupposes than for what it states, namely that improving one's attractiveness is a reasonable objective in that culture and that acquiring a tan is one recognized way of attaining it. Reasons, through referring to public norms, allow us to represent individual behavior in terms of acknowledged practices, thereby helping us to understand it.

Another kind of example is that of the judge who resigns from the bench in order to enter private legal practice. The reason given, that he believes (correctly) that he can make substantially more money as an attorney than as a judge, is explanatory only if both the agent and the investigator grasp the norm according to which high salaries are valued less than higher ones. In order for the action to be explained as rational, it is not enough to establish that it seemed rational to the agent; one cannot be said to explain an action in terms of reasons if one does not think they would be good reasons for anyone else in a similar situation. Thus we would probably not consider it an adequate explanation of the judge's behavior if we were told that his reason was that he was tired of wearing black.

Social norms represent an important element in the background of the explanation even of irrational actions. If a rational action is one that is appropriate to a certain set of circumstances and beliefs and desires, an irrational action is one that is inappropriate in one way or another. Such

66

an action is not necessarily one that is done for no reason, but may be one that is done for bad reasons. A bad reason is one that does not justify the action in question. Such a reason will go part of the way in explaining the action, however. Having someone cut into a gasoline line ahead of one is not a good reason for shooting him—the response is obviously a disproportionate one—but knowing that that was the reason does help to explain a killing under those circumstances. We could not even begin to understand such an action if we did not know the reason that motivated it. What makes the reason explanatory for us at all is that we are familiar with the norms that determine when anger is justified and what counts as an appropriate response. We can understand the extreme reaction because we can understand a moderate one.

When the reasons that are given for an action fail to explain it completely, it is because those reasons do not suffice to show the act to have been something that a person in that situation might reasonably be expected to do. When this happens, we assume either that the reason stated is not the real or true reason, or that the explanation needs to be supplemented by other information that has not been provided. We know, for example, that the reason that explains why someone has canceled a magazine subscription after ten years cannot *just* be a change in the magazine's format. Benefiting from a neighbor's testimony in a successful civil suit is a reason that explains why one takes that neighbor out to dinner; merely receiving directions to the nearest post office is not. Rational explanation requires there to be a proportionateness between actions and their antecedents, and this proportionateness is determined by culture-based standards of rational response.

It has sometimes been remarked that reasons are typically cited to *justify* actions, whereas (other kinds of) causes are invoked to explain them. The account of explanation in terms of reasons that is being presented here accords with the spirit of this observation, but only to the extent that it implies that reasons explain in a different way than (other) causes do, and that the former kind of explanation involves an element of appraisal. To accept a reason-explanation for an action is to accept a justification only so far as one accepts the norms on which the explanation rests. I have argued that reasons explain only through implicit reference to norms, and that they are unintelligible in the absence of such reference. It does not follow, however, that the norms need to be shared or accepted by the investigator in order for them to be identified. Therefore it is not necessary to justify an action in order to explain it in terms of reasons, but only to see how it might be justified by someone who did accept the social norms on which the explanation rests.

Explanations of actions that give the agent's reasons for acting presuppose norms, and these norms are what make the connections between the agent's wants and his actions intelligible. It is important to notice that the norms themselves do not occur as elements in reason-explanations; their place is rather in the background. They are like the background assumptions that are required for any successful act of communication in that they must be grasped in order for what is said to be comprehended. Rational norms are what a listener must tacitly invoke as the means of completing the connection between actions and the reasons that are offered to explain them.

It also deserves to be pointed out that these norms of rational intelligibility serve not to explain the actions themselves but only to provide a backing for rational explanation. Since a given action may be in conformity with any of several norms, and since often there are conflicting norms, citing a norm cannot explain why that action was done, even if that is the norm that the act was done in conformity with. All that I am claiming is that reasons must be backed by norms if they are to explain. When giving a reason explains an action that has occurred, it does so not in virtue of an empirical generalization that may be invoked, but rather because there is a norm, a principle of acceptable action, that any plausible reason-imputation must implicitly appeal to. The part that norms play in the rational explanation of actions is not to explain why what was done was done, but rather to set constraints on what can count as a reason for acting.

To investigate actions rationally means looking for reasons. One of the most salient features of the task of imputing reasons for actions is the fact that in order for an assigned reason to be explanatory, it must be a reason *for* the agent. The purpose or end of the action must be *his* purpose or end, and the beliefs that connect the act to its objectives must be *his* beliefs. If a person goes with his family to a park on a Saturday afternoon and thereby enables another person to burglarize his house, facilitating a burglary was presumably not his reason for going to the park. Nor will an investigation of why he went to the park pursue someone else's reasons for enticing him there. When we look for reasons, we concentrate on the agent, not on things outside the agent.

One of the things that seem to follow from the proposition that reason-explanations must be agent centered is that only the agent is in a position to know his reasons for acting, and therefore the best way we can discover what these reasons are is by paying attention to what he has to say about his actions. Although we are often able to infer a person's reasons for acting on the basis of observations of his behavior and its environment, the only way we can be sure of his reasons, so it might be argued, is to have access to his own sincere testimony. The assignment of reasons for actions would then appear to rest on the incorrigibility of first-person reports, so that a social science that is concerned with discovering reasons must pursue a method of eliciting direct testimony as the means of understanding people's reasons for their actions.

Social science does devote a good deal of attention to interrogating individuals as to their reasons for behaving as they do. It is not only journalists who are interested in reporting what people give as their reasons for voting a certain way or for joining or rejecting a particular movement, but sociologists and political scientists as well. Historians, who are not ordinarily in a position to conduct interviews, often rely heavily on their subjects' written expressions of their beliefs as indications of reasons for acting.

If people always knew what they were doing and why they did it, social science would be extremely easy. Unfortunately, a number of considerations make it impossible to have a social science based on professed reasons. In the first place, it is often the case when an action is performed that either no reason at all can be elicited or else the reasons that are given are so banal as to be uninformative. People are not usually called upon to justify or rationalize their actions, and when they are, the "reasons" that are brought forth typically include such responses as "because I was told to" or "because it seemed like a good thing to do." Second, since a given action may be done for several reasons, testimony, even when it does not involve deliberate misrepresentation ordinarily involves a selection based on extrinsic considerations, with the result that a person may give a different reason for performing the same action on different occasions even though the circumstances may be the same. A person may even offer mutually incompatible reasons for performing a single action.

A third problem associated with accepting professed reasons as reasons that explain actions is that the agent may simply be mistaken as to what his real reasons are. A young man who courts a woman of higher social station may honestly believe that enhancing his position is not a reason for his having chosen to pursue this particular woman; statistical studies of such cases, on the other hand, may suggest that he and many others like him are simply mistaken as to their reasons or motives. A judge who decides a lawsuit in favor of a firm in which he holds stock may believe that he has made his decision solely on the merits of the arguments presented; yet an investigation of his susceptibility to similar arguments in other cases may indicate that the real reason he decided as he did was to favor one party to the dispute. Agents, even when sincere, are notoriously unreliable sources for discovering their own reasons for acting because they often do not know what motivates them.[13]

Looking for reasons is the way we try to explain actions that we take to be rational. If reasons must always be present to the agent's consciousness, and first-person ascriptions of reasons are necessarily incorrigible, then the search for reasons will yield only very meager accounts of human action, and the range of reason-explanations will be quite limited. Since there are, as I have tried to show, serious objections to basing explanations of actions entirely on agents' own accounts of their reasons for acting, either reasons will need to be interpreted as capable of operating on an unconscious as well as a conscious level or else explanations in terms of reasons will have to be relegated to a minor role in accounting for why people act as they do.

An argument against recognizing unconscious reasons has been presented by Peter Alexander, who tries to show that psychoanalytic explanations that appeal to them are not properly understood as a species of rational explanation.[14] In order to explain a piece of someone's behavior in terms of a reason, Alexander reminds us, the reason must be *his* reason. He takes this to imply that the agent must be able to discover the reason or to recognize it when it is suggested to him as having influenced his behavior. It is implausible, he argues, to maintain that a patient undergoing psychoanalysis can be said to *recognize* the reasons that he may (reluctantly) come to accept as a reason of the psychoanalytic process. It is more plausible, he believes, to suppose that the reasons that he "discovers" were not really his reasons at the time and that the behavior they are invoked to explain can better be explained in causal rather than rational terms.

Lurking at the core of Alexander's objection to acknowledging unconscious reasons seems to be the implicit rhetorical question: What can it possibly mean for a reason to be *his* reason, if he cannot recognize it as such? An answer, which Alexander does not consider, is that it is a function of the agent's beliefs and desires. Whether or not such things as unconscious desires ought to be acknowledged depends, first, on whether humans exhibit purposive behavior of a kind that is similar to that which expresses conscious desires but is unaccompanied by such conscious states, and second, whether ontological commitment to such explanatory posits is warranted. The former is an empirical matter, and the latter is not relevant to the question at hand: the issue is whether unconscious desires, and hence unconscious reasons, can explain in the way conscious ones do, not whether we are justified in postulating their existence. There is no *logical* reason why a reason that one has forgotten or repressed cannot be identified as one's real reason for performing a particular action.[15]

Unconscious reason, it should be noted, plays an important part not only in psychoanalysis but in everyday affairs as well. It is a commonplace that people are sometimes mistaken as to their reasons and motives and that they undergo self-deception. It is not at all odd, for example, to find a parent who sends his children to an exclusive private school because (he thinks) of the superior academic training it affords when he is in fact motivated by a desire for prestige, or a politician who takes a certain stand on an issue concerning the allocation of tax reductions because he thinks that that is the fairest arrangement, when in fact the reason is that he believes that taking this stand is most likely to help him gain reelection. We do say, after all, that there are some things that people cannot admit even to themselves.

What makes certain explanations that cite considerations of which the agent is unaware a species of reason-explanation is that these considerations explain in the same way that conscious reasons do: they *rationalize* the action by pointing to relevant wants and beliefs that, given the background of norms, show the action to be appropriate. Because the paradigm of rational explanation is one that shows an action as having been performed for a reason of which the agent is conscious, explanations in terms of unconscious reasons are parasitic upon explanations in terms of conscious ones. In order to ascribe unconscious reasons to someone—say, to a professor who sincerely believes that the reason he demands no written work of his students is that he doubts the educational value of such assignments (when his real reason is that he does not want to be bothered with having to read them)—one must be able to understand the unconscious reason as though it were a conscious one.

What makes a reason the real or correct reason if not the honest testimony of the agent? The answer is that it must be the reason, or one of the reasons that got him to do something. If reasons are a kind of cause, the real reason is the one that *caused* the action. It is the one that made the difference between performance and nonperformance of the action *in that instance*. A professed reason is not a real reason if the act would have occurred even if what was professed was false; a professed reason is not the complete reason if there are other reasons that were also necessary for the act to occur.

How can we know that something is a reason for an action, if the agent himself cannot? We can know by seeing whether it in fact explains why he did it, as opposed to merely appearing to explain it. Suppose a man were to take steps to prevent his wife from accepting an attractive job offer, believing that his reason for doing so was concern for the welfare of their children. If it also turned out that he would allow her to take a less prestigious or less high-paying job, or that there is other evidence that shows he does not believe the children would in fact suffer as a result of their mother's being employed, then it is likely that there is a reason for his actions other than the one he professes—such as wanting to maintain his position of dominance within the family. To ascribe a reason for an action is to offer an explanatory hypothesis, the test of which is its consistency with other things the agent does and with his own established patterns of beliefs and desires.

All explanations must be based on evidence, if they are to be believable. Whether or not a person can be convinced that his true reasons for performing a particular action are not the reasons he has professed will depend on how he weighs whatever behavioral evidence may be adduced, or whether he accepts such evidence as relevant at all. Someone who is willing to admit that the reason he originally gave may be incorrect necessarily concedes that external evidence, including his own utterances, may be relevant. If he fails to be convinced by the evidence, he may possibly be mistaken. If, on the other hand, he denies that anyone else can possibly know what his real reasons are, then he is a candidate for irremediable self-deception. In either case, there is the possibility that a person may be unaware of his reasons for acting as he does.

Reasons are a subject for investigation, therefore, to be studied not merely by examining first-person reports as dreams are, but to be investigated more in the manner of physical causes. The way to find out why the man in our earlier example tried to keep his wife from taking a certain job is to try to discover, by considering other aspects of his behavior, what his desires really are, and to see whether the behavior he exhibits is consistent with the desires he professes. There is an important difference, however, between looking for reasons in this way and looking for causes in other domains. When we identify relevant desires, we do so by appealing to a rational paradigm, that is, by seeing what desires enable us to see the behavior as rationally intelligible. We do not need to recognize empirical regularities, as we would, for example, in the identification of smoking cigarettes as a cause of lung cancer. What makes a desire to maintain one's position as chief earner in the family a plausible reason for a man's efforts to dissuade his wife from taking a job that pays as much or more than his own is not the existence of a lawlike regularity between such desires and measures but rather the (cultural) fact that this might seem an appropriate response for a male whose sense of well-being, as is not unusual in that society, is tied up both with his earning power and with his role as chief provider for his family.

Finding a person's reasons for acting involves more than simply identifying the specific wants and beliefs that gave rise to the action. In the first place, as we have seen, the explanation of an action in terms of reasons implies a recognition of certain social norms that determine what counts as a reason. Second, in the case of many of the things that people do, giving an explanation in terms of reasons may require grasping a wide range of norms and concepts. One has to know a great deal about a culture if one is to understand that the reason someone regularly brings his lunch to work and eats at his desk is to save money, which he hopes to use toward the purchase of a sailboat; or that the reason a child spends several hours a week making sounds on a piano is that he is preparing for a weekly piano lesson. Reasons are often determined by practices, and practices are typically defined in terms of other practices or institutions. Understanding reasons for someone's behavior may presuppose comprehension of a whole way of life.[16]

The view I am defending has a certain affinity to Max Weber's doctrine of *Verstehen*. What social science requires, according to Weber, is "interpretive understanding," wherein it is necessary that the investigator be able to see the phenomena as if through the eyes of participants.[17] In maintaining that understanding a person's reason for acting depends upon being able to see the connection between reason and action as reasonable and plausible, I am also saying that the behavior that the reason is supposed to explain must be made to appear to be just the sort of thing one would do if one shared the beliefs, desires, and norms that acting for that reason implies. Seeing an action from the agent's point of view is part of what it takes to make his action appear reasonable.

The notion of *Verstehen* that social science needs to rely on may be seen to operate both as a method of discovery and as a requirement for validity. It is not merely a technique or heuristic device, as some of Weber's critics have insisted;[18] it implies a particular analysis of what it means to understand another person's social behavior. The thesis of *Verstehensoziologie,* as I am construing it, makes a specific aim about the logic of social understanding: that rational explanations must conform to cultural norms of plausibility. A reason cannot explain an action unless it succeeds in showing the action to be a reasonable one.[19]

One of the criticisms that has been lodged against *Verstehen* as a method of understanding actions and other social phenomena is that it is too narrow, that it leads to excluding all motives, wants, and values that go into producing a person's behavior other than those he is aware of.[20] Indeed, *Verstehen* would yield a very nearsighted view of social action if it were interpreted as implying that the agent's is the only viewpoint from which actions can properly be scrutinized. If spectators' views can be ruled out altogether except when they coincide with those of the actors, then the investigator will be at the mercy of the agent both with respect to how action is to be described and the way it is to be explained.

This objection is met by interpreting *Verstehen* in accordance with the decision not to regard agents as the sole authority as to the reasons for their actions. To understand why someone does something is to be able to assign reasons that can be ascribed on the basis of evidence that may be gathered either from direct testimony *or* from observation of behavior. Interpreting *Verstehen* in this way allows the spectator to explain actions, within the proper constraints of reasonableness, without having to grant the last word to the agent. It implies, for example, that it may not be necessary to elicit testimony from any particular National Guardsman to learn the reason why he, along with a score of others, fired into a crowd of demonstrating students. There is no guarantee that the spectator will come up with a correct explanation, of course, but then neither is there a guarantee that the agents themselves will either.

One may ask how close to an account that an agent might himself give of his actions an assignment of reasons must be in order to provide a rational explanation. Winch makes the point that in expressing reasons we need not be restricted to the vocabulary of the theoretically unsophisticated participant in a social situation: the exercise of a liquidity preference may be a reason for certain actions on the part of a businessman, for example, even though it is unlikely that he would have such a concept.[21] All that is required is that the concepts used in expressing a person's reasons for acting be connected with those that he would correctly use in explaining the behavior in question. We can extend this principle to unconscious reasons, both in cases where a person would accept the reasons imputed to him and in cases where he would not. So far as neurotic behavior is seen to have rationale in terms of unconscious reasons, we do not ordinarily expect a person either to understand or to agree—initially, at least—with the imputations of reasons to him, though we do base our assignments on concepts that he is familiar with. We do need to view human actions as though from the "inside," though it is not the mind of the agent that we must penetrate in order to know why human individuals do as they do but rather the ideas of the culture or subculture.

The reason social behavior is so difficult to understand for anyone unfamiliar with the culture is that proper interpretation of it requires mastery of a whole system of rules and concepts. It would not be easy for someone with no prior knowledge of the game of chess to come to understand the moves merely by watching. When an interpretation is a good one, observed patterns of subsequent behavior serve to confirm it. Observing behavior within a culture is like watching a game. When the culture or the activity is a familiar one, we already have the relevant concepts that enable us to assign meaning to what we see. When we are confronted with actions of an unfamiliar kind, we must resort to conjecture as to the significance of what is going on. These conjectures can be derived only from concepts we already possess and must be tested by subsequent observations. Communication with agents offers a more direct means of learning what is being done and why: given the range of shared concepts that even a minimal knowledge of the language presupposes, one can learn through conversation further rules and concepts that will enable one to acquire participant understanding (*Verstehen*) of the activities being carried out. It is the need to depend on this "shortcut" that explains why some people might want to accord interviews and first-person reports a central position in social science. It is because testimony is so notoriously unreliable that other methods need to be used as well. We have to rely on behavioral data to suggest, support, and discredit possible interpretations of action and imputations of reasons, but since acting is not simply behaving and reasons do not explain in the way natural causes do, interpretations of action can only be guided by the study of behavior, and never established by it. One can, after all, totally misconstrue an activity without contravening any of the statistical evidence.[22]

Assigning a reason is like giving advice: it is worthless unless it takes into account the agent's point of view, his aims and objectives, and the background of norms of rational action that he accepts. Good advice, like a good reason, makes an action appear rational. What determines the rationality of the reason or the advice is not just consistence with certain goals and beliefs, but also conformity to standards of acceptable action in the circumstances. A rational person is one who acts on advice only if it is good, and who acts only for reasons that are good.

We need to investigate reasons for actions because understanding why people behave as they do requires knowing how they perceive and assess the situations in which they act. But in order to know how reasons explain we need to know what it means to be rational in these situations. We need to know the cultural norms that make the rational rational and the irrational irrational. Therefore the study of actions is the study of culture as well. The fact that reasons depend on norms guarantees that there can be no science of action that regards actions as separable from the culture in which they are performed.

# 5. Rationality and the Methods of Social Inquiry

Giving reasons, we have seen, explains actions by showing how what was done was appropriate to the circumstances. Sometimes knowing a person's reasons is sufficient to enable us to understand what got him to act in that way at that particular time. What shall we say, however, about behavior that is irrational, or behavior that no one had any reason to do? Clearly where there are no reasons, we cannot cite reasons as explanations. If in fact there are among social phenomena other kinds of occurrences than rational actions, these must call for other modes of explanation than rational explanation. The aim of this chapter is to briefly consider some of these alternatives. What I shall argue is that none of these alternatives, so far as they are explanatory of specifically human phenomena, escape dependency on the rational paradigm. Though reason-explanations have a limited reach, they are, I maintain, central to the understanding of human society.

Let us first consider the problem of deviance. Deviant behavior, so far as it is comprehensible as a form of intentional and voluntary behavior, is behavior that is seen as departure from the rational norms that govern behavior within a given culture. Some types of behavior are deviant only with respect to certain cultures, while other types are deviant in virtually all cultures, depending on the pervasiveness of the particular norm. Besides those activities that are deviant in virtue of being designated as crimes, candidates for deviant behavior include suicide, psychopathologies, and various kinds of sexual practices.

Because deviant behavior is a form of voluntary action, it can be examined from a rational point of view. It is possible to explore the rationale of any deviant act, and one way of understanding the nonconforming individual is to discover what that person's reasons are

77

for what he does. Some investigators, such as R.D. Laing, who has pursued this approach with schizophrenics, have tried to show that even psychotic behavior makes rational sense, given certain sets of perceptions.[1] Sociologists have sometimes tried to represent various forms of criminal deviance as rational responses to an irrational world. Certainly there is a sense in which the understanding of a deviant personality entails grasping the person's reasons for behaving as he does.

On the other hand, there is, at least in some cases, an aspect of deviant behavior that seems to call for more than rational explanation can provide. This aspect is revealed by the apparent compulsiveness of some deviant actions, the fact that some people seem neither able nor inclined to control their actions. Knowing a person's unusual beliefs and intense desires does help to explain his extraordinary behavior, but the acquiring of these beliefs and desires is left unexplained by a rational account. We need to know, furthermore, why certain individuals rather than others deviate from norms, why some people take extreme risks, become violent, or develop peculiar sexual attractions. Whatever the determinants of a person's behavioral propensities, there is no basis for assuming that they will be found in his reasons for acting. If a person is different, he is not likely to have reasons for being different, whether his differences are congenital or are the result of things that happened to him in his childhood.

Consider the case of the visitor to the zoo who deliberately and intentionally shoots and kills the zoo's celebrated polar bear. Let us suppose that we are able, through psychoanalysis and interviews with people who know the person involved, to discover what the particular fears and anxieties were that made this particular act seem appropriate for that agent at that particular time. Most people, I think, would feel that we still lacked an adequate explanation of the event. There appears to be more to explaining an action than showing how it made rational sense to the actor. (Notice that acts like these are commonly called "senseless" by officials who are asked to make statements to the press.) It is an important pragmatic feature of action explanation that beliefs and desires do not provide satisfactory explanations unless these beliefs and desires are themselves plausible. The deviant's reasons are not sufficient to explain his action because the peculiar conditions against which the reasons are offered are themselves in need of explanation. When an action has been identified as a deviant one, a rational account gives us only part of what we want to know.

The sociological and psychological study of deviance is based on the principle that testimony and the individual's rationale are not an adequate source of information for understanding why such behavior occurs. A deviant act, if it is not one for which an adequate rational explanation can be adduced, must be regarded as an act for which the person's reasons, even those that might be uncovered through psychoanalysis, are at best of limited value in enabling us to grasp what made him act as he did. If a sociological approach is pursued, what are important are social variables, facts that the agent would not himself cite but that are presumed to exert a causal influence on the behavior that occurs. Thus the relevant data for Durkheim's classic study of suicide were found not in suicide notes or in interviews with kin, but rather by examining the circumstances of family membership, religious affiliation, and economic conditions—facts that Durkheim saw fit to correlate on a statistical basis with greater or lesser suicide frequencies.[2] For Durkheim these correlations served as indices of the presence or absence of social factors that are, in his view, the real determinants of events that might otherwise have been seen as isolated acts of a more or less rational character. He was thus able to represent suicide as a failure of social integration, as an effect of causes that can be found by examining the objective conditions that obtain in the society in which it occurs.

However, individual acts, whether deviant or not, are not explained by statistical correlations. What Durkheim's findings provide is not a determinate account of acts of suicide, but rather a way of showing that the relative likelihood of such acts occurring is a statistical function of the presence or absence of certain features in the life contexts of individuals. Identifying the social factors that give rise to the highest incidence of particular forms of deviance no more explains why any individual performs the deviant act as he does than does a probability calculation explain why any particular poker hand or roll of the dice comes out the way it does. Such research never makes contact with the question of what makes some people perform the act in question whereas others do not.

The problem with sociological attempts to explain deviance is that such explanations cannot cross the gap between the conditions of social life and individual human actions. How shall that gap be bridged? On this question sociology is necessarily silent. On the other hand, we also lack any deterministic psychological accounts that permit us to link social circumstances to behavioral acts by means of causal laws. What we do have is a way of understanding the individual acts that at the same time can be used to explain why the sociological generalizations have as much truth as they have: these acts are rational or quasirational social responses to situations whose nature is fixed by the conditions that are reflected in sociologists' observations. Thus suicide can be seen as one way of responding to the absence of the ties of family and community that sustain so many of those who belong to groups having low suicide rates. It is not that suicide is a rational act, but that its likelihood appears to be increased by the presence of conditions under which its occurrence is more rationally intelligible.

There is a further respect in which the explanation of deviant actions is dependent on the paradigm of rational explanation. Deviant actions, however compulsive or irrational they appear, nonetheless have the logic of intentional action: such acts are purposive and they presuppose an agent's grasp of the meaning of his behavior. The distinction between a suicide and a self-inflicted accidental death is one that the agent must be credited with understanding; he must be presumed to intend the outcome and to believe correctly that he is acting in such a way as to achieve it. Furthermore, in order for any social fact to have an effect on behavior it must have entered the cognizance of the agent. The fact that a person is an urban Protestant or an unemployed fatherless youth can make a difference to his behavioral propensities only if it affects his assessment of the range of plausible actions for him to take. If being a divorced executive threatened with a loss of job at a time of economic recession makes suicide more likely, it must be that awareness of these circumstances or their consequences makes suicide a less unreasonable course of action than otherwise. The act may still be irrational, in the sense that it is not an appropriate response to the situation, but if it is intelligible at all as a voluntary action, it must at least be made to appear more reasonable than some of its alternatives, given those circumstances.

The person who commits an act that we cannot rationally comprehend has behaved in a way that we cannot understand at all. The extent to which we do understand acts that we perceive as crazy or irrational is determined by how effectively we can represent them in terms of a rational paradigm. The pont of citing a person's past experiences or mentioning social or psychological variables is that these may help us to see how the behavior might seem appropriate to that agent. The fact that a deviant act is an act that is done for insufficient or unacceptable reasons does not mean that it is done for no reason. And bad reasons can be identified only because good reasons can. When we look for objective conditions as a means of trying to explain puzzling or anomalous actions, what we seek are sources of reasons, good or bad, that will help us understand why certain courses are pursued rather than others. The external or nonrational study of deviance is therefore at most a *supplement* to a rational account of behavior.

What is true of deviance is also true of seemingly irrational phenomena on a larger scale. The European witch-craze of the seventeenth century, for example, and the American anti-Communist crusades of the 1950's, if they can be understood at all, must be seen as results of certain beliefs and desires, and fears and anxieties, that affected people in those situations. We need to investigate the conditions that gave rise to those states of mind, but it is important to realize that we are looking at the reasons that made those actions appropriate for those who performed them. When we look upon such actions as irrational, it is because we take them to have been based on bad reasons—bad, in these cases, because they depend on beliefs that were inadequately supported. What was irrational about the conviction and execution of the Rosenbergs in 1953 for espionage and for allegedly helping the Russians build a hydrogen bomb was not that the United States' action did not follow from the reasons given, but that there was hardly any evidence to support the belief that the Rosenbergs had done things that were sufficiently dangerous to national security to warrant the peacetime use of the ultimate punishment. It is an important task of social science to explain how people come to hold the irrational beliefs and desires that many of them have, but the reasons that move them to action still have to be understood against the background of a rational paradigm. Attempts to explain deviant or aberrant behavior represent efforts to locate actions that are seen as not fully rational within a universe in which the norms of rational action are already understood.

There are other kinds of social explanation besides those that seek to illuminate individual actions. One of these is functional explanation. A functional explanation is one in which the existence or persistence of an item is explained by indicating a beneficial effect it has in the system within which it occurs. In biology, the assignment of function explains by showing how a given structure or process contributes to the survival of an organism or class of organisms. Functional explanations in social science are supposed to explain the occurrence of an action, practice, or element of social structure by showing how it contributes to the maintenance of a social whole. According to the classical statement by Malinowski of the functionalist position in anthropology, "in every type of civilization, every custom, material object, idea and belief fulfils some vital function, has some task to accomplish, represents an indispensable part within a working whole."[3] The function of any religious institution, for example, is that it is a means of achieving social cohesiveness; the function of a system of higher education is to provide a hedge against destructive forces. Every identifiable feature of a society is assumed by the functionalists to have a function and to be subject to a functional analysis that will reveal why it exists.

Societies do indeed consist of mutually adapted parts. But it is surely a mistake to insist that *everything* in a culture is necessary for a society's continued survival, and it is doubtful that it is reasonable to see the social system, as Radcliffe-Brown did, as a unitary whole in which all parts work together and every social usage contributes to the "total social life."[4] Societies, unlike organisms, are not the sorts of things whose survival depends on having all of their components maintained in their current state. Social order is compatible with a number of possible configurations of social elements. Not even radical upheaval ordinarily causes a society to disintegrate. While it may be useful to view small-scale, nonliterate societies as integral wholes, it is hardly plausible to suppose in larger, industrial societies every element is needed for the contribution it makes toward maintaining the social system. Since this way of looking at the elements of social life carries with it the implication that any kind of social change will be undesirable, it is no wonder that functionalism has been held to support a conservative ideology.

The functionalist approach has at least to some extent been rescued from the charge of conservatism by Merton, who pointed out that although functional analysis does have to relate an item to some end or need served, this end does not have to be the perpetuation of the existing social system.[5] A cultural element or institutional practice, in order to be functional, must have consequences that contribute to the adaptation or adjustment of a complex system, but that system need not be the society as a whole. The unit could be a class, an institution, a profession, or other subgroup whose interests may be served by social practices that are functional within the context of those interests but are antithetical to the goal of perpetuating the existing type of social order.

82

Sociologists who have adopted the functionalist orientation have generally followed Merton in taking the functionalist approach to allow analyses in terms of contribution to units that are usually much smaller than the society as a whole—so much so, in fact, that as Ryan has put it, the dominant sense of "function" in recent sociological literature has come to be "good consequences."[6] It seems that any item is considered functional if it can be shown to contribute in some unexpected way to somebody's welfare. Thus American machine politics has been represented as having served the function of providing certain kinds of support for new immigrants in a society that had no other means of looking after their welfare.[7] Participation in voluntary service associations has been seen as having the function of allowing those permitted to belong to such associations to gain a certain social status.[8]

A functional analysis is explanatory only when the account it gives of an item's beneficial effects is also an answer to the question why that item exists. This requirement holds regardless of the range of units for which a putatively functional item is supposed to have beneficial consequences. The way that a function statement explains, when in fact it does, is by showing that an item is in place because it has those consequences, that that is the reason why it is there. To assign a function to something is, in effect, to give the reason someone might have had for putting it there. Thus to assert that the function of the white collar and cuffs of a gentleman's dress is to show others that the wearer does not have to work with his hands is not merely to suggest a likely effect of dressing in that manner; it is to point to something that could have provided an explanatory reason for doing so. Functional explanation is therefore not an alternative to explanation in terms of reasons, but rather an extension of it.[9] It is important to notice that functional explanations are parasitic on reason-explanations even in the case of machines and organisms. With respect to the former, knowing the function of any functioning part is equivalent to knowing the designer's reason for having it placed in the machine. In the latter case, function is similarly tied to reason, regardless of whether there is actually a designer or merely a theory, such as the theory of evolution, that explains why the parts of an organism look *as if* they were designed to function as they do. Functional explanation is not an alternative to rational explanation, for it is itself based on the rational paradigm.

The functional approach to social phenomena offers an essentially pseudorational account, one that extends the search for rational understanding to certain elements that *could* serve as reasons for adopting various practices but do not actually comprise anyone's reasons. An approach that can be seen to have nothing to do with reasons, even in this extended sense, is that of structuralism. What the structuralist seeks to do is to set forth the observable characteristics of cultural life as particular manifestations of a constant underlying structure. This structure is supposed to determine relationships among cultural elements such that any structural features that are discernible in a given culture can be seen to reflect structures that are universal throughout human cultures. The structuralist's program is of a piece with that of structural linguistics, according to which the grammatical form of a language is interpreted as the result of a particular filling in of a universal substructure. In anthropology, the program consists of studying and analyzing the relationships within a culture—as in systems of kinship, for example—and trying to determine what kinds of transformations and permutations are possible. Structuralism aims to discover what structural relationships exist, what natural constraints there are on cultural variation, and how universal structures are revealed in the social life of particular cultures.

The way structural anthropology attempts to illuminate particular cultural phenomena is by ordering them in terms of cross-cultural universals. It does not show how anything came about or what its presence helps to achieve; it rather allows us to fit specific items into patterns of phenomena both within a culture and with respect to their alleged counterparts in other cultures. It aims at discovering constancies behind diversities: thus Lévi-Strauss offers a new way of looking at our interest in visiting historical sites by comparing it with the Australian *churinga,* a kind of ancient artifact that is cherished because of the tie it represents to a tribe's ancestry.[10] Another illustration is his presentation of psychoanalysis as a variety of shamanism and sorcery.[11] There are, according to Lévi-Strauss, certain fundamental polarities that occur in every culture and reflect a common structure of the human mind. That is why the variety of arrangements of elements within human cultures is severely limited.

For the structuralist it is not necessary that society be viewed as a system, and thus he does not have to insist that everything fit together in a functional order. "To say that a society functions," Lévi-Strauss says, "is a truism; but to say that everything in a society functions is an absurdity.''[12] A society, for Lévi-Strauss, is defined simply as individuals and groups that communicate with each other.[13] The descriptive task of the structural anthropologist is to find the rules that govern social relationships within a culture. The foundations of whatever order can be discovered at this level are believed to exist at a lower level, that of the innate organization of the human mind or brain. Cultural phenomena, including all of social life, are seen as super-structures for which anthropology is supposed to provide a theory.

If there are cultural universals and these can be used to explain particular customs and practices, then there exists a kind of social explanation that competes both with explanations in terms of reasons and with explanations that call upon social variables. If, for example, there are universal constraints on the structures of kinship, or there are in every society ceremonial meals that have a number of successive courses that exhibit increasing geometricity and increasing dessication, we do not need reasons to explain why certain behavior conforms to these patterns. So far as structural anthropology explains behavior and social relationships, it explains by subsuming them under general descriptive principles.

What then is the connection between structural and rational explanation? Two possibilities suggest themselves: structural explanations are essentially in competition with explanations in terms of reasons, or the two types of account are compatible; either they explain the same phenomena in different ways or they explain different things. If the first possibility is correct, then what a structuralist must be trying to show is that reasons are irrelevant; reasons and rationality are explained away. If the second possibility is accepted, then we have to say that structural and rational accounts explain different phenomena, that they explain different aspects of the same phenomena, or that they are complementary in some other way. Either a structural account of the way humans behave wipes out the claims of reason to explain the phenomena of human social life or else there is a way that the two modes of understanding can be reconciled.

The latter possibility is the one that I believe can best be defended. The behavior that the anthropologist is concerned with, we need to remind ourselves, is rational behavior: it is behavior that is voluntary, intentional, and subject to rationalization by those who engage in it. The structures that are considered, whether they are features of language, kinship relations, or the treatment of foodstuffs, are the structures of cultural productions. What are represented as revealing universal structures are the products of human action, individual and collective. They are supposed to fix the outlines of the customs people adopt and the kinds of institutions they establish. The result of studying them, therefore, will be knowledge of the constraints that exist on what rational persons or groups of rational people can be expected to do in the conduct of social life.

It is clear that common underlying structures, if they exist, cannot explain why individuals or groups living within those general constraints behave specifically the way that they do; nor can such structures explain why certain practices have arisen rather than others, or why they persist or change. Structural principles may reveal the shape of human production, but not the content of it. A structural anthropology that indicates constancies in the structures of myths, for example, might be likened to an aesthetic that tells what shape paintings have or what size sculptures take. Analogies like these are very weak, of course, but they do serve to illustrate the point that structuralist social science seeks to provide answers to questions different from those that are supposed to penetrate matters of why one rational or irrational action rather than another is performed. A structural account does not explain rationality away but rather represents the limits within which it occurs.

Before turning to the possibility that biological inquiries may provide a valuable source of knowledge that may increase our understanding of human social behavior, there is one further area of social research that I want to consider that appears to call for explanations in terms other than reasons: the investigation of institutions and other social wholes. Social inquiry comprises more than the study of individuals and groups; it also includes the study of political entities and social institutions, as well as such collective phenomena as wars and liberation movements. Not everything that social science examines is a human being.

The first point to stress about institutions, already mentioned in Chapter 3, is that social institutions may be regarded as having lives of their own: they typically seem to maintain their identities beyond and independent of the actions performed by any particular individual or set of individuals. It should not be surprising, therefore, that the study of institutions involves the consideration of indicators of a nonpersonal nature, such as tables of numbers and lists of goods. Institutions do things that individuals cannot do, and these call for special means of

86

detection. Nations, not persons, make war; parliaments pass laws, corporations merge, and stock markets fall. The evidence upon which descriptions of institutional behavior are based, though it is always derived from what individual people do and what happens to them, owes its significance to the fact that the individual performances are indicators of the performance of entities that may outlive the people on whose actions they confer meaning.

Someone who takes these points seriously may be tempted to view institutions as independently existing real entities. One can, after all, enter into a relationship with an institution: one can join the Navy or become a depositor at a bank. We might also say that institutions are what we apprehend whenever we identify actions that presuppose institutional roles and practices. We refer to institutions, it can be said, every time we identify such an action as getting married, buying a home, or fighting a war; whenever we know enough to recognize these actions we can be said to have knowledge about institutions.

A person who looks upon institutions in this way may even regard them as objects on a par with naturally occurring things, as targets for objective study. The view has a certain plausibility, and it does accord with a number of things we say about institutions. If a nation rearms itself, or a government nationalizes an industry, we detect these occurrences in the same way that we detect occurrences at the submicroscopic level: by observing indicators and instruments that we treat as objective measures. We monitor the state of a nation's economy by examining numerical indicators and we follow the progress of a war by noting battle lines and body counts. There is indeed a part of social inquiry that is concerned with the behavior of institutions and that tries to emulate that part of scientific investigation that looks for quantities to measure and items to count.

Looked at thus abstractly, institutions appear to occupy a domain of social life in which individuals play no part. Economics can be studied by focusing solely on quantities such as interest rates, level of government expenditures, and gross national product. Sociology is concerned with, among other things, relationships among such items as the establishment of value patterns, the institutionalization of role expectations, and the stability of social systems. Neither the formulation of principles nor the testing of hypotheses may require attending to any but macro-level variables.

I insisted in Chapter 3 that, although social understanding demands a recognition of the existence and role of institutions, institutional behavior can always be represented in terms of the behavior of individuals. It does not follow from this fact about institutions that they cannot be studied as if they were irreducible wholes with characteristic properties. It is true that a stick of butter is composed of molecules whose random motion is a function of temperature, but it is also true that butter melts into a pool of liquid when placed in a heated oven. The study of macroeconomic phenomena can be seen as similar to the study of the gross features of ordinary physical objects.

One consequence of conceiving of the institutional sciences in this way is that they turn out to be human sciences only *per accidens.* Economics, for example, can be understood as a means of systematizing the movements of objects whose connections with human actions are quite incidental. Supply and demand, costs and prices, the flow of capital, the production of commodities—all of them are treated in ways that are independent of how and by whom they are created. As economists deal with money, goods, and services, they could just as well be studying pinball machines. The same kinds of considerations can be applied to studies of political institutions. The fact that the subunits within the gross phenomena studied by these sciences happen to be human beings is of no account.

The reason we are able to treat social wholes as entities whose behavior can be described and predicted is that human beings, at least in certain situations and in certain respects, tend to behave as if they were interchangeable mechanical elements. It is a fact of the world that human beings often behave just as properly functioning parts would be expected to. For many areas of behavior the methodological practice of reducing human activity to a few simple assumptions appears to be vindicated. In economics, for example, there are principles that have application to human affairs—because people can, sometimes, be counted to act like *homo economicus,* to maximize their expected self-interest and to share certain conceptions of what that consists of. If there are true empirical principles that govern the behavior of bureaucracies it is only because human behavior within these institutions reveals a sufficient degree of predictability to make it methodologically fruitful to treat it as movement rather than action. Social wholes comprise a set of investigatable objects only so far as there is enough coincidence with respect to what different people do in similar circumstances to allow humans to be perceived as uniformly determined by outside events and circumstances.

The study of institutions does have a certain autonomy. Yet there is something very strange about treating these objects as essentially removed from the sphere of human action. Institutions and social wholes are not just contingently human. They have an intentional character; they are what they are only because they are conceived as having certain properties and roles. It is not merely that there is no institutional relation or state of affairs that fails to make a difference to the life of persons, but that there are no institutional events that can occur without someone doing things that require certain conceptualizations on the part of the agent. There can be no such thing as a corporate merger or the decentralization of a school system without individuals acting with knowledge of these institutions and their roles within them. Institutional behavior always presupposes rational, intentional action.

People are the means by which institutions operate, but not in the sense that neurons are the means by which human motor and sensory processes operate or that men on ponies were the means by which the U.S. Postal Service once operated. To say that an institution is the people who participate in it is not a reduction but an identification: of institutions with people acting in institutional roles. The explanation of institutional occurrences is therefore ultimately the explanation of actions—and vice versa.

While there are ways of studying institutions that regard them as objects that are scientifically interesting in themselves, it is impossible to study the workings of institutions—not to mention their effects—without at the same time studying human social existence. Just as you cannot understand religious practice and economic activities without understanding religious and economic institutions, so you cannot understand the nature of these institutions without knowing what they mean in terms of human social life. Knowing about institutions means knowing about the lives of people, and knowing about the lives of people requires knowing something about the institutions that give their social existence the character it has.

As objects, institutions are neither rational nor irrational; like tables and mountains, they just *are*. Their behavior, however, is often scrutinizable from the point of view of rationality. Institutions are like human beings in that they behave in both rational and nonrational ways: they undergo nonrational changes such as growth and fragmentation and also behave in ways that can be judged rational or irrational. Institutions have policies and objectives, the pursuit of which is assessable in terms of

89

ordinary standards of rationality. The moves that an institution makes can be examined to see if they make sense relative to its goals and to its social role. Popper and the methodological individualists have insisted that institutions and social wholes cannot have aims and intentions that are not the aims and intentions of individuals. The claim is correct, strictly speaking, but it carries very little weight, for it is only as occupiers of institutional roles that these individuals can be said to perform the actions that are ascribed to them. There are such occurrences as government and corporate actions, and individuals are accountable for them because they are acts—institutional acts—of individuals.

Institutions can thus be conceived under two aspects, as objects and as rational beings. As nonrational objects, their connection with human rationality lies in their effects on the structure of the world in which people act, and in the fact that any behavior or changes that occur that involve institutions are explainable in terms of what individuals do. Institutions shape one's universe, but the way they do it can be explained only by citing what other individuals can or have done. The rationality of an institution is nothing but human rationality, institutionally positioned. Institutions are essentially impersonal, but because they are also essentially human, there is no comprehending them apart from the comprehension of human rationality.

Facts about institutions, like facts about customs, practices, and deviant behavior, call for explanations that go beyond the search for reasons for actions. None of these explanations replaces rational explanations; rather they extend or supplement them, or else they presuppose them. Many things contribute to making the social world what it is, and not all of them find expression in people's reasons for acting. Understanding why human beings constitute their social universe the way they do depends on grasping factors that are frequently unknown to those who act and are acted upon. Individuals do not make themselves the way they are, nor do they create the conditions under which they act. But there are no explanations of social phenomena that do not presuppose the existence of rational agents, and there are no explanations of what rational agents do that do not rest on the paradigm of a person doing something for a reason. All social explanation is ultimately rational explanation.

90

# 6. Biology and Social Inquiry

In the last chapter several ways of approaching social phenomena were considered that have been alleged to provide explanations of human behavior that reach beyond the search for agents' reasons for acting. What we found was that all of these, so far as they are explanatory of actions, still presuppose the rational paradigm, according to which any action, in order to be explained, must be rendered recognizable as appropriate with respect to the norms governing the social context in which it occurs. A piece of behavior is intelligible as human action only if it can be given a rationale; otherwise it is either inscrutable or else treatable as merely a mechanical movement.

There is still another approach to human social behavior that needs to be examined, one that appears to cut across the question of rationality by stressing underlying determinants. This is the biological approach, the effort to discover how much of what people do is the result of the biological features of the human organism, and the extent to which patterns of human social behavior can be explained in terms of these features. If what people do in societies has a significant basis in biology, then it ought to be possible to explain a considerable amount of what happens in human society in terms of biological factors. Rational accounts will have been shown to be irrelevant, or to lack application, to the extent that any causal biological account is correct. Whatever can be explained in human society as determined by a person's or his species' biological makeup will turn out to be explainable in a way that bypasses the notion of human rationality.

The most obvious way to begin trying to apply biological science to understanding human social behavior is with the commonplace that the human being is an organism and that its behavior is a kind of animal behavior. As such, human behavior can be seen as a product of evolutionary processes and hence as subject to biological explanation. Humans are similar to other creatures, not only in many of their anatomical and physiological features, but also in a number of aspects of overall behavior. Because many animals, like humans, are social, their social behavior could provide a valuable source of insight into human sociality.

If a biological approach is going to be useful for explaining human social behavior, such behavior must be representable as the result of biological forces. What people do that counts as social behavior will have to be explainable in terms of their inherited biological nature and their environmental adaptation. What is peculiar to the biological account is that it requires that the adaptive behavior be determined by the creature's biological nature; otherwise it would not differ significantly from other environmental accounts. All behavior is presumed to be influenced by environment somewhere along the line; what is distinctive about the biological explanation is the fact that it tries to appeal to features that evolution has fixed in the creature's genotype.

Before considering the project of using a biological approach to study human social behavior, it will be worthwhile to remind ourselves just what sorts of phenomena need to be explained. I shall assume that human social phenomena consist of actions plus certain events and states of affairs that are the results of actions. These phenomena include social practices, institutions, and patterns of voluntary behavior. They do not include reflex movements and other bodily processes not subject to voluntary control. Nor do they include capacities, which only fix the limits of action. The capacity to learn a language or write a sentence is not a social phenomenon, though the delivering of a sermon or the writing of a letter is. It will not, therefore, count as an explanation of a social action or practice to provide an explanation of the occurrence of structures or capacities, even though without these no performance of the phenomenon in question would be possible.

It is obvious that not all animal species behave alike; if they did, it would not be necessary to study the behavior of more than a single species in order to determine the way all species behave—including human beings. Ethology, the study of animal behavior in zoological contexts, is based on a recognition of the need to take this fact seriously.

To the early ethologists, the study of animal behavior meant the study of instinct. They concentrated on behavior that could be seen to be rigidly stereotyped, such as nest building among insects and mating dances among tropical fish. While the methods were easily extended to birds and mammals, including the higher primates, the paradigm remained the same: behavior that is uniform throughout the species, is triggered by specific environmental cues, and is stable under otherwise changed environmental conditions. The project was to identify and explain the things that animals do as a result of their inherent natures.

Later ethologists, more aware of the fact that animals do not behave in their native environments in all of the same ways that they do under controlled and restricted conditions, have construed the study of animal behavior more broadly and have allowed it to include the study of learning and other environmentally induced modifications of behavior. There is a tendency among modern students of animal behavior to avoid the use of expressions like "instinct" and "innateness." Behavior, they point out, is always a joint product, a result of interaction between a genotype and an environment, and the role of hereditary factors is a matter of degree. And since animals possessing a given species inheritance live in a variety of environments and in fact exhibit different behavior depending on the features of the ecological niche they occupy, the study of their behavior should not be restricted to what can be identified as instinctive. If, as often seems to be the case, there is no inherent structure that rigidly and specifically determines a unique type of behavior, independent of the nature of the environment, then it is at least misleading to say that the behavior is programmed by heredity. The biology of behavioral adaptation turns out to be a good deal more complicated than is suggested by an approach that concentrates on trying to find out which behavior is instinctive or innately determined.

Nevertheless, what reliance on an ethological perspective typically signifies when human behavior is being considered is that an effort is being made to show that human biological inheritance must be invoked to explain why people and societies behave as they do. Thus the point of Lorenz's attempts to extrapolate to humans the results of his studies of aggression in animals was to show that humans have an instinctive aggressive drive that leads them to kill members of their own species.[1] Similarly, the principal thrust of recent attempts to offer biological accounts of phenomena such as human altruism, xenophobia, the sexual division of labor, and homosexuality has been to suggest that it is the genetic structure of human populations, not environmental influences, that is mainly responsible for the patterns of social behavior that we observe.[2] Instead of trying to reveal the way biological structures and environmental conditions interact to produce human behavior, the aim seems rather to demonstrate its dependence on the species' genetic constitution. Examination of human behavior from a biological perspective has been thought to be capable of helping us discover human biological nature.

If there is such a thing as human nature and if biology can be used to investigate it, the biologist is in an important position to help us to discover why human societies are the way they are. If we could find out what is natural for the human species, what people are really like, independent of cultural influences, we would know what is fixed by biology and what needs to be explained as the result of environmental contingencies. Such knowledge could serve as a foundation for social science. A conception of human nature that is grounded in knowledge of biologically inherent tendencies would provide a base for sociological and psychological explanations. It would constitute a background against which the things people do, including those that are environmentally influenced, could be displayed. Just as in Newtonian mechanics the concept of motion at constant velocity (of which rest is merely a special case) yields a standard with reference to which all other types of motion are explained, so a genetic or ontogenetic conception of human nature would enable us to know which social phenomena we ought to seek explanations for and which, because they flow directly from human biological nature, we ought to regard as intelligible in themselves.

A science that can establish which human social patterns will remain invariant through major cultural change and which patterns can be modified could have considerable social importance. If we knew how deeply—or how shallowly—rooted human aggressive or territorial behavior is, for instance, we would have a better idea of the significance of social institutions as means of maintaining peace. It could be very useful to know whether or not there is a genetic basis of competitiveness, whether xenophobia is a universal, heritable characteristic that arises in every society, and whether moral commitment is entirely learned or is subject to genetic programming. If we could discover the human species' natural propensities, we might then have better insight into why various social practices are adopted and what sorts of alternatives are possible.

The science that has been heralded as holding the promise of satisfying these aims is sociobiology. This relatively new discipline, whose practitioners look upon ethology as merely an adjunct, is supposed to offer "the systematic study of the biological basis of all social behavior."[3] Its program is to investigate animal  populations using not only the methods of comparative ethology but also the conceptual frameworks of genetics, including population genetics, and ecology.

What have the ethologists and sociobiologists achieved thus far with respect to gaining an adequate biological conception of human nature? In fact, the results have been extremely meager; at best, they are highly controversial. The problem is not that animal behavior has not been adequately investigated, but rather that what has been discovered has not shed much light on humans. Lorenz's studies of geese, wolves, and rats,[4] for example, have definitely not succeeded in demonstrating the presence of an instinctive aggressive drive in humans, nor have the studies by Schaller on gorillas[5] and Goodall on chimpanzees[6] indicating a general lack of aggression in the higher primates proved that humans are not innately aggressive. Sociobiologists have speculated that behavior such as human altruism, social conformity, and even creativity and entrepreneurship is controlled by genetic factors, but there appears to be no direct scientific evidence that this is the case.

In order to grasp the reasons for the lack of success of the project of discovering a genetic or biological basis for human social behavior, we need to consider what one would have to do to establish that a human behavioral trait is based on species inheritance. First, one would have to become convinced that the trait is universal. A way of finding out whether a trait is universal is to make cross-cultural comparisons and determine that there are no counterinstances within the species. But would this show that the trait is genetically based, rather than a result of common environmental influences? Edward O. Wilson, in *Sociobiology*, suggests that it would, especially when the trait is found in all, or nearly all, other primates.[7] Although he allows for the possibility that some traits that are present throughout the rest of the primates "might nevertheless have changed [i.e., mutated] during the origin of man," he does not seem to consider seriously the possibility that they may be environmentally induced in humans. The fact that Wilson has said of qualities that are "distinctively ineluctably human" that "they can be safely classified as genetically based"[8] indicates that he simply *assumes* that whatever is universal in humans is fixed by a common genotype. Another possibility, not ruled out by the evidence, is that what is most distinctive in humans, beyond their "distinctively ineluctably human" traits, is their adaptability, their capacity to learn what in other animals is already programmed into the genes. Humans have no instinct to eat only edible food or to drink only potable water, but must acquire these tendencies on an individual basis in order to survive. It is very likely true that whatever is universal in humans is biologically significant, in the sense of contributing to the perpetuation of the species, but it does not follow that any of these qualities must be genetically determined.

What is needed in order to prove that a trait or behavior pattern is innate is to demonstrate that its development is stable under widely varying environmental conditions. A method commonly used for establishing that a trait is not a product of environment is the "deprivation experiment," whereby it is supposed to be shown that a creature will develop and exhibit the behavior in question even if it has been isolated from all of the factors that are thought important in leading to its acquisition. A difficulty with relying on such experiments, however, is that one cannot exclude *all* environmental influences and still have the behavior persist. At the very least, an environment must be maintained within the limits wherein life itself is possible. More to the point so far as social behavior, especially human social behavior, is concerned, we cannot expect the deprivation conditions to include absence of social context, at least of a rudimentary sort. Humans, so far as is known, have always lived in cultural environments. Not only do they shape their environments by cultural means in terms of normative conceptions, but they define their environments conceptually, that is, in terms of categories that are themselves cultural artifacts.[9] The range of behavior that can be investigated using deprivation experiments is necessarily extremely narrow.

One of the most general and striking features of social behavior in humans and in at least certain other animals is its susceptibility to modification. Almost any kind of social behavior can be inhibited or provoked by means of sufficiently drastic manipulation of the creature's environment, often well within the limits of viability. We know, for instance, that dogs can be domesticated, that ordinarily peaceful monkeys can be trained in aggressiveness, and that birds can be gotten to ignore their young by introducing extraneous sounds. Behavior that it is plausible to designate as innate or instinctive must be stable throughout a range of environments. Whether or not social behavior can be said to be determined by the creature's biological nature will therefore depend on whether we are able to classify the conditions under which the behavior fails to appear as deviant or unusual.

We cannot justly characterize as instinctive or as rooted in human nature any kind of social behavior for which exceptions are known, unless we are prepared to explain away the exceptions as results of abnormal or unnatural conditions. We can justify calling eating instinctive, but only because we recognize as extraordinary the conditions under which a person will voluntarily starve to death. We could not, on the other hand, maintain that human aggression is innate in the face of evidence indicating the existence of nonaggressive tribes; to do so, simply on the basis of the aggressiveness exhibited by our society and by other societies with which we are familiar, would be a form of ethnocentrism. There is no conceivable evidence that would decide between the hypothesis that aggression is a basic drive that is sometimes masked or repressed and the hypothesis that it is something that is produced only when other drives are thwarted or when certain types of stimuli are present. So far as the way people act is variable across cultural lines, there is no discoverable human nature that can be said to underlie human social behavior.

If it is possible to investigate human nature, the only way this can be done is to concentrate on aspects of human behavior that either do not vary at all or whose variations may uncontroversially be exhibited as a result of bizarre conditions. In fact, a number of cross-cultural universals have been at least tentatively identified. Male-male competition, for example, has never been specified as absent in any culture that has been studied. Another universal seems to be the avoidance of incest by taboo. Others that have been mentioned include sexual inhibition and shyness, play, male dominance, and territoriality.

There is no evidence that characteristics such as these are genetically based, but neither is there any evidence that they are not. Since it is not clear what *would* show such universal features to be part of a species' genetic inheritance, the dispute is essentially a philosophical one. Where the traits in question fail to exhibit continuity with traits of other species in structure and function, it is impossible to demonstrate homology, and as a consequence, there can be no convincing argument that the traits are products of Darwinian evolution. What is clear, in any case, is that the present defenders of the genetic interpretation have not presented evidence sufficient to justify their claims.

Let us assume, nonetheless, perhaps on the grounds that no alternative assumption is better supported, that behavioral universals such as the ones that have been suggested are genetically based and that they do reveal certain characteristics of human nature. I would like to argue that even if this assumption is made, the generalizations that would be yielded would still not be of much help in understanding why people and societies behave as they do. One problem is that the principles by which we represent the patterns we observe—as variations on common themes, perhaps—are likely to be true only at a level of abstraction that renders them trivial or commonplace. Human social behavior does not consist of rigidly determined, fixed patterns that are uniform throughout the species; it rather varies considerably from one social group to another. Social science is typically interested in explaining these variations. The kinds of phenomena that we expect a social theory to explain include items such as racial prejudice, juvenile delinquency, war, individual and group rebellion, and social control. Whether or not these can all be seen as manifestations of biological drives or tendencies, it is still the differences among them as social phenomena that interest us. The enunciation of underlying biological generalizations, even if possible, will not be of much use. If the determinants of the specific differences among a widely disparate range of behaviors are not biological but sociocultural, it will not explain any of them to subsume them under a common biological rubric.

As an illustration, consider the notion of human territoriality. If we observe the variety of ways in which humans maintain more-or-less exclusive occupancy of an area, we realize that territoriality, at least in humans, is not a matter of turning away unwanted visitors by means of a pattern of signals and responses common to the whole species. The rules regarding property and land use are culturally determined and vary widely among human populations. The phenomena that social science undertakes to explain include the variety of forms that human concern for property and territory takes. But if the concept of territoriality that sociobiology employs is made so broad as to allow senses as disparate as the ones that apply, respectively, to capitalist societies and to nomadic tribes, then it is not clear that very much is explained by citing territoriality as a driving impulse. It is doubtful whether anything substantive would be said if one were to assert that the human species is territorial if this concept is made to fit—as at least one sociobiologist wants it to—not only societies that contain legal institutions that govern private property, but also societies that do not allow exclusive use by tribes or families of any resource except for the richest sources of vegetable foods, and even societies that under some conditions exhibit no territorial behavior at all.[10] Because the thesis that territoriality is a general human trait fails to signify a single unitary feature of either individuals or groups, it lacks explanatory force with respect to any of the multifarious behaviors that have been called territorial.

In order for a cross-cultural generalization to explain an observed practice or pattern of behavior, it cannot be as loose or abstract as the sort we have been considering. On the other hand, even when the generalization is at the level of the phenomena to be explained, it will not go very far as an explanation of why people and societies exhibit the traits they do. The discovery that something is a universal human trait will show only that it is a general feature of human existence, that it is not merely the result of particular events and circumstances. It remains to be shown that the feature is a biological one, that it derives from the creature's genetic inheritance. Furthermore, in order for a generalization to be used to provide a biological expansion of the trait in question, it must be possible to show *how* certain biological characteristics are responsible for the behavior. If that can be done, however, then the argument that the behavior is biologically determined no longer depends on its being universal. The problem of showing how a creature's biological inheritance can account for a behavioral trait is the same whether the trait is universal or variable. In fact, we find that defenders of the biological approach tend to treat at least some of the variation that is found among human societies as due to genetic differences. Thus Wilson has suggested that "the genes...maintain a certain amount of influence in at least the behavioral qualities that underlie variations between culture," and that "we can heuristically conjecture that the traits proven to be labile [i.e., traits that shift from species to species or genus to genus] are also the ones most likely to differ from one human society to another on the basis of genetic differences."[11] In other words, any behavioral trait, whether it is common to all societies or a feature of only some societies, can be seen as revealing the genetic basis of human behavior. The gene hypothesis at this stage appears to be capable of explaining any distribution of traits whatever—and thus it explains nothing.

In order for a human trait to be explained biologically, it must first be "biologized," that is, represented in terms that befit the study of organisms qua organisms. The problem with such biological reduction is that it is likely to sacrifice precisely those features of human social behavior that give it a socially and philosophically interesting character. A case in point is the treatment of altruism. When Wilson defines an act of altruism as one that occurs "when a person or animal increases the fitness of another at the expense of his own fitness,"[12] he is specifically ignoring the distinction between acts that are performed with the intention and for the purpose of benefiting others and acts that merely *turn out* to have this effect. Using this definition, Wilson is able to label as cases of altruism not only the behavior of dolphins cooperating to rescue their wounded, but also the labors of sexually neuter workers among the social insects, the warning calls of small birds, the defense of the colony by the soldier caste of termites, and even the behavior of bees that lose their stings and their lives when attacking a predator, thereby leaving a chemical deposit that serves as a signal to summon additional defenders. (It is interesting that Wilson chooses to characterize this type of apian behavior as "kamikaze attacks."[13] One would be unlikely, I think, to call an actual kamikaze attack a case of altruism unless the mission were a voluntary one.) By disregarding what makes the creature do the beneficial acts it performs—its reason, if you will—the sociobiologist is likely to miss the entire point of designating a piece of behavior as altruistic.

A sociobiologist might reply that he is not interested in what the *point* is of calling a type of behavior altruistic; rather he is concerned to offer an explanation of how the behavior we call altruistic arises and why it persists. Indeed, what Wilson and others have tried to show is merely that such behavior, whether it occurs in humans or in dolphins or in the social insects, serves to promote the transmission of a species' genetic material. The fact that Wilson is willing to concede that, as far as human altruism is concerned, the specific form of the acts performed is to a large extent culturally determined does not at all prevent him from insisting that the impulses that give rise to these acts are themselves the products of evolution through the genes.[14]

Nevertheless, I think it can clearly be affirmed that whatever is explained by the sociobiologists' speculation, it is not altruism as the concept is ordinarily understood but rather something much more general, of which human altruism is a special case. Not everything we do that benefits others more than it benefits ourselves is a case of altruism. And just as we would not be willing to accredit a putative study of suicide that failed to distinguish it from accidental death, it is difficult to imagine anything but confusion resulting from trying to explain the social phenomenon of altruism without distinguishing it from the unintentional or incidental conferral of benefits. To the extent that understanding human institutions and human social interactions requires grasping distinctions that have to do with reasons and intentions and these are part of the residue that biobehavioral reduction leaves behind, the social behavior of humans will not be biologically explainable.

Anyone who proposes, as an explanation of why people engage in fights, perform altruistic acts, or enter into social arrangements, an account that appeals to their inherent biological characteristics is proposing an account that is in competition with one that sets out the reasons people had for acting. Reasons are viewed as irrelevant on the biological account, except as they are themselves part of an innate response pattern. Acting for biological reasons, it should be pointed out, does not imply that the behavior is explainable by the actor's genetic constitution: we take medicine for biological reasons, but we would not try to explain the taking of medicine as a genetically determined response. If biological elements are the causal basis for social behavior, there must be some way that they work their effects other than merely by figuring in people's reasons for acting.

If there is a way that human biology can be said to influence voluntary human behavior, other than by setting the limits that fix human capacities, it must be through the determination of a person's feelings and inclinations. The idea is that what people do in any given situation depends on their natural urges, their inborn desires, and the tastes and preferences that are part of their biological makeup. All of these features are supposed to be fixed by the genotypes; the genotypes are the result of natural selection; and the natural selection is based on the adaptive advantages that the genotypes confer, or did confer at an earlier time, either on the individuals who perform the actions to which these genotypes lead or on populations in which these actions occur.

What the theory—if that is what it may be called—implies is that social practices that persist do so not because they are adaptive or because of the weight of cultural tradition but because of propensities that reside in the genes. The fact that cultures exhibit certain common features would be explained by the occurrence of specific genes among the human population. These innate factors are supposed to be what cause people to choose the behavior that finds expression in their culture. Culture becomes the reflection of humans' genetic inheritance.

There is no way to support this biological hypothesis, however, that does not equally well support the idea that it is culture, rather than biological nature, that determines what behavior persists in human culture. Suppose, for example, that there were a xenophobic gene that could be invoked to explain the cultural fact of racism. Now in order for any gene to flourish it has to be adaptive, which means in this case that its manifestations would have to be supported by the culture. A racist gene, in other words, can flourish only in a racist culture. But since a racist culture is one that not only supports the expression of racist tendencies but also engenders racist attitudes among its members, a culture must already contain and be capable of producing—by whatever means—racist individuals if it is to provide a hospitable environment for the posited xenophobic gene to survive in. The evidence for the existence of a genetic determinant of racism is therefore no different from the evidence for the existence of racism in any culture. The difference the biological hypothesis makes, given its lack of independent evidential support, is essentially ideological: it suggests that any change in conditions that might make cultures cease to foster racism would require an evolutionary time span.

One way of assessing the adequacy of an explanatory scheme is to consider the way it tries to cope with apparent exceptions. In the case of sociobiology, the problem seems to be especially acute: whenever there is found a counterinstance to the suggestion that social practices can be explained in terms of innate preferences and tendencies, it must be supposed either that the tendency is one that can be overridden, in which case the factor is too weak to provide a satisfactory explanation of the behavior, or else an ad hoc postulation of a genetic difference must be made in order to account for the exception.

102

The attempt to provide a biological explanation of the apparently ubiquitous incest taboo is a case in point. There is evidence, albeit indirect, that the avoidance of the dangers of excess homozygosity, namely physical and mental defects, could very well be the basis of the taboo. But this giving of a biological reason would not show that incest avoidance has a genetic basis. There would have to be a biological mechanism, one that works through natural preferences to make individuals not want to mate with kin. But it is doubtful whether such a mechanism is operative. For, as a number of people have pointed out, if incest avoidance were instinctive, incest would not have to be illegal. Some people do (knowingly) commit incest, and unless we introduce the utterly wild assumption that these people are genetic variants, we must suppose that, whatever basis there is in human biological evolution for the fact that humans do tend to avoid incest, it is not enough to explain the taboo.

Wilson has suggested that the way a cultural tradition may become established is by means of social reinforcement of natural tendencies that have been selected for because of the adaptive advantages they confer. With regard to the incest taboo, a mechanism that has been supposed to operate involves what has been called "the precluding of bonds": kinship relationships such as between fathers and daughters, mothers and sons, and brothers and sisters seem to exclude the possible formation of other types of bonds.[15] Evidence cited for this hypothesis includes studies in Israeli kibbutzim, where it was found that, among unrelated members of the same kibbutz peer group who had been together since birth, there were no recorded instances of heterosexual activity, despite the absence of formal or informal pressure, and that all of the marriages that occurred were with persons outside the kibbutz. The inference drawn is that social prohibitions on incest may have arisen as a result of evolved natural inhibitions, which have persisted because those who have them tend to leave a larger number of fertile offspring than do those who lack them.

The model is not an implausible one, and could be extended to cover other sorts of cases. Cultural rules and social beliefs could very well have arisen as rationalizations of people's natural preferences. The difficulty, apart from the lack of direct empirical support, is that these preferences, since it is known that they can be overridden, are again too weak to provide any significant explanatory power. Human beings are capable of

103

internalizing a number of quite different norms, as many anthropological studies have shown; innate preferences of the sort invoked are clearly not strong enough to prevent some tribes from drawing the incest line between what anthropologists call matrilateral and patrilateral cross-cousin marriages (i.e., between marrying one's mother's brother's daughter and marrying one's father's sister's daughter), for example. It is tempting to suppose that norms may be derived from natural tendencies, but it impossible to say which norms *must* be so derived. A norm is something that governs voluntary behavior, and there is no norm that is not susceptible to replacement by a substitute.

As a final example, we might consider the matter of the sexual division of labor, whereby, as Wilson puts it, "women and children remain in the residential area while the men forage for game or its symbolic equivalent in the form of barter or money."[16] Wilson has suggested that the basis for this division of labor, which he takes as revealing a genetic bias, may lie in the fact that males are, on the average, demonstrably more aggressive than females from the beginnings of social play in infancy, and that they tend to show less verbal and greater mathematical ability. If these differences exist, they may help to explain why some people dominate others, and also why certain professions have a disproportionate number of men in them. They do not explain the institutionalization of male/female dominance patterns and the resulting role distributions, however, nor do they explain the extent to which the social patterns that are actually observed reveal polarizations that are much more pronounced than the essentially statistical findings would dictate. A basketball team may dominate another team whose members are on the average shorter, but only because each team is organized as a unity for the sake of demonstrating its collective dominance. One cannot derive a culture of male/female dominance, or deduce a strict or nearly strict sexual division of labor, from a set of statistical differences between males and females.

What the biologist who seeks a basis for understanding human social behavior in the study of nonhuman animals is trying to show is that some of what we know about some animals is also true of human beings. Since human behavioral traits, unlike anatomical features, cannot, for the most part, be established as homologous, as based on common phylogenetic descent, the ethologist is forced to rely on analogy. But analogies that concern patterns of human social behavior and similar displays among animals are unconvincing because the behavior is typically either disanalogous or not known to be analogous just at the point where analogy is the most crucial: the way the behavior is mediated. If behavior that is rigidly determined by a mechanism whereby a specific releaser triggers off an internal response has as its counterpart in humans behavior that is subject to nothing like such rigid causal determination, we are not licensed to infer anything whatever concerning the biological basis of the human behavior in question. It is also presumptuous to suppose, in the absence of any evidence pointing to a specific kind of mechanism, that a universal feature of human societies is a biologically inherent characteristic of the species, regardless of how many other species exhibit behavior that is analogous. When similar behavior is observed across species lines but the biological mechanism shown to operate in one species is known not to operate in the other, it is not reasonable to argue that there must be some *other* biological mechanism that can be assumed in order to explain the effect in the second species. Human behavioral tendencies *could* be species characteristics having significant genetic components, but they could also arise in other ways; and since we know that the behavior is in any case subject to environmental modification, biological conjectures are extremely unlikely to make any sort of contribution to understanding why the behavior occurs.

A behavioral trait that is common to all human societies must be shared by some other animals, all other animals, or no other animals. As far as behavior that is unique to humans is concerned, it is clear that comparative studies involving other species will not provide such illumination, regardless of whether the human behavior is thought to be biologically determined or not. On the other hand, studying behavior that is performed by some other species as well as by humans, even by all closely related species, is also not going to yield results that can automatically be extended to humans. If what is true of animal societies is also true of human societies, this can be established only by studying humans on their own. We cannot *assume* that animals in different species will behave in similar ways under similar circumstances, nor can we assume that behavior that is common to two or more species and has a genetic basis in one is equally heritable in the others. We simply do not know what to make of our observations of animals. So far as social behavior is concerned, there is not enough force in any conclusion that could be reached regarding nonhuman animals to give its extension to humans a significantly higher antecedent probability of being true than could be assigned to the proposition that people are exceptions.

Because discoveries about the way animals behave are often so *interesting,* it is tempting to believe that there must be something that we can learn about humans as a result of these studies. One can easily be impressed by seeing the way monkeys or wolves avoid destructive intraspecies fighting by means of dominance hierarchies, or by observing the effects of crowding on social harmony among rats and hippopotamuses. It is fascinating to discover that female baboons do not compete directly but rather vie with one another in terms of the position of the males associated with them in the dominance hierarchy, or that rats, who will try to kill an intruder when it cannot escape, will not (unlike the Royal Canadian Mounted Police) pursue it into the wilds. By telling us a lot about animals that we did not know, animal behaviorists can perhaps help us to discover that we are more like animals than we thought we were.

It has been suggested that, although animal behavior studies do not prove anything concerning natural human tendencies, or even that there are any, they may provide a source of ideas for subsequent studies that could be carried out on humans.[17] Perhaps noticing that crowded conditions among cats give rise to the emergence of a despotic leader, or that young male African waterbucks, who are not tolerated by the older, territorial males, form roving "bachelor herds" can serve as a guide to looking for connections among elements within human societies. Biological studies may serve as means of generating important questions and of providing tentative answers that might then be examined as to their relevance for humans. We can ask, for example, how other animals avoid bloodshed, and then try to find out how ritualization serves this function. We can observe the way some species preserve social stability through adherence to dominance hierarchies that are rarely if ever challenged, and we can see what happens to previously peaceful animal colonies under conditions of higher population density. While no legitimate inferences may be drawn as to what results would be obtained were these ideas to be tested on humans, studies such as these do represent a considerable source of possible experiments to be carried out within the human domain.

Nothing that is a possible source of ideas deserves to be summarily dismissed, of course, and animal behavior studies may be a particularly rich source. They may also be no better a source of ideas about human behavior than might be afforded by travel to foreign lands or by reading imaginative fiction. The role of a source of inspiration is a very important one, but it is also very limited. I suspect that what makes animal societies a particularly attractive source is not so much the wealth of illustrations that they afford as it is the unsupported notion that what is true of animals and can be applied to humans is likely to be true of them. But like the free play of fantasy, knowledge of the ways animals conduct themselves does not tell us anything about what happens in human life.

Citing ethological discoveries in the context of considering human social behavior has an effect that is largely rhetorical. Like Aesop's fables, facts about the ways animals behave are often thought to provide us with "lessons" as to how we ourselves might behave, quite apart from whether or not they reveal the way we do in fact behave. Specific findings with regard to animals, like stories or myths, neither establish nor refute assertions concerning what human behavior is or ought to be; the most they can do is serve to counter other claims that have been made based on other examples. Finding that higher primates seem to lack intraspecies aggression does not lead to any reliable conclusion concerning humans, but it may serve as an antidote to the claim, based on analogies between humans and certain animals that do fight, that human beings are innately given to fighting. The popularity of the sort of popular ethology that is associated with the names Konrad Lorenz, Desmond Morris, and Robert Ardrey is mainly due to these rhetorical effects. What these works offer are essentially anecdotal accounts of animals and human behavior enshrined within a general ethological perspective.

There is in these accounts a definite undercurrent that suggests that people do what they do not for reasons or as a result of conditions that are brought about by other people or by cultural influences, but because of internal forces that we have all inherited from our remote animal ancestors and that cannot easily be resisted. Thus Lorenz urges that "humanity must give up its self-conceit and accept that humility which is the prerequisite for recognizing the natural laws which govern the social behavior of men."[18] The reason "why reasonable beings...behave so unreasonably," he believes, is that human social behavior "is still subject to all the laws prevailing in all phylogenetically adapted instinctive behavior."[19] The lesson being taught is that we ought to resign ourselves to accepting a nonrational basis to our social behavior, and acknowledge the truth of such propositions as one that Ardrey affirms, that "man is a predator with a natural instinct to kill with a weapon."[20]

We have seen that none of these conclusions is warranted by the evidence ethologists have presented or are ever likely to turn up. Failure to realize how limited is the reach of their discoveries has led some of these researchers to think they can derive socially significant results having a strong normative content—such as the inference that there is a basis in nature for private property or for an authoritarian family structure, a basis so strong that it would be futile to attempt to avoid these institutions. Others have been more cautious in their suppositions, but are not always willing to deny that their investigations could yield results of a prescriptive nature. Thus Wilson, although he explicitly warns against the dangers of committing the naturalistic fallacy—the supposed mistake of trying to infer what ought to be from what is—nevertheless maintains, for example, that if the theory of "innate pluralism" is correct, then "no single set of moral standards can be applied to all human populations, let alone all sex-age classes within each population."[21] He also suggests that lessons can be derived, albeit not deductively, from discoveries such as those concerning the connection between crowding and aggressive behavior in cats and rats.[22] The important issue, however, is not whether Wilson or any other sociobiologist has been completely faithful to the antinaturalistic stricture, but rather whether even the allegedly factual inferences regarding human beings are warranted. *Of course* facts are relevant for what ought to be done; the major question is whether the sorts of facts that sociobiology comes up with are ones that shed any light on the social behavior of humans.

Although I have been arguing that conclusions drawn from studying animal behavior concerning human societies lack adequate scientific basis, I do not wish to suggest that ethologists and sociobiologists can never turn up significant insights about people. Scientific inference need not be regarded as the sole vehicle of truth. Myths and fables, as well as true stories about other people and other animals, often are repositories of truths of a very important sort. What I am denying is that what can be learned about people or the human condition from observing animals is any more scientifically warranted by the evidence adduced than is the "sour grapes" phenomenon by Aesop's fable. So far as elucidating human actions is concerned—as opposed to human bodily functions—animal studies are more like literary works than they are like scientific experiments. The author may have "gotten it right" for people as well as animals, but there is nothing in his presentation itself that assures us that he has.

As an illustration of this aspect of ethological discovery, we may consider an example from the work of Konrad Lorenz.[23] One of the things that he found in studying pair-formation in ravens is that it is the sex of a newly introduced prospective sexual partner that determines whether an individual that has been raised in isolation will act like a male or a female: regardless of its own biological sex, the isolated bird will adopt the courting behavior appropriate to the sex opposite to that of the introduced bird. Lorenz's finding, though intriguing, offers no basis for inference concerning any possible human situation. Any suggestiveness is merely implicit, part of the rhetorical effect of the example, though it could very well express something that is also true of human beings. The suggestion is not altogether dissimilar to one that is found in D. H. Lawrence's story, *The Fox,* in which the role that a young woman has assumed in a homosexual relationship is seen to change abruptly from that of a male to that of a female when a young man enters the scene. The writer and the ethologist have both hit upon something significant about the way the human creature behaves, that neither is in a position to prove.

Biologically inspired claims concerning human social behavior, though lacking empirical validation, ordinarily do have a grounding in what has been scientifically demonstrated. They are in that respect not unlike science fiction, wherein plausibility is conferred upon speculative propositions through showing them to be consistent with, but not entailed by, an established body of scientific theory. Unlike most science fiction, however, ethologically based propositions concerning humans commonly have a moral or political thrust, one that is all the more effective because of the illusion that these propositions have scientific backing. So far as biologists pretend to have shown that human behavior and human societies are constrained by biology to fall within limits that make it impossible, except through organic evolution, for human social patterns and social arrangements ever to be very different from what they are now, the only way to interpret the project of attempting to use biology to understand human social phenomena is as a way of rationalizing or defending the status quo. When a science is alleged to set forth for us what we can and cannot do because of our inherent nature, its pronouncements amount to either sound counsel or ideological preaching, depending on how well grounded in evidence the advice is. In the case of biology and human social behavior, it is both a scientific and a philosophical error to believe that the evidence warrants any conclusions either of a normative or descriptive kind concerning biological determination of either the form or the content of human social life. It is not by studying animals that we shall gain understanding of why people do as they do.

# 7. The Place of Causation in Social Science

A familiar way of explaining an event or circumstance is by citing a prior occurrence. We look for antecedents to tell us how things got to be the way they are and why occurrences happen as they do. When these antecedents are believed to have influenced or contributed to the event in question, they are ordinarily called *causes*, at least in the domain of natural phenomena. Explanations that enable us to understand phenomena in terms of their causal antecedents are called causal explanations.

The purpose of this chapter is to consider whether human actions and other social phenomena have causal explanations. We know that many things happen, in the social domain as well as in nature, because of other things that precede them: there are crimes of revenge, strikes that stem from past grievances, and changes in the birthrate that are the result of economic conditions. The question is whether the "because" of social explanation indicates causal explanation. We need to consider the forms of explanation that the mention of antecedents provides.

An explanation is an answer to a "Why" question. But the question "Why?" is often ambigous, and there is a corresponding ambiguity in the word "because." Bradley distinguished a causal from an epistemic sense of "because": when I say that the furnace went out because we ran out of oil, I am using the "because" of causation; when I say that a certain geometrical figure can be expected to have interior angles of 128 degrees because it is a regular pentagon, I am using "because" in a different sense: I am indicating the ground of my knowledge.[1] Nor do these exhaust all the senses of "because": there is a usage according to which we say that the flags are up because it is a national holiday, and that someone is entitled to sit in the front row because he is a member of the board of trustees. We also may say that a person has pushed a certain knob on the dashboard of his car because he is planning to light a cigarette, the knob being part of a cigarette lighter. In none of these cases does there appear to be an assignment of cause, at least in any straightforward sense. "Because" begins to look less like a means of signaling the imputation of cause and more like a rather general, nonlogical sentential connective that is used to indicate that what follows it is supposed to explain what precedes it.

Talking about social phenomena thus seems to be one area in which "because" is used in other than a straightforward causal or epistemic sense. There are, on the other hand, many cases of events within the social domain for which explanations in terms of prior events and circumstances would be identified as causal. Certainly one speaks of the causes of a war or of an economic depression, and social scientists are often concerned with the causes of such things as social unrest, election outcomes, and changes in dress styles. One also speaks of the causes of individual human actions, such as an official's resignation or a parent's writing an angry letter. Certain things that happen to people cause them to act, and often the way we try to explain actions is by seeking to identify these causes.

Since Hume, the problem of causation has been the problem of either specifying what there is that connects the events in a causal relation other than regular association between event-types, or else reconciling the conclusion that there *is* no causal nexus, that all there is is constant conjunction, with the familiar conviction that there must be a further sense in which the cause *produces* the effect. Followers of Hume have held that there is nothing but constant conjunction. As Bradley pointed out, however, constant conjunction is neither necessary nor sufficient for a causal relation to exist.[2] If a single instance of succession may not amount to causation, mere repetition will not either. But if repetition does not constitute the causal relation, then the causal connection, if there is one, must be present in the single instance. Constant conjunction is thus merely a *consequence* of causation. While it is true that we often depend on demonstrations of constant conjunction as means of identifying or confirming putative causal connections, it neither follows nor is it true that constant conjunction provides an analysis of the causal relation.

112

Philosophers in the empiricist tradition have generally believed that what makes the connection between events that are perceived as constantly conjoined a causal one is the existence of a lawlike regularity. Laws of nature that "cover" the events are what are supposed to explain the observed conjunctions. Thus to offer any singular causal statement is taken to imply that there exists some true universal statement, a discoverable law that ties together the events under considerations. Laws of nature are supposed to be what make singular causal statements true.

The thesis that causal connection presupposes laws has important application with respect to the attempt to provide causal explanations of human actions. It implies that if these occurrences are causally explainable, they must be connected to their antecedents by true generalizations. But since there appear not to be any such laws—it is simply not true, for example, that persons always respond in the same way in similar circumstances—it would seem that we are not entitled to suppose that actions are caused by the occurrences that prompt them. If causal explanations require laws, and there are no laws connecting actions with their antecedents, then these antecedents cannot causally explain actions.

A way of avoiding this consequence, as we saw in Chapter 4, is to argue that explanations of action can be causal even though no general law can be formulated, as long as there exists a general law connecting events of a kind to which the antecedent belongs with events to which the act belongs. We do not need to know what the law is or in what terms it can be formulated. All we need to assume for there to be causality is that there is a law, at some level, such that every time a prior event of a kind that we say causes an action actually sets off an action, the latter event occurs as a consequence of there being a lawlike connection. The fact that we may not observe regularities between action-types and antecedent event-types does not have to be taken to imply either that there exists no causal connection or that causality does not require laws.

This way of reconciling lack of knowledge of laws with wanting to regard antecedents of actions as their causes still implies that there have to be causal laws that connect the occurrences under some description or other. The trouble with this idea is that it places the assignment of causes on a very shaky foundation. For while it is true that we have knowledge of lawlike regularities that we can use to back up our assignments of cause in some matters of a physical or biological nature, we have no such

113

knowledge with respect to the domain of human action. The conviction that there *must* be a law linking any two events that we take to be causally related may be no more than a reaffirmation of faith in determinism, as Scriven has put it.[3] Davidson, who is responsible for the suggestion that the laws needed to support causal explanation need not be statable but only presupposed,[4] offers no argument for the assumption that every singular causal statement implies that there exists a law covering the events at hand. The widespread acceptance of this assumption may very well be, as Anscombe has characterized it, one of "the dogmatic slumbers of the day."[5]

If it is impossible to identify a causal connection without supposing that there exists a law, then only those who share this assumption should be able to assign causes. Someone who holds a different view of causation, or someone who claims not to know that there are laws where none has been formulated, would be disqualified from making any ascriptions of causal connection at all. But as Davidson himself concedes, we are usually far more certain of a singular causal connection than we are of any causal law governing the case.[6] Furthermore, it is often much easier to establish a causal claim—that leaving the milk out will cause it to go sour, for example—than it is to discover a relevant general law. If it is not inconsistent to assign a cause in some particular instance and at the same time to deny that there is a law that connects the events thus associated, then it must not be the case that one has to believe that where there is causality there also has to be law.

What is needed is an alternative view of causation, one that does not require the existence of laws. Fortunately, one is available: the view that causation is a basic concept, not reducible to others.[7] A cause is an event that produces a difference in the train of occurrences or states of affairs that would otherwise obtain.[8] It neither refers to nor implies constant conjunction or lawlike regularity.

The idea that causation is a basic category is one that is deeply rooted in Western philosophical thought, despite the influence of more recent positivist and empiricist attitudes. Descartes, Spinoza, and Locke all treated causation as a concept not subject to further analysis, and Kant specifically identified it as a fundamental category in terms of which objects of experience *must* appear to the human mind. Like light, which physics has never succeeded in reducing to anything more basic such as waves or particles, causation represents one of the basic ideas in terms of which we make sense of the world. It follows that the concept of cause does not depend on the concept of law, even though the existence of lawlike regularities is what enables us to discover causes. Laws do not explain causation; causation rather explains why there are such things as causal laws.

Anscombe has pointed out that causal concepts are acquired directly with the learning of language: to know the meaning of such words as "scar," "frighten," "sharpen," "tickle," "burnt," "intoxicated," and "squeeze," we must already have mastered the concept of causality.[9] One does not have to know a law in order to know the cause of something, nor does one have to know even whether there *is* an exceptionless generalization that connects cause and effect. I may know that someone's telling a joke is what caused me to laugh, or that my leaving a newspaper out in the sun is what caused it to turn yellow, and yet not know if there is any necessary or universal connection that is operating—even though I may very well assume, especially in the latter case, that there is a lawlike principle at work.

The fact that one particular occurrence is what made the difference in one particular case does not imply that it would have made a difference in other, similar cases. Causality does not have to entail determinism. It is true, of course, that often what makes a particular causal claim *believable* is that the thing that is designated as the cause in any given instance is recognized as the sort of thing that is known to make a difference in that sort of case, but this is merely an epistemic requirement. We do not have to accept determinism to the extent that we believe that causes and effects are identifiable as repeatable types. But the fact that causal uniformities must be presupposed in order for particular causal claims to be validated does not mean that these claims must be universal in character.

Even if nature is uniform and similar effects can be expected to follow from similar antecedents, this still is not enough to guarantee that causal explanations will presuppose causal laws. In order for there to be causal laws that are discoverable, it must be possible to abstract from those antecedent conditions that gave rise to a given occurrence a set of principles that can be generalized to other, different situations. Merely having the same causal conditions always produce the same effect will not suffice, if this requires that *all* of the original conditions obtain and nothing intervene. For if all of the elements in the domain are interrelated in such a way that if *any* of them had been different, a designated cause-effect would not have produced its effect, this would be a case of causation without causal laws. (An illustration of this might be an artist's bringing about a particular effect by adding a certain brush stroke.) Causation according to laws of nature requires something else: that only some of the world's repeatable conditions be relevant with respect to whether particular types of occurrence give rise to particular kinds of effect. In order to infer the existence of causal laws from the existence of causal sequences, one has to make the additional assumption that these sequences are repeatable independently of variations in other conditions.

One of the pragmatic traits that any explanation, including causal explanation, must exhibit is generality. If an explanation contributes understanding, it must convey information that can be used to illustrate more phenomena than just the one that is to be explained. The assignment of a cause is not explanatory unless the cause is generalizable to other situations. The fact that causal explanations have generality does not mean that they always presuppose universal laws, however. For as Anscombe has pointed out, if you take a case of cause and effect and try to form a universal proposition that is supposed to connect all instances of events picked out by relevant descriptions of the cause and effect, you usually will not get anything true, because there will be an indefinite number of circumstances in whose presence the causal sequence does not obtain.[10] When we explain why the eggs broke on the way home from the grocery store (they were packed under some tin cans), or why a student failed an examination (he was extremely nervous), we do not expect to be able to indicate what all the conditions are that had to obtain and what ones had to be absent in order for the effect to take place. Nor is it unreasonable to doubt that there *are* any true generalizations of the desired scope that will cover the cases being considered. What we know is that certain things tend to happen unless something else happens that causes them not to happen—which is to say that our notion of causation is prior to our notion of natural law.

Once the assumption that causation always requires laws is rejected, there is no longer any obstacle to accepting our ordinary intuition that giving a person a reason often does cause him to act. If we do not have to assume that reasons have to be connected with actions by causal laws, then there is no problem in regarding the hearing of the sound of bombers overhead, which is a reason for someone to run for cover, as the cause of that action. We do not have to believe in the existence of what Scriven has called "phantom laws" in order to recognize the sequence as a causal one.

Freeing causation from dependence on law also allows us to resist the idea that causes always necessitate, that it is not possible that the cause-type event occur and the effect-type event not occur without the intervention of anything to prevent it. Thus treating reasons as causes is entirely compatible with the fact that it is not obligatory to assume that, when a person is given good reasons for acting but nevertheless fails to act, something must have interfered that kept him from acting or else there were additional reasons that caused him not to act. A large and unexpected inheritance may give me a reason for canceling my life insurance. If that is what I do, we may say that receiving the inheritance is what caused me to do it; but if I decline to do so, we do not have to believe that there is a causal explanation of my not acting.

Causal explanation, when of the Humean type, explains by showing how the thing to be explained and the cause that it succeeds instantiate a regularity. An event *a* causally explains an event *b*, according to this model, when *b* can be seen to be a member of event-species B and *a* a member of event-species A and there is a regular succession between A-type and B-type events. But if reasons explain actions, and there are no causal laws under which these phenomena can be subsumed, then it is not clear how it is that reasons do explain actions. That is why Davidson and others have tried to show that reason-explanations may very well rest on causal laws even though no such law is statable. How else can reasons explain, if not by appeal to underlying regularities?

The answer, of course, is that reasons explain in some other way. Davidson, though he insists that reason-explanations presuppose causal laws, in effect acknowledges this when he says that reasons explain by "rationalizing" actions, that a reason "leads us to see something the agent saw, or thought he saw, in his action—some feature, consequence, or aspect of the action the agent wanted, desired, prized, held dear, thought dutiful, beneficial, obligatory or agreeable."[11] The problem that needs to be dealt with is that reasons have a more intimate connection to the events they explain than do other kinds of causes. A reason, if it explains my action, must be a reason *for me*; I must act *for that reason*. It is not enough that my reason be what caused the outcome that I desired. An example of Chisholm's illustrates the point: a man wants to inherit a fortune, and believes that he will do so if he kills his uncle. This desire and belief throw him into such a state of agitation that he drives excessively fast, with the result that he accidentally runs over and kills a pedestrian, who turns out to be none other than his uncle.[12] The reason he had for killing his uncle is what caused his uncle's death, but he did not kill his uncle for that reason.

If reasons cause the actions they explain, they must cause them in the right way. Davidson has suggested that the way to eliminate counterexamples such as Chisholm's is to lay down additional conditions about *how* the attitude and belief cause the behavior in question. He has to concede, however, that he is incapable of identifying all those conditions that will eliminate what he calls "quaint causal chains." Unable to find causal laws that will reveal how reasons rationalize actions, he is forced to conclude that his search for a causal analysis of acting for a reason is a failure.[13]

When we act on a desire, or for a reason, it is not, strictly speaking, the reason or the desire that causes our action. They are not the sorts of things that can function as causes, any more than the content of a thought can. What may or may not be a cause is accepting, adopting, or coming to have a certain reason, or the acquiring of a reason or desire. A desire is nothing more than a particular state, characterized in terms of its propositional content. To act on a desire is for that desire to become a reason—which is to say that it is representable as a component in a reasoning process—and for that reasoning process to culminate in action. If the reason I have placed my house key under the mat is that I want my brother, whom I am expecting to come for a visit, to be able to let himself in, I am acting on the basis of a desire that he should be able to gain access to my house and a belief that he knows where the key is and is likely to use it for that purpose. By indicating the reasoning I am explaining the action without specifying anything as its cause.

Since Aristotle, reasoning that leads to action has been called practical reasoning. It is a kind of reasoning that shows how wants and beliefs are brought together to give rise to intentions. A reason-explanation of an action is one that represents the reasoning that a rational agent might go through in forming the intention to perform the action. The agent himself does not, of course, actually have to deduce the conclusion that he will act in such-and-such a way. A restaurant owner who decides to fire a kitchen employee for not covering his face when sneezing does not have to arrive at the proposition that he will act in that particular way by means of an explicit process of deductive inference. One does not have to deduce one's actions in order for them to reveal a logic of practical reasoning.

According to one fairly representative account of practical reasoning, a person's action is rationally explained if the intention to perform that action can be shown to follow from the fact that the agent intends to bring about a certain end and that he believes this action to be necessary for the achievement of that end.[14] Thus my act of putting the key under the mat is explained by my intending to make it possible for my brother to gain access to my house and my believing that that will not happen unless I leave the key in that place. The link between premises and conclusion in an argument of this kind is represented as one of logical entailment.

Some philosophers have considered practical reasoning to be a causal process. Goldman, for example, who treats practical inference as a process whereby wants and beliefs come together to cause new wants, sees reasoning as a process in which a person moves from one psychological state to another.[15] The intention to act is thus a causal result of something that happens within the agent. This account does not indicate how practical reasoning *works*, however. The explanation of practical reasoning is not a matter of explaining why one psychological state succeeds another; rather it is one of showing how the occurrence of one such state explains the occurrence of the other, and this depends on how these states are characterized. Wants and beliefs explain actions in virtue of their *content,* as it is represented in a practical argument, not in virtue of any causal role that may be played by the psychological fact of *having* them. The acquiring of the intention to perform a specific act may very well be a causal process, but a reasoning process is not such a process, and if the reasoning process is one that explains why one has that intention, then the explanation is not a causal one.

In order to see why practical reasoning is not the same as causal reasoning, it may be helpful to consider an example. Suppose we learn that someone has just killed his horse by shooting it. We seek an explanation that will represent the reasoning carried out by the agent that led him to perform his action. We are informed that the reason he killed his horse is that his horse had broken its leg. Finding this inadequate as an explanation, we press further and learn that the horse's owner believed that the break would never heal and that the only way to relieve the horse, which he loved, of long and pointless suffering was to dispatch it as soon as possible. We now have an explanation, or at least the sketch of an explanation, one that shows the action to be something that a person with that belief might plausibly do.

If this is a case of causal reasoning, then there must be a causal principle under which the behavior that is being explained is subsumed. The principle that appears to operate, if there is one, states, in effect, that people who care about animals try to reduce their suffering. This is not an empirical causal law, however; it is rather a quasi-necessary, noncontingent truth that derives from the conceptual connection between caring about a creature and not wanting it to suffer. What links his attitude toward the horse with the action of shooting it is a series of rational or logical connections, given the beliefs he has. That people tend to perform those actions that they believe will further their ends is not an empirical causal principle; it is a defining principle of rational behavior.

But didn't the fact that the horseman wanted to end the animal's suffering cause him to act as he did? In a sense this is true, though it would be more accurate to say that coming into this situation is what caused him to do what he did. But to say this is not to provide an explanation, for that would require showing how the agent's wants and beliefs were rationally brought together to form the intention to act at that time. The task of such an explanation is to chart a course. It is no more a species of causal explanation than is the explanation of why a military commander has positioned his troops for battle as he has. What we want to know is the plan or scheme, not a sequence of events.

When something happens that gives a person reason to do something and he does it for that reason, we ordinarily would say that giving him the reason caused him to act. The sort of causation that is involved does not require the existence of any law or general regularity that can be discovered. A peal of thunder may cause someone to run out of the house and close the car windows; we do not need to assume that there is a true empirical generalization in order to find this singular causal proposition intelligible. The sort of principle that we do need is rather something like, "Events that produce in a person the belief that an undesired situation is likely to occur will lead him to try to prevent that situation from occurring." This is not an empirical generalization, but is closer to a tautology: it is an instance of a necessary truth: that people who have reasons to act are likely to act. To identify the giving of a particular reason as the cause of an action is not to show that the act and its antecedent comprise an instance of an empirical regularity; it rather serves to inform by revealing what it was whose occurrence prompted the act to be performed.

The only role that causation plays in the explanation of actions in terms of reasons is as a relation between the occurrences that give people reasons for acting and the actions that they do for those reasons. Receiving a telephone call can cause someone to write a letter, and receiving a letter can cause someone to make a telephone call. The connections between these occurrences, I have argued, are mediated not by causal laws but by processes of practical reasoning, which do not themselves need to rest on causal inference. I have also argued that in order for something that happens to be the cause of an action it is not necessary for there to be a causal law that the sequence in question may be seen as instantiating. Whether or not there are regularities between actions and their antecedents, the way we recognize these causal connections is by being able to discover what is reasonable. What is familiar with respect to actions is always reasonable, but not everything that is reasonable is familiar.

That explanations of actions are not causal in a Humean sense but are based on practical reasoning is illustrated by an example von Wright discusses: the assassination of the Austrian archduke at Sarajevo in 1914, an event said to have caused the outbreak of World War I. What the killing is recognized to have led to was the issuing of an Austrian ultimatum to the Serbian government, resulting in Russia mobilizing its army, Serbia refusing to comply with the ultimatum, Austria's declaration of war on Serbia, and so on. Von Wright considers the first step, the connection between the assassination and the ultimatum:

> Why did the Austrian cabinet issue it? Would it have issued a similar ultimatum to Denmark, if the archduke on a pleasure trip to Greenland had been killed by a mad eskimo? Hardly. The Sarajevo incident affected the aims and interests of Austrian politics quite differently. One of the traditional pursuits of the Habsburgs had been to maintain and extend Austrian influence in the Balkans. This influence might have been seriously weakened unless those found guilty of the murder were punished, the conspiracy behind

the assassination tracked down with all its possible ramifications abroad, and an assurance given that the interests behind the assassination would not be allowed to interfere with current Austrian plans to organize an independent Croatian kingdom to counterbalance the influence of Russia in the Balkans. These considerations provided the raw material of motivations for the Austrian cabinet in making the "practical inferences" which terminated in the issuing of the ultimatum.[16]

It is important to note that there exists no regular empirical association between assassinations and ultimatums, or even between politically motivated acts of violence and harsh governmental response. Although the killing and the ultimatum are logically independent events, they are linked not by a set of general laws but by a series of rational connections that are made clear by statements indicating the apposite beliefs and attitudes held by persons involved. Revealing the motivational background serves the explanatory goal of showing the issuing of the ultimatum to be logically necessitated, in that its nonissuance would have been taken as grounds for believing that the Austrian cabinet did not have the aims and conception of the situation that von Wright's explanation ascribes to it. The way that such an explanation shows that the event was to be expected is by showing that its occurrence followed logically from its perpetrators' beliefs and desires.

When an event is cited as a cause of a major historical event such as a war, revolution, or migratory movement, it does not have to be meant to explain in the way Humean causes do in natural science, namely by showing how the *explanandum* is linked to its antecedent by a lawlike regularity. The way that an event such as an assassination, bank failure, or drought makes a difference is by altering the situation that human agents have to assess when they perform the practical reasoning that culminates in their actions. These things explain by virtue of the fact that they give people reasons for acting that they did not previously have. When an action is explained as the outcome of a process of practical reasoning, what provides the explanatory power is not an empirical principle that links actions with prior occurrences, but a logical principle that expresses the connections among a person's wants, beliefs, and intentions.

Explanations of human actions in terms of causal antecedents, I have argued, do not require that these events be subsumed under universal empirical statements, nor do they imply that there exist laws that govern the phenomena in question. But even if there are no laws that can provide the backing for Humean explanations of human actions, it does not follow that there is no place within social science for causal explanations of precisely that kind. Indeed, much of social research, especially on the level of institutions, is carried out under strict Humean assumptions. The aim is to discover regularities of which specific occurrences of social and economic change can be seen as singular instances. A social or behavioral classification is regarded as effective if it expresses the terms of a causal law. The search for regular patterns of association plays a large part in social inquiry.

Every assignment of cause involves an act of abstraction. To identify a cause-and-effect relationship is to pick out some pair of elements in experience such that one can be seen as that which makes the difference with respect to the occurrence or nonoccurrence of the other. Whether or not it is possible to provide Humean causal explanations of phenomena within a particular domain will depend on whether or not one possesses or can invent concepts that will enable one to find lawlike regularities under which one can subsume particular instances of succession that one wishes to have explained. A class of phenomena for which that approach has been thought to be useful is made up of all human behavior that can be interpreted as typical or characteristic responses to internal or external stimuli. If a person writes his name upon hearing a certain command, or if a number of people cast their votes in opposition to a previously popular candidate whose involvement in a scandal has just been disclosed, the connection between the event and its antecedent is presumably a causal one. The conjunction, furthermore, would seem to indicate the existence of an underlying regularity, which can then be invoked in order to explain other instances of the same behavior. A Humean account may be quite adequate for explaining those parts of human behavior in which we respond as if we were blind mechanisms.

Humean causation is also a useful and relevant concept in explaining human behavior with respect to understanding the *conditions* of human life. Human actions are affected not only by physical conditions of sickness and health, heat and cold, rain and drought, and jungle and plains, but also by social conditions of poverty and wealth, war and peace, and tolerance and repression. Though we may not be able to explain the things people do as a result of such conditions in terms of causation according to law, we can often account in that way for the production of these conditions. The study of urban crime or juvenile delinquency, for example, often amounts to the attempt to identify the conditions under which certain types of action tend most frequently to occur *and* to learn what brings these conditions about. Similarly, the investigation of economic and technological conditions—the conditions that structure human life-situations and determine what the behavioral options are—involves conceiving them as effects brought about by antecedent circumstances in accordance with law. The same applies to the attitudes and emotions from which actions arise, for these are also caused by things over which the agent ordinarily has no control. Humean causation is ordinarily presupposed in an account of why, for example, someone is politically frustrated, though not in the attempt to explain what the frustrated person actually does.

The gap that exists between the conditions that serve as the springs of action and the actions themselves is one that we often justifiably ignore, for essentially methodological reasons: the interpretation of behavior as inevitable consequences or predictable responses is warranted just so far as it allows us to discover order in the relations between actions and what has gone before. There is indeed a gap that causal law cannot close between being in intense agony and performing an act of submission, between acute depression and active self-destruction, and between extreme frustration and violent rebellion. But it is a gap that is routinely crossed in practice, a point attested to by the fact that people are so often able to wield power over others, that they are able to get others to do their will. A great deal of human behavior, both individual and collective, does look like responses to stimuli, or like the movement of interchangeable pieces. We do act like automata to a considerable extent, and our behavior is often susceptible to prediction, just as it would be if it really were governed by causal law. It appears that, for many practical purposes, the gap between what is determined in accordance with causal law and actions that people perform may be assumed not to exist.

If there truly is such a gap, if human action is theoretically beyond the reach of Humean causal explanation, how is it that the gap can be crossed so easily in practice? How do we account for the appearance of causal regularity between so many kinds of actions and their antecedents? The answer is one that takes us back to the theory of practical reasoning: what we mean when we say that a person has been caused to act in a certain way is that he has been given a reason for acting in that way and that he has acted for that reason. When the same reasons produce similar actions in different people, we do not have to believe that these elements are linked by causal laws. Similar conditions give rise to similar actions because people appraise their common situations similarly and because the desires they have or have produced in them incline them toward making similar choices. The gap—which is a logical gap—is always there, however, even when the sequence of circumstance and act is most reliable, as in the case of a person's yielding to a coercive threat or irresistible urge. Extreme conditions may not literally destroy one's capacity to act, but by so limiting the choices and structuring the consequences, they destroy any effective difference between autonomous action and behavior that is causally necessitated.

The fact that rational individuals make similar appraisals and act in the same ways in similar situations—especially when the options are limited and the choices are heavily weighted—is what gives the pattern of conditions and responses the appearance of law-governed regularity. But that is not a way actions can be conceived and still retain the character of human actions. *You cannot infer from the fact that people make similar choices that their choices are determined in accordance with causal law.* Humean causation and free action are necessarily incompatible only to the extent that the former implies that there are deterministic laws linking actions with their antecedents. If actions are free—that is, if there are events that could have been otherwise even if nothing else were different—then it is logically impossible for there to be natural laws that connect them with determinate conditions.

Considering the role of cause in social science, one of the things we find is that the more a given investigation is oriented toward discovering lawlike regularities among actions and other social phenomena, the less it has to do with that which is specifically human. The extent to which causal explanation, of the kind that bases itself on causal law, gains a purchase on human behavior appears to vary in inverse proportion to the degree to which humans are regarded as moral agents. The fact that we do not ordinarily refer to our own actions as caused (though we may allow that they are suggested or influenced)—because we tend to think of causes as necessitating and as determining in accordance with causal law—can be seen as reflecting this point. What a person is caused to do, in this sense, is something for which he can receive neither praise nor

125

blame. Thus a plea of insanity entered in criminal proceedings is supposed to imply that what occurred was not a responsible act but rather a consequence of a process governed by causal law. To represent one's actions as causally determined is to disclaim responsibility and hence to derogate their status as free human actions.

The fact that we find nothing problematic about treating the behavior of institutions deterministically is an indication that we do not view them as responsible agents. Whether or not there actually are causal laws to be discovered that govern institutions and other social structures, it is generally a presupposition of the attempts of sociology and economics to explain behavior at this level that there exist such laws. The methodology of institutional social science does not require that the constituent elements of a social or economic system have to be human agents who are free to do other than their roles dictate.

How shall we understand the relation between that which appears to operate in accordance with causal laws and is effectively impersonal, and that which seems to elude such a characterization and is distinctively human? On the one hand there are large-scale events to which we seek to apply principles of Humean causation; on the other hand there are individual human actions for which we have no such causal explanations. Social change, whether of a political, economic, or general cultural nature, always consists of changes in a pattern of human actions. Democratization, industrialization, urbanization, revolution, and social disintegration, as well as changes in life style, manners, and customs, all imply that numbers of human agents will come to perform different actions from those they were performing previously. Many of these changes, as Popper has stressed, have come about as unintended and unforeseen consequences of intentional actions. But not every socially significant event happens without anyone's having intended to bring it about. People do, after all, often strive successfully to produce policies and legislation, effect reforms, make revolutions, and start and end wars. It is important to recognize that events of this kind are brought about not merely by people acting in direct pursuit of their goals but also by getting others to act in ways that they believe will contribute to these goals. Agitators, politicians, and reformists all play a role in promoting (or retarding) social and political change. It is the nature of this role that is problematic with respect to the matter of how social phenomena are caused.

126

In a discussion of the causes of a war or revolution, one does not ordinarily cite the actions of those who sought to rouse the others to action. Such behavior is *always* present when there is a self-conscious political movement. Where one looks for explanations of such phenomena is at the conditions and circumstances and the key events that give rise to the actions that constitute the change. Yet it may not be clear how these economic and political factors that are cited as causes produce the specific individual and collective actions that make up the fabric of the large-scale event that is to be explained. Just how is it that economic changes produce political effects, and socioeconomic events and circumstances cause armed struggle?

When Marx said that "men make their own history, but they do not make it just as they please," he was reminding us that people do not choose the circumstances that determine their options and condition their choices of action."[17] It is the "circumstances directly encountered, given and transmitted from the past" that are what explanations need to consider if history can be made intelligible. But Marx was also calling attention to the fact that human actions are what history is about, that history is constituted by people doing things, not as passive automata but as active participants. It is people who deliver speeches, read and write pamphlets, and man the barricades; and it is in virtue of their ideas and reasons, the way they think, that they perform the acts they do.

According to a Hegelian idealist interpretation of history, social changes are stages in the progressive realization of ideas (or the Idea). Individual acts are conceived as the concrete expression and working out of the ideas that are embodied in a tradition and in the institutional structures that provide the framework in which the acts occur. The process of history is seen as a unique process of organic growth. The problem of causation does not even arise when such a view is maintained, at least so far as causal understanding implies the possibility of isolating causes and effects. Certainly that way of conceiving history does not suggest a search for regular conjunctions of kinds of historical events. The way in which succeeding events or stages might be said to be caused by preceding ones would not be subject to causal analysis in terms of laws. Nor would the role of human agents be recognizable in causal terms. Those who work to move others to act would not be construed as active participants, as initiators of sequences of events; rather their role would be more like that of midwives, ensuring that the changes with which the times are pregnant are delivered. Any causal understanding of the role of human individuals would be ruled out.

There is another version of historical idealism, one that is associated with John Stuart Mill and the liberal tradition. Historical and social events are conceived as composed of individual acts that are caused by the ideas that people derive from the situations in which they find themselves. New ideas are generated by new situations and cause changes in the pattern of actions. A way that individuals are supposed to make a difference in history is as creators and purveyors of relevant ideas by which they try to convince others to act in pursuit of certain ends. Social causation, which need not imply here the existence of laws, is taken to operate through the causation of ideas by circumstances and by the causation of actions by these ideas.

This view of the mediation of social processes, unlike Hegelian idealism, acknowledges the active role of human individuals as contributors to historical processes. The picture it delivers of the relation between ideas and actions, however, is mistaken. An action is not to be conceived as one thing and an idea that drives it as something else. Actions are as it were infused with the ideas that are supposed to produce them; ideas cannot be the causes of actions whose essential character they define. The idea of democracy can no more be regarded as the cause of a rebellion against an autocratic ruler than can the idea of writing one's name be the cause of an act of signing an autograph; the rebellion is an act that is itself informed by that idea. Ideas give rise to actions that are done in the name of them, but these ideas are connected to the actions by an internal or logical connection, not an external or causal one. It requires a special act of abstraction to separate ideas from the behavior they give meaning to, not unlike that required to separate the taste of chocolate from a piece of chocolate candy. The importance of ideas in meaningful social action lies not in their causal efficacy but in the character they bestow on what occurs.

In order to account for the apparent determination of macroscopic social change by holistic and impersonal factors without either ignoring ideas and reasons or treating them as Humean causes, a different answer is required to the question of how they bear on the formation of changed patterns of individual actions. I want to maintain that the sort of causal analysis that seeks to subsume phenomena under covering laws is appropriate at the level of gross phenomena but not at the level at which individual actions are influenced. The use of a Hempelian or covering-law type of explanation to explain institutional or cultural changes does not imply that the same type of explanation will be applicable to the actions that constitute the substratum of these changes. Not only physics, but also economics, sociology, and political science study processes whose microstructure does not always yield to deterministic causal analysis. In none of these domains is there any conceptual obstacle to the causal investigation of macroscopic phenomena.

We have seen that institutions typically have lives of their own, but have neither aims nor ends apart from those of the individuals whose actions they govern. Their behavior is not, accordingly, to be designated as action. Their coming into and passing out of existence, as well as any other changes they undergo, are reasonable candidates for causal analysis according to the empiricist model. It is a contingent matter whether there are any regular associations among holistic social phenomena, but if there are, a strong case can be made for treating such associations as causal relations. So far as we can treat economic measures and features of social structure as facts whose human underpinnings are invisible, we can approach their interconnections the same way we do the facts of astronomy or chemistry.

Actions, on the other hand, though often illuminated by pointing to circumstances and prior events with which they are associated, are not capable of being causally explained in the way that other kinds of events are. I have tried to show that the sense in which actions are caused by things that happen that induce the agent to perform them does not require the existence of causal laws, and that practical reasoning, the reasoning that goes into explaining why an agent performs an action he does, is different from causal reasoning. The process whereby one gets another person to act in a certain way should equally be expected to demand a different kind of explanation from that afforded by deduction from causal laws. When a person is moved to act either by moral suasion or by appeal to rational self-interest, we do not, I have argued, need to suppose that there exists a causal law in order to acknowledge the action as having been caused. What we do when we try to cause others to act is provide premises for practical inferences that we hope will culminate in the performance of appropriate action. The way that urgings, pleas, and threats influence behavior is by introducing beliefs and desires that will lead, by a process of practical reasoning, to the formation of an intention to act. Effective persuasion makes people act: not by supplying causally sufficient conditions but rather by providing conditions that give them reasons to act.

Whenever a systematic change occurs in a society, it is reasonable to assume that people within that society are responding to influences and pressures that are what lead them to alter their ways of acting. The influences that affect people's intentions, and hence their actions, come from a variety of sources. Some of these influences are incidental or haphazard; others are created with the deliberate intention of promoting the actions to which they lead. Persuasion is merely one of the ways of shifting the ground of action; force is another. What makes any of these means effective, so far as concerted action is concerned, is the background of common beliefs and desires. It is this commonality of background that accounts for the tendencies toward uniformity of human behavior and for the fact that the results of exposing people to various social influences tend to be orderly. The extent to which it is possible to discover empirical regularities within the domain of large-scale social phenomena is a direct reflection of the degree to which this orderliness exists.

I have been arguing that there is no incompatibility between an investigation on the macroscopic level that looks for explanations of social phenomena in terms of general causal laws and a conviction that the constituent subphenomena, namely individual human actions, are not themselves governed by such laws. The situation is in some ways analogous to that of modern physics. The science of mechanics is both causal and deterministic on the level of perceivable objects, and yet we know from quantum mechanics that there is a small but nonzero probability that any object, say a ball on a pool table, will behave contrary to the laws of classical mechanics. Since there is an indeterminacy that is built into the theory of particles on the microlevel such that it is impossible to give a causal account of the behavior of any single particle, there is always the remote statistical possibility that enough of the constituent particles might happen to behave in such a way during a given time interval as to confound the principles of molar physics. The fact that the deterministic laws of physics are found to hold on the macroscopic level is a reflection of the unlikelihood that such a situation will actually occur. What it shows, however, is that an indeterministic microphysics does not rule out the possibility of a deterministic macrophysics.

This relation between levels may be presumed to exist in the human sciences as well. It is not as inconsistent to maintain that human actions are insusceptible to complete causal analysis, but that there may be general causal laws concerning collective or institutional phenomena. The analogy is a superficial one, of course, and ought not to be taken to imply that human behavior is itself ultimately indeterminate. To make that assumption would be to confuse the claim that actions cannot be adequately explained by means of deterministic laws with the view that not all of the movements of the human body are causally determined. Since, as I have argued earlier, actions cannot be identified with bodily movements, and the set of concepts in terms of which actions are explained are radically different from those used to explain bodily movements, there is no reason to *assume* that there are no deterministic accounts of movements. What I have argued above is that causation at the level of actions does not imply that there have to be laws on any level; nothing that has been said *precludes* that there be laws on the physiological or any other level.

Neither should the analogy between macro-determinism and micro-indeterminism in the physical and the social sciences be taken to imply that the indeterminacy of human actions amounts to admitting the presence of an element of randomness. To make that assumption would mistakenly rule out the possibility of conceiving of behavior as neither random nor as causally determined. Events that we recognize as actions are anything but random, whether they are predictable or not. One is not behaving randomly when one does as one intends to do; nor is one behaving randomly when one does what one does not intend to do. What is essential to our understanding of human actions is that they be conceived neither as random nor as determined in accordance with causal laws.

The model of explanation whereby phenomena are explained by subsuming them under covering laws does not, I have argued, provide an adequate analysis of the way we explain why people do as they do. Causation does, nevertheless, deserve a central place not only within the social sciences but also with respect to explaining human actions. In the first place, if we reject the claim that all causation presupposes the existence of causal laws, we may accept the fact that it makes perfectly good sense to say that actions often do have causes, provided we do not insist that these must be Humean causes. Second, even if we deny that actions themselves have causes, there is still the need to explain the production of those influences to which actions are subject. Though it may be a mistake, or at least an oversimplification, to represent human actions as effects of Humean causes, we ought not to repudiate that approach when trying to explain the coming about of the conditions from which certain identifiable (and to some degree predictable) types of action come forth. Many social phenomena are not actions at all, but rather are things that happen to people. Others do not concern persons directly but affect them only through institutions or collectives. The explanation of such phenomena may involve a search for lawlike regularities just as it does in the nonhuman domain. To the extent that the social sciences focus on events that happen and conditions that arise rather than on what people do to make them come to pass, their success may be just as dependent on the discovery of causal laws as is progress in the natural sciences.

The existence of causal regularities is what makes human 'action, including social action, possible. If there were no regularities, nothing that anyone did could have any reliable effects: you cannot murder someone without assuming that your actions have certain consequences, nor can you send a letter, cast a vote, or sell a piece of property without presupposing regular causal connections. On the other hand, the fact that some things are subject to causal explanations does not imply that all things are. Actions are certainly not known to be caused in the sense of being explainable in terms of known laws. That they are caused in accordance with unknown laws is an assumption that I have tried to show is unwarranted. All we are entitled to say is that at least some actions are caused. But that statement, since it implies neither that actions are causally necessitated nor that they are determined according to natural laws, tells us nothing about how their antecedents produce them.

# 8. Theory in Social Science

The mark of a mature science, at least if it is modeled on the most successful physical sciences, is the possession of a body of laws and theories. Sciences gather facts, but they also attempt to explain those facts. If an explanation is a scientific explanation, it must enable us to understand in terms of general principles. The best scientific explanations are ones that accord with theories that express invariant relationships among general or fundamental features of the world. A scientific theory provides explanations of both empirical regularities and particular facts.

It is a notorious fact about social science that its achievements have been rather meager so far as obtaining well-confirmed general laws and theories is concerned. There are not many general propositions of sociology or anthropology that hold true of all human groups and societies, and there are virtually no theories that command universal assent. In physics, there have been a number of cases in which a lawlike regularity, such as Boyle's law or any of Kepler's laws, has been discovered and subsequently embedded in a theory that explains not only the regularity but also many other findings as well. Nothing comparable exists in the realm of sociology, anthropology, or political science. Only economics, which, along with demography, appears to be the farthest removed of any of the social sciences from the study of specifically human behavior, has produced a sizable body of propositions of its own that have shown significant explanatory and predictive power. Theories of society and of history have been put forward, but none has the kind of unequivocal support that would serve to establish it as correct or as undeniably superior to its competitors. Although social science has accumulated many ideas and much specific information concerning human social life, it has definitely not provided the sort of theoretical knowledge in that sphere that we have with respect to the world of nature.

A common response to this situation has been to declare that the social sciences are in their infancy. The assumption behind this response is that the social sciences, given enough time (and support), will ultimately achieve a maturity in which they will enjoy the same predictive success as the natural sciences. These disciplines have not yet been able to produce their Newtons or Darwins, but when they are ready to do so, it is maintained, we can look forward to a systematic and predictive ordering of social phenomena. In the meantime, the social sciences are accumulating data, trying to discover uniformities, and looking for explanations of basic observations and generalizations.

Others have challenged the assumption that there is a general theory to be discovered, or even a number of theories that will cover the various areas within the social domain. Perhaps the lack of theoretical development in the social sciences is the consequence of a "deficiency" of the subject matter. The theoretical poverty of the social sciences may be a reflection not of their immaturity, but of a real impossibility: that there is no system that can be adduced that will organize social facts and provide a means of explaining them in terms of a uniform set of fundamental entities or states. It is conceivable, after all, that the phenomena just simply are the way they are and are not susceptible to being explained by relating them to anything else. The subject matter of social science may simply not exhibit enough stability and uniformity to permit the sort of ordering that the development of a theory would require. Thus one of the reasons why we do not have universally accepted theories of criminal deviance or child development may be that human beings are not sufficiently alike for there to be general principles that will reveal how certain personality types are produced. There may not be any general correlations between environmental factors and particular behavioral traits. If there are no regularities, there is nothing for a theory to explain.

There is no way of proving that there is no theory still waiting to be discovered. Certainly there exist within the sphere of social behavior a number of uniformities of at least an approximate nature. Behavior is, after all, classifiable, and we have some general ideas, correct and incorrect, concerning what kinds of circumstances produce what kinds of outcomes. A theory, if we had one, would tell us which popular generalizations are true and why. We know that a certain amount of order in human affairs is necessary for human social life to occur at all; the question is whether there is enough to found a theory on, and whether the order that exists is of a kind that submits to scientific theorizing.

Before the study of any part or aspect of the world can begin to develop a body of scientific theory, it must exhibit the character of a discrete discipline and satisfy three requirements. First, it must contain a number of descriptive statements that embody a set of classifications that enable it to represent the phenomena in its domain using a restricted number of general terms. Second, it must contain categories of varying degrees of generality that allow the arranging of the things it describes in an order whereby certain classes of phenomena can be grouped into more inclusive classes. Third, it must have a number of propositions having some degree of generality that express traits common to certain classes of phenomena. A scientific discipline must have a structure and a typology, and must exhibit a body of truths not all of which are particular in character.

All of the social sciences meet these requirements. Economics, sociology, and psychology all have vocabularies of their own, a great deal of descriptive material, and a number of general or quasigeneral statements that reveal correlations between features of certain kinds of social structures and indicate the ways individuals and institutions act under certain conditions. Social scientists have discovered relationships between kinship rules and modes of economic production, between voting patterns and ethnicity, and between interest rates and unemployment. Nevertheless, the social sciences lack established theories that enable us to give effective and noncontroversial explanations of these and other findings. The principles we have tend to be narrow in scope and/or riddled with exceptions, or else they are too imprecise either to yield definite predictions or to allow adequate testing. We simply do not have the kind of theoretical understanding of the phenomena of human social life that we have in the domain of biological and physical phenomena.

The failure of the subject matter of social science to lend itself to rigorous theoretical comprehension shows that either the subject matter

135

is "deficient" in the sense that it refuses to behave in ways that can give rise to a theoretical ordering, or else social scientists have not been patient or clever enough to discover what the proper ordering should be. Whatever the situation, the problem anyone trying to do social science has been faced with is the difficulty of finding divisions than can be reliably correlated with those aspects of social behavior that we are interested in studying. The result is that we lack a clearly articulated pattern of lawlike connections that a theory can be devised to explain.

It is important to note that the kind of deficiency it is suggested that social phenomena may exhibit is not something that is in principle restricted to the human domain. Any set of phenomena that science sets out to investigate could conceivably turn out to resist all efforts to systematically order it. It should also be pointed out that the fact that it is impossible to order human responses perfectly with respect to the effects of any particular disturbing influence does not entail the truth of any particular philosophical view of the nature of man or of the problem of freedom and determinism. It is no threat to scientific determinism that some people will not lose their willingness to resist external aggression in the face of heavy bombing, or that a certain type of soil additive helps some plants to grow but harms others; it is merely technically and scientifically inconvenient. It is, after all, a contingent matter whether numerically distinct individual insects or people or plants should be similar to one another with respect to their susceptibility to certain applied influences. Science develops the classifications it does because these enable it to coordinate its subject matter with the explanatory and predictive ends toward which it is used. If it turns out that social science is unable to generate theoretical and empirical principles that can be used to explain and predict the behavior of human individuals and collections of individuals on the basis of knowledge of prior circumstances, it may be the case that there exist no discoverable correlations between the controllable variables and the behavior patterns in which we are interested. As Scriven has suggested, there may be so many crucial variables operating in even the simplest interesting cases that it is impossible to discover the simple laws that would enable us to develop a theoretical framework capable of yielding effective explanations and predictions.[1]

To many social scientists, the apparent lack of theoretical achievement in their disciplines indicates merely the complexity of the subject matter and the presence of a large number of important and often uncontrollable variables. On this view, the social investigator must simply do the best he can, trying to answer specific questions such as why the birthrate is declining in a particular region or why a certain election was lost. Scientific progress, it is argued, can come only from dealing with manageable topics, ones that lend themselves to minute study and permit effective control of the relevant variables. Piecemeal investigation may be the only way that social research can hope to achieve scientifically valid results.

One way that social scientists whose research consists of such restricted studies have sought to provide intellectual justification for their work is to suggest that the result of accumulating a large number of microscopic studies may ultimately be an integrated social science, one that will afford a broad and comprehensive knowledge of societies and their problems.[2] The idea is that if we can establish enough correlations of a limited but uncontested nature, these can be put together to form a single comprehensive scheme that will amount to a realization of the goal of a unified social science. Our current inability to understand social behavior and to anticipate societal changes is interpreted as reflecting our not having acquired all the pieces we need in order to grasp the way all of the elements in a society can be expected to behave.

For such a synthesis to be possible, it is, of course, necessary to assume that the entire field of social phenomena can in fact be systematically ordered and is in principle subject to scientific explanation. Even if we grant this assumption, however, it is not clear why we should believe that any sort of integrated theory could come forth from the microscopic studies that are being carried out. One rarely gets any more scientific ideas out of a piece of research than one has put into it, and highly detailed research is likely to embody only very narrow ideas.

One of the reasons we cannot expect to build a comprehensive social theory out of the results of piecemeal research is that it is simply false that data, whether on the level of single observation or of empirical correlation, will organize themselves into higher-level conceptual patterns. Theories do not spring from data like a Phoenix from ashes, but must be fashioned by someone who brings more to the phenomena than is required to perform any single isolated study or set of studies. It takes someone whose ideas range beyond what is contained in any of the specific investigations to put together the pieces.

137

A second reason why particular studies may fail to lead to the development of a comprehensive theory is that the findings that are obtained may not be the proper ingredients. The data that get considered tend to be limited to items that exhibit the methodologically desirable features of being numerous, measurable, and amenable to statistical treatment. These are also the features that serve as criteria for selecting studies to be carried out. The only kinds of questions that can be answered scientifically are those that can be put in a form that will generate empirical data that can be handled by statistical techniques. An investigation of people's reasons and attitudes, for example, if it is carried out on the model of research in the physical sciences, will require a reduction of these features of human existence to things that can be counted—items such as bathtubs, hours spent watching television, and boxes checked on questionnaires. Both the questions and the answers in such a research program are set by the methodology. We may wonder how much bearing this type of research can have on understanding human societies and the human condition.

To illustrate the problem associated with attempting to investigate social questions by gathering quantitative data, let us consider the built-in limitations of questionnaires. If opinions are measured by counting subjects' responses to questions whose answers must be chosen from a short list, there is a strong possibility that, for many respondents, the choices will not effectively reflect what they would say if given a different kind of opportunity to reveal their views. If more expansive replies are solicited, on the other hand, the researcher is faced with the problem of dealing with the variations in subjects' articulateness and in their willingness to respond, as well as with the general difficulty of trying to reduce a large number of disparate responses to a limited set of categories. By restricting usable data to what can be recorded in tables and displayed in graphs and matrices, those researchers whose method of operation is to ply their subjects with questionnaires will inevitably prejudge the nature of the distillate by identifying what is significant with what can be counted.

In fact, a large proportion of this piecemeal social research is carried out without concern for laws and theories. One does not have to have a social theory in order to look for empirical connections between types of social phenomena, just as one does not have to have a theory of matter in order to discover and classify a series of repeatable chemical transformations. Some of the experimental findings and correlations that have been discovered by social science even have a modicum of predictive use. Entire fields have been developed, for example in the area of psychological testing, based on research that seeks to establish nothing more than regular conjunctions between certain personality traits and tendencies to certain kinds of behavior.

Since knowing the causes or correlates of something does not require knowledge of laws, there is certainly much that can be learned about the relations among various social phenomena without having a grasp of law or theory. A social scientist, like a dramatist or a novelist, can have a great deal of practical knowledge of human affairs without having any sort of theoretical understanding. On the other hand, because such knowledge is essentially fragmentary, it does not offer any systematic way of accounting for exceptions to any generalizations that may be put forward. A mark of a well-developed science is its ability to explain its predictive failures as well as its predictive successes; that is one of the things that a good theory is supposed to do. Without a theory that will explain why certain generalizations are true, a social science can have no way of explaining why they are sometimes false.

A theory of social phenomena, like a theory of chemistry, would enable one to explain why the regularities that are discovered exist. Among those social scientists who do not see their role as contributing to a theory of society at all, some are not interested in that kind of explanation. Others believe that the explanations of social phenomena can be given in terms of laws and theories belonging to other disciplines. Just as the theoretical principles that explain many of the regularities of a biological or geological nature are found in more basic sciences such as chemistry or physics, the generalizations of sociology and political science may be explainable in terms of general propositions at the level of individual behavior. The claim that in order for a discipline to be recognized as a science there must be laws and theories that allow its phenomena to be explained and predicted does not imply that the laws and theories must belong to the discipline whose subject matter is to be explicated. As Morgenbesser has remarked, we should no more expect sociologists to explain small-group behavior by looking for small-group laws, or political behavior by looking for political laws, than we should expect to explain accidents by accidental laws or to predict and explain snow by snow laws.[3]

139

A number of social scientists believe that all social phenomena can be explained in terms of individual psychology, and that the only laws that govern human social behavior, whether individually or in groups, are psychological laws.[4] This belief needs to be examined. We have already seen (in Chapter 3) that not even individual social actions can be explained in terms of psychological concepts alone. As Lukes has pointed out, no one has given the slightest clue as to how one would go about explaining social and political attitudes exclusively in terms of predicates that make no reference to any feature of any social group or institution.[5] We are not able to explain historical, economic, sociological, or anthropological contexts in such terms, nor do we have any grounds for believing that these contexts are simply backdrops against which psychological or neurophysiological forces are the sole causal influences at work. Psychological considerations, at least of a trivial sort, are relevant for every explanation of action, but they will not account for the differences among specific actions and practices that different social situations give rise to. The fact that *all* events and conventions of social life are dependent on the psychological propensities of individual human beings does not imply that psychological principles alone will explain the panoply of phenomena that comprise the domain of the social.

Another reason for being skeptical of the prospects of accounting for all human social phenomena in terms of psychological laws and theories is that the situations in which human behavior is seen to exhibit the kind of lawlike regularity that would indicate the operation of psychological law turn out to be rather narrowly defined. Psychological predictions and explanations tend to be most reliable under rather restricted conditions, such as the ones under which psychological experiments are typically carried out. We know what the behavior of an organism will be in a Skinner box, for example, but we can afford to have much less confidence with respect to whether the psychological principles we identify will manifest themselves in ordinary life situations. It is only when the behavior studied is under severe constraints or when choice is heavily weighted in favor of one alternative that we find strict adherence to psychological laws. (It is worth noting that Skinner, in his studies of operant behavior of pigeons, had to starve them to seventy-five percent of their normal weight in order to get workable results,[6] and that a paradigm that he has cited to illustrate the model of conditioning that he espouses is that of patients in a mental institution who were made to respond more promptly to the call for dinner by refusing to feed them when they were late.)[7] Behavior of human beings in less structured situations and under less stressful or restrictive circumstances is in fact much less subject to effective prediction. The closer we get to situations where more than one reasonable option exists and where social interactions reveal a multiplicity of possibilities, the less we can expect from an attempt to explain social phenomena in terms of psychological processes.

If the social behavior of human individuals and groups is susceptible to complete rendering in terms of psychological laws and theories, either the life of humans in society is like that of creatures in cages, or else all differences in individual behavior, regardless of socialization or institutional setting, are fully explicable in solely psychological terms. Neither of these alternatives has much plausibility. Not even John Stuart Mill, the very apostle of psychologism, believed that the order of human social development or the general facts of history could be derived from "the principle of human nature and from the general circumstances of the position of our species."[8] So far as human behavior is both governed and constituted by social practices and institutions, it can only appear chaotic from the point of view of individual psychology.

If there is order among social facts, it will not be discovered by psychology. Societies are either unordered configurations of natural, societal, and psychological elements or else they have an order that is determined in accordance with laws that exist on a social and not an individual level. Popper, despite his attack on psychologism, essentially accepts the former alternative; he is content with a form of individualism according to which societal facts are explained in a nonsystematic way, as the unintended consequences of intentional actions.[9] What Popper is unable to explain about phenomena on the societal level is that they appear to exhibit at least traces of order at their own level. It is this order that sociological and historical theorists have sought to account for.

If there is an explanation of regularities among gross social phenomena that is not reducible to an account in terms of the nonsocial properties of individuals, it must be one that appeals to an underlying structure or set of laws that provides a basic framework for understanding the range of behavior and social process that are observed. This is not the sort of framework that could be discovered by studying the psychology of individuals, nor can it emerge directly from specific studies so far as these are narrowly and nontheoretically conceived; it requires "thinking big." Such a theory of society would be analogous to Bohr's theory of the atom, a highly theoretical model that was devised to explain something directly observable, namely, the existence of regular patterns of lines in the electromagnetic spectrum. If it is possible to understand patterns of social phenomena in similar fashion—as manifestations of theoretically cognizable processes of a general and pervasive kind—they, like the spectral lines, will have been systematically explained.

There has been no dearth of speculation concerning what the basic structures and underlying principles are that allegedly determine the nature of social life on the level at which it is experienced. The works of Comte, Marx, Durkheim, Weber, and Levi-Strauss all represent attempts to delineate features that characterize a social order, features that can neither be simply read off the surface of social reality nor directly learned from the testimony of individuals. The aim of sociologists and anthropologists who are thus oriented, as well as that of certain economists and political scientists, is to understand societies at a level different from the one at which either behavioral description or introspective report operates. By looking for theoretical underpinnings, they hope to grasp the "big picture," and to answer questions of a sort that can scarcely be formulated, much less satisfactorily dealt with, by piecemeal social science—questions like "How does society (or a particular society) hold together?" and "Why do social changes occur?" Their goal is to discover order where others have seen only diversity.

Proponents of these large theoretical conceptualizations are sometimes attacked as being insufficiently concerned with data, with having a cavalier attitude toward "the facts." Defenders of rival theories all claim considerable evidential support for their interpretations, however, based on often quite detailed examinations of particular societies and periods of history. Social research carried out in this manner consists of the performance of two tasks: providing descriptions that present the phenomena in a certain perspective, and explaining why the phenomena thus described occur as they do. The fact that these theories operate at a high level of abstraction does not preclude their being grounded in facts and being subject to empirical confirmation.

The problem that besets theorizing about societies is not that these broad theories lack empirical grounding but rather that confirmation may be so readily available as to support a number of very different ways of conceiving the phenomena. One of the major differences between the relatively low-level hypotheses employed within the context of a more restricted empiricism and the propositions of theories having a wider scope is that it is frequently impossible to decide on observational grounds alone among several competing conceptualizations. Alienation, anomie, class, social integration, and internalization of institutionalized values have such a wide variety of manifestations that almost anything that happens is likely to provide confirmation. Descriptions of phenomena, furthermore, being pregnant with whatever theory is employed, may be so disparate as to make the comparative assessment of theories virtually impossible. Someone investigating human societies with a broad theory in hand may never find anything that actually puts his theory to test.

Later on I shall consider the implications of this feature of social theorizing with respect to the practical and intellectual value of social science, and I shall also consider the extent to which the situation is different in the natural sciences. Here I wish merely to illustrate the problem by briefly considering two sorts of attempts at broad social theory, both of which exhibit the difficulty pointed to. One of these is represented by the social theories of Talcott Parsons, wherein a general solution is offered to the problem of what holds a social structure together. Parsons' answer, briefly, is that social stability is determined by the existence of a set of commonly accepted values that fix both the expectations people have of one another and the tendencies of individuals to behave in accordance with these expectations.[10] Whatever the merits of this principle in giving us a perspective on what we can recognize as a social system, it has the disadvantage of leaving no possibility of discovering any society, any continuing group of interacting persons, in which this feature is absent. When Parsons says that "it is only by virtue of internalization of institutional values that a genuine motivational integration of behavior in the social structure takes place,"[11] he is saying no more than that individuals must comply with the wishes and expectations of others as embodied in social institutions if the society is to hold together at all. Since no empirical fact could show this statement to be false, Parsons' claim must be a conceptual one, not an empirical one.

Another sort of social theory that yields only a loose fit to the phenomena is historical materialism. Although it is a theory of social change rather than, like Parsons' theory, one of social stability, it too

143

can be accused of sacrificing falsifiability for generality. Such is the indictment that can be made against any form of historical materialism that seeks to enunciate a general thesis. Thus Plekhanov, in maintaining that "there is no historical fact that did not owe its origin to social economics,"[12] can defend the claim only in a very weak form. For he needs to reconcile his thesis with the fact, which he acknowledges, that the histories of law and of political institutions, as well as those of literature, art, and philosophy, are preceded by and depend upon definite states of consciousness. The way he achieves this accommodation is by concentrating on the "totality of phenomena," which he allows may be either *directly* or *indirectly* determined by social economics. In the case of law, for example, which he says is always a defense of some definite interest that is created by economic relations, the way he is able to keep his thesis from being falsified by the manifest variety of legal forms and institutions is to insist that only its (economic) content be governed by his principle.[13] In this way Plekhanov tries to justify ignoring the fact that ideologies of all sorts influence the nature of law. The distinction he draws is between the form and the content of law; only the former, he insists, is determined by social consciousness. But since the content of the law, as Plekhanov interpets it, refers only to the interests that either gave rise to the law or are protected by its preservation, it appears that virtually any kind of law could be enacted and said to support Plekhanov's thesis. It seems that historical materialism, thus construed, is insulated against any possible empirical refutation.[14]

The general theorist, in searching for a broader and, by his lights, deeper understanding of social phenomena, tries to view each event or state of affairs in its appropriate context and at the same time to conceive of it on a level of abstraction at which it can be perceived as similar to other phenomena in quite different contexts. There is a level at which all wars and all revolutions and all technological changes fall together, and it is at this level that broad historical generalizations are possible, if they are possible at all. One adopts a certain perspective, and if this results in the blurring of details, the loss is supposed to be made up for by the gain that is gotten by the discovery of a unity that ranges over a number of contexts. The order that is discerned is one that is identified as a result of perceiving broad, repeating patterns.

An important consequence of viewing human social life in this way is that it allows for an infinite number of possible behaviors on the part of the individual that are compatible with the overall conception of society. Virtually any action-type that an individual does repeatedly can be labeled a case of role fulfillment, and anything that is not can be classed as nonconformity. Political conservatives can be said to embody perfectly the interests of the ruling classes, but there is also a way of accounting for those whose liberal ideologies lead them only to adopt modified means of working toward the same ends that conservatives seek, as well as for radicals and revolutionaries, who, regardless of their class origins, may be seen as engaged in the class struggle. Nothing any individual might do could count as a refutation of any of these general social theories. If there are grounds for choosing among competing conceptual schemes, they must be sought elsewhere than on the level of individual behavior.

The fact that the empirical evidence has not led to the emergence of a single general social theory does not mean that none of these theories deserves to be counted as a scientific theory, however, nor does the failure of general social theories to be directly falsifiable by itself disqualify them as scientific theories. For it is not in general true that scientific theories are automatically subject to refutation by single disconfirming instances. Scientific practice does not demand that refractory observations be allowed to upset an entire theory; the procedure more typically is either to ignore them or to accommodate them by making no more than minimal adjustments to the theory. Furthermore, when there is more than one theory that can be rendered consistent with the data at hand, the choice of one theory over another is dictated by nonfactual rather than factual considerations. Economy, simplicity, and accordance with prevailing extrascientific (including metaphysical and ideological) assumptions all play a role in determining the ascendancy of one theoretical scheme over its competitors. The fact that the data do not permit any one theory to be singled out does not imply that the existing theories are empirically inadequate, and the fact that no general social theory has achieved worldwide dominance may reveal nothing more than that there is no consensus with regard to the nonfactual criteria for accepting proposed conceptual schemes.

The major inadequacy of general social theories derives not from their lack of empirical content but rather from the limitations that are imposed by their selectivity. A social theory cannot be all things to all

145

people. Explanations are keyed to interests; the answers that an acceptable explanation provides must fall within an anticipated range of explanation *types*. It is our interest in certain kinds of considerations that determines what counts as a satisfactory explanation of, for example, an accidental death. With regard to social phenomena, it is similarly our interests and preconceptions that dictate the kind of explanation we look for. Whether we seek to understand a particular happening in terms of individuals' personality characteristics, organizational needs, the class struggle, or the requirements for social integration will be determined by which aspects of the social environment we choose to focus on. Different ideologies and different explanatory purposes will influence what gets accepted as the proper or "truest" theory.

One of the concerns that a general theory cannot satisfy is an interest in having the specific mechanisms of social processes explained. Another is the interest in these processes at the level at which people feel themselves affected and at which they conceive their intentional actions. Durkheim's conception of religious life, for example, presents us with a picture of specific practices perceived only as the means whereby a social group is held together.[15] Their significance to members of the society is not elaborated. The general theory is concerned not with the particular form that religious practices take in a given society but only with the fact that, as sacred institutions, they function in certain ways and they comprise a number of general types. The theorist makes a decision *not* to consider these institutions at the level that individual practitioners find most important. The level at which the general theorist operates is not that of theological debate or of moral dilemmas.

A general theory, because of its commitment to a particular level of abstraction, dictates the choice as to what is counted as significant. The point can be illustrated by considering an aspect of the Marxist interpretation of history. Thus Plekhanov argues that if Napoleon had not existed, or had been a peaceful man ("or had possessed the musical gifts of Beethoven instead of his own military genius"), it would not have made any difference to the internal life of France as a whole.[16] Influential individuals, he contends, "can change the individual features of events and some of their particular consequences, but they cannot change their general trend, which is determined by other forces." The implication is clear: whatever else might have transpired as a result of changes in the personality of the leaders is not important, compared with the kind of social changes that would have occurred quite independently of these changes. The claim is only partly an empirical one, for it rests on the ascription of greater significance to certain sorts of eventualities than to others. Since anything that an individual does that is socially or historically important depends on the social context in which he acts, whatever he does that is recognized as significant can necessarily be seen as a result of these social elements. The individual can *always* be bypassed in explaining important social occurrences, so that one is never required to identify specific indivduals as perpetrators of those events that the Marxist picks out as important.

Not everyone's interest in history is the same as that of the orthodox Marxist historian, of course, and there are many whose interest lies in understanding just those "individual features of events and some of their particular consequences" that Plekhanov mentions as depending on the specific character of persons and events. As Sartre points out, the consequences that even Plekhanov acknowledged would have ensued had Napoleon been killed in battle and his place as a dictator been occupied by a more peaceful man—that the Bourbons would not have returned to France at all and that the liberal movement that arose might have placed Louis-Philippe on the throne five or ten years earlier than it in fact did—comprise the whole life of men.[17] For they also include the terrible bloodshed of the Napoleonic wars, the slowing down of economic and social life that marked the return of the Bourbons, and the widespread misery that afflicted those who suffered and struggled under the Restoration. The level on which Plekhanov is right in asserting that things would have come out the same even if Napoleon had not appeared is not the level on which other historians are interested in events of that period.

No general-theoretical aproach to social phenomena can satisfy an explanatory interest in anything seen as unique. So far as the historical disciplines are conceived as idiographic, as aimed at understanding the unique and nonrecurring, they are not concerned with the same aspects of events that a general theory is supposed to capture. The historian who tries to explain why Hitler was able to come to power when he did, or why there was a revolution in France and not in, say, Spain, by concentrating on the circumstances that are peculiar to the event being studied has little or no use for theoretical abstractions. The point of view that focuses on discovering unique combinations of factors and circumstances that allowed a specific event to happen is clearly at odds with one that tries to represent each event as one of a general kind.

It is worth pointing out that Marx himself, who wrote more than one kind of history, acknowledged that every historical situation, every nation and every era, has a character of its own that makes it impossible to predict with certainty the outcome of the class struggle and what kind of revolutionary development will occur. What takes place in France will be different from what takes place in the United States, and what happened in 1871 should not have been expected to be the same as what happened in 1848, because the historical circumstances were so vastly different. It follows that a general theory, even one that is highly successful in providing a broad framework to which a wide range of phenomena can be found to conform, may be incapable of yielding accurate prophecies on the level at which it is supposed to be most useful. If every nation's history and every social milieu is unique in a sense important enough to affect some of the major features of its subsequent development, then there can be no general social theory or theory of history that will enable us to form true nontrivial generalizations about the ways societies can be expected to develop. The contribution of a general theory such as Marxism seems limited to providing a perspective from which to view human society and to giving explanatory insights after the fact.

The feature of abstract theorizing to which I have been calling attention is not one that is peculiar to a Marxist theory or to theories of history, for it applies to synchronic theories as well. There is no theory of society that explains what holds a society together that is capable of encompassing the many ways in which social entities that cohere do cohere and also of yielding predictions as to whether a given group will or will not disintegrate. No theory that is general enough to explain both why the Mafia holds together and why nineteenth-century America held together is going to enable us to anticipate, for any given social creation, whether that entity will remain whole or come apart and dissolve. General understanding appears to be possible only if it is not expected to offer specific predictions.

Students of human social life have failed to deliver the promised goods because what has been wanted could not be properly packaged and what could be packaged is not wanted. Science can investigate only what is repeatable or what is capable of being broken down into what is repeatable. With social phenomena, the problem is that what is repeated is often not significant, and what is significant is not capable of being rendered systematically. There is no social theory that resembles the theories of physical science in the respect of being both general and specific.

Social knowledge, like knowledge of the natural world, serves a wide variety of interests and conceptual orientations. A science may contain theories on a number of levels that satisfy different explanatory purposes; chemistry, mechanics, and atomic physics can all be applied to the same object without confusion, according to the kind of information that is wanted. With respect to social phenomena, there is often a dispute as to the proper level on which to seek an explanation. The reasons for this competition are in part ideological, in the sense that they are determined by a concern for the level at which one would like to ground one's explanations, but it is also a result of the failure of the objects studied by social science to conform unequivocally to laws and theories on *any* level at which people wish to understand them. The phenomena of human social life are not like mountains and metals and muscles; they might have been, but they are not. It is difficult to decide what theory to employ when none of them fits the data with any degree of precision.

Lack of consensus with respect to explanatory interests is by itself sufficient to account for the existence of controversy regarding the level at which social theories ought to be sought, or even whether they should be pursued at all. But that is not the only ground for believing that the goal of a "complete" social science may never be achieved. If a proper theoretical ordering of social phenomena can be obtained, human social behavior must be capable of being placed under laws and theories that will provide an adequate explanatory account of it in all of its various manifestations. If no such principles can be discovered, we may be left with only a plurality of competing and not fully adequate conceptual schemes, each vying for the center of the stage. Should that turn out to be the case, then no amount of "progress" in the social sciences will alter our current situation.

149

# 9. Objectivity and Social Inquiry

A social science, even if it is not systematic, is nevertheless supposed to be objective. If anything is objective, science is; hence if the social studies are to qualify as scientific disciplines, they must be capable of providing accounts of human affairs that are as free of bias and independent of the values held by the investigators as the natural sciences are. This chapter is concerned with whether a social science can be objective in the way the natural sciences are supposed to be. Such objectivity, I shall argue, is not even a coherent ideal for social science, but is at best a procedural value.

The notion of objectivity, so far as it is associated with the statements and methods of science, has generally been tied to the notion of truth. An objective account is one that is free of such distortions as could be the result of biases on the part of the person offering the account. An objective procedure is one that is least likely to yield false statements. It is supposed to be reliable, regardless of the value preferences of the person who uses it. The paradigm of such a method is scientific method; that method, by definition, is the best guarantee of objectivity with respect to any domain in which it may be employed

The answer to the question as to whether a social science can be objective that was given by Max Weber is that it can, but only in a very limited sense.[1] Whereas Weber was a staunch advocate of a "value-free" social science, he also denied that there is any absolutely objective scientific analysis of social phenomena. A social science, according to Weber, can and should adhere to the strictest standards of scientific proof in its analytical ordering of empirical reality. On the other hand, what we choose as subject matter for study will be determined by our values, as will our assignment of causes to specific events. Weber points out that social science only first arose in connection with considerations of public policy, and hence its practice is inextricably tied up with the assessment of social ends and means. The selection of certain facts as significant and worthy of study is inevitably determined by the investigator's values and goals. Furthermore, the way we select, analyze, and organize factual evidence in order to explain individual social phenomena depends on the significance we impute, based on our value-ideas, to particular features of cultural situations. "All knowledge of cultural reality," Weber affirms, "is always knowledge from particular points of view."[2] There is, accordingly, not one objectivity but several objectivities in social science, each embodying a set of significance criteria derived from a way of approaching the social world.

Of course, the social sciences are not unique in having their selection of problems reflect the concerns of the scientist. As Ernest Nagel has pointed out, the things that any scientist selects for study can be determined by his interests as a human being and as a member of a particular culture, whether he is studying marine biology, projectile motion, or the motions of the planets.[3] If these investigations are objective, then the reasons one has for studying something must not necessarily affect the objective character of the inquiry.

Nor are the social sciences unique in having the selection of the cause of a specific event influenced by the investigator's interests and values. An event has many causes, in the sense that there are a number of antecedent events and circumstances that may correctly be cited as determinants of the occurrence in question. This is true whether the event is an election victory, an automobile accident, or the appearance of a rainbow. But as Brodbeck points out, even though the cause selected as "significant" depends upon our interests and values, whether or not it is *in fact* a cause does not depend upon them.[4] If a cause is any event that makes a difference with respect to the outcome of a series of occurrences, not everything that can be identified as a cause has to be the most important thing, from our point of view.

There is, it happens, far less consensus with respect to the assignment of causes of social phenomena than there is for natural phenomena. Social explanations are often much more controversial than explanations in the physical sciences. There is not the agreement regarding the merits of explanations of student uprisings or political apathy, for example,

151

that there is regarding the chemical basis of inheritance or the physics of the aurora borealis. What we need to explore is the nature of the disagreement as to the proper scientific explanation of social questions. Assuming, as I shall do for the purposes of this investigation, that the consensus that tends to occur in the natural sciences is not merely a matter of shared preconceptions but is based on common use of independently reliable methods, I would like to consider why it is that the methods of scientific investigation have generally not yielded authoritative and uncontroversial accounts of the phenomena of human social life.

Weber attributed the lack of consensus in the social sciences to the role of cultural values in social research, particularly in the matter of assigning causes. His position is in sharp contrast to the empiricist view, according to which a failure to reach agreement is only a sign of the immaturity of the social sciences, and it is only a matter of waiting until we discover all of the relevant causal laws before we shall be able to assess fully the causal significance of each of the factors that might be cited in an effort to explain a given phenomenon. Where Weber's argument cuts more deeply than the empiricist rejoinder is in his insistence that, whereas in natural science the only criterion for causal significance is whether or not a particular feature is connected by causal law with the effect to be explained, this is not the criterion that operates with respect to explanations of social phenomena. What we need in order to explain particular cultural facts, Weber insists, is knowledge of the phenomena in their concreteness, which depends not on knowledge of abstract, general laws, but on our ideas of the significance that these particular social constellations have for us.[5] Every social explanation, for Weber, is at least to some degree concerned with a unique configuration, the significance of which depends on one's value orientation. Those aspects of a cultural phenomenon that are picked out as worth knowing, and those features that are selected as essential to a causal understanding of the particular case, are determined by the evaluative ideas or cultural values of the investigator.

The problem of cause selection for explaining social phenomena is thus not the same as that of deciding which of a number of causal factors should be chosen as significant when explaining a natural or nonsocial occurrence. To assign a cause implies identifying a facet of an event to be explained. Competing causal explanations differ with respect to what it is about the event to be explained that needs to be accounted for. With nonsocial or inanimate phenomena such as the collapsing of a bridge or the flooding of a town, different causes are assigned depending on one's concern: whether it is why the event occurred at that particular time, why it occurred at that particular place, or why its effects were as severe as they were. Each of these accounts represents a causal story. Weber's claim with respect to cultural phenomena is that our explanatory needs can never be adequately satisfied by citing causal generalizations, because of our concern with the unique character of the event. It is not a matter of these cultural events not being governed by laws—Weber in fact believes that they are—but rather that our interest is directed toward their individual character. What we take this character to be, what unique feature we consider most worth explaining, will depend on our aims and values. Causal analyses can therefore not be objective because there is no way that one value-imbued account can be shown to be empirically superior to another one.

Weber did not believe that the cultural variability of the ideas that determine the kinds of explanations that are put forward implies that the results of research in the social sciences are subjective in the sense that they are valid only for some people and not for others. Only the degree to which these results would interest different persons was held to vary. We can trust the findings of social scientists to be fair and objective, therefore, once the choice has been made as to the object and the extent and depth of the investigation. Furthermore, since we are to some extent interested in the general and repeating character of cultural phenomena as well as in their particularity—Weber is mistaken if he believes that we are never interested in having social occurrences represented as instances of general principles—it looks as if social science can, on Weber's terms, offer a large number of causal analyses that should in principle be no less objective than those achieved by natural science.

A more far-reaching assault on the objectivity of social-science research was mounted by Karl Mannheim.[5] According to Mannheim, what one says about social affairs is shaped by one's social perspective, the manner in which one views any object, what one perceives in it, and how one construes it in one's thinking. Every point of view is limited by the concepts one employs and omits, the way one breaks up the totality of experience, the level of abstraction adopted, and the structure of one's categorial apparatus. There is no freeing oneself from the dominant models of one's thought, from what is implicitly in one's mind when one proceeds to reflect on an object.

Many of Mannheim's claims are similar to ones made much later by Thomas Kuhn about science in general.[7] According to Kuhn, the life of science is characterized by a succession of mutually incompatible paradigms. A paradigm is a broad theory or set of theories that provides the framework for explaining phenomena within its domain. It fixes the relevant variables, determines what observations shall be counted as significant, and limits the range of items that may be invoked in an acceptable explanation. The ruling paradigm, furthermore, determines not only the way facts are selected but also the way observations are reported. What we say we see depends on what theory we hold. In representing the orthodoxy of the scientific community, a dominant paradigm establishes the proper way of thinking about the "objective" world.

The particular implications of this view for social science should be especially significant. It has been suggested that, on a Kuhnian analysis, the social sciences are in a "pre-paradigm" condition, in the sense that there is no single dominant conceptual framework that permeates all thought about social life and determines the way they are to be interpreted and the research questions that are to be asked.[8] On the other hand, it can also be argued that there are competing paradigms in the social domain, and that the fact that the way things are represented is bound up with paradigms is all the more critical because of the class antagonisms and other social conflicts on which the results of social science often have considerable bearing. One finds in the social sciences not a single dominant paradigm but a proliferation of budding paradigms. There exist models of explanation such as behaviorism and transactional analysis in psychology, or functionalism and materialism in anthropology, that predetermine the questions that are asked and the answers that are considered. These conceptualizations are what determine the approach to such problems as urban decay and juvenile delinquency, and the differences among them account for the fact that disputes over proper explanation often are not resolvable by collecting additional data. What the claim that social science is in a "pre-paradigm" state amounts to is that it fails to exhibit what Kuhn calls "normal science," wherein there is full agreement within the scientific communtiy as to what the puzzles are that need to be solved and what the

154

proper explanatory devices are. If there is ideology in natural science, in the sense that perceptual evidence is organized in accordance with significance criteria and a world view that has already been established by one's community of investigators, the same is certainly true for social science.

This is not the place to explore the validity of recent challenges to the idea of scientific objectivity in general.[9] Two points deserve to be mentioned, however. One of these is that, *if* there are such things as scientific standards of truth and validity, then the fact that the form scientific knowledge takes is subject to influence by the investigator's social and historical perspective need not render the knowledge any less objective, so long as it measures up to these standards. Even if there is not *an* objective account, there may be several objective accounts, in the sense that what is affirmed is controlled by evidence. Second, it is important to be aware of the distinction between bias in an approach or way of conceptualizing a set of phenomena and bias in assessing its effectiveness. Social conditions may be responsible for the form a theory takes and for the time and place of its appearance, but these are not what determine its ultimate success or failure. It was, indeed, more than a coincidence that the setting in which the biological theory of natural selection was put forward was a nineteenth-century England whose dominant political ideology was laissez-faire capitalism, but it was not the theory's ideological implications alone that accounted for its having prospered. Similarly, we know what social forces prompted the rise of Lysenkoist genetics in the Soviet Union, and we also know that its failure was not the result of bourgeois attitudes infiltrating the domain of science and technology. If there is at most one theory that the empirical evidence will effectively validate, then the social origins of the theory cannot be what determines the character and quality of science's greatest achievements.

The thesis that the way we seek to describe and explain the social world is determined by features of the conceptual set we bring to it has, as we have seen, a counterpart in the case of attempts to develop a natural science. Mannheim offers a more radical thesis, however, one that entails placing the social sciences in an entirely separate category. In the case of social propositions, he maintains, the historical and social genesis of a proposition is not always irrelevant to its truth. What philosophers have called the genetic fallacy—the mistake of thinking that the way one comes to believe something is relevant to the truth or falsity of what is believed—is a fallacy, Mannheim argues, only "if the temporal and social conditions had no effect on its content and form."[10] If we recognize a distinction between a statement's "meaningful genesis" and its "factual genesis," he points out, we should see that, because the meaning of a statement may very well depend on who says it and in what historical circumstances, its truth value will equally be determined by these elements. Whether or not "p" is true depends on what "p" means, and if history or social context is what gives "p" its meaning, then its meaning depends upon its historical or social genesis.

Examples used by Mannheim to illustrate the relevance of genesis to meaning are the use of such words as "freedom" and such designations as "liberal position," and the use of what he calls a counterconcept such as *Volksgeist* in opposition to the progressive concept of *Zeitgeist*.[11] Even a mere date such as 1789 has a meaning that encompasses a considerable amount of social history on which the truth of many statements in which it occurs can be seen to turn (consider: "It was 1789 all over again"). Other illustrations may be provided by cases where differing traditions give what appears to be the same concept different meaning in different social contexts. Among these are the concepts of pride (which, MacIntyre points out, has important connections with honor in Italy but not in England),[12] political parties, and land or territory. Differently situated people call different things by the same names.

Someone may object that what is at stake here is merely a matter of ambiguity, and that all that is needed for objectivity is to identify the appropriate meanings. It may very well be true that social and historical perspectives determine the meanings employed by individuals in societies, so it can be argued, but once this meaning is known, the historical and social genesis becomes irrelevant to the truth of any proposition. Furthermore, there is only a causal or contingent connection between one's social situation and the meanings one adopts, so it appears that truth and social condition are logically independent after all.

In reply, it may be granted that *if* the meaning of a statement is properly comprehended, then *how* it came to have that meaning is indeed irrelevant, as is the story of how the speaker came to believe it. Mannheim need not be interpreted as denying this. His point is rather that there is an important class of statements whose meanings cannot be grasped without a knowledge of certain facts concerning their origin. Nor must he hold that the connection between a person's social or historical perspective and the meanings he imparts is logically necessary; all that need be claimed as necessary is that truth depends on meaning and that a given sequence of words can have a meaning that depends on who utters it and under what circumstances. The "sociology of knowledge" that Mannheim calls for is the empirical study of how propositions come to have the meanings they have; its concern is "the varying ways in which objects present themselves to the subject according to the differences in social settings."[13]

It is therefore a mistake to regard the "sociology of knowledge" as a misnomer for the sociology of belief, as some critics have done.[14] Mannheim was not primarily concerned with false beliefs, and he in fact distinguished between the sociology of knowledge and the study of ideology, whose task, he said, is "to unmask the more or less conscious deceptions and disguises of human interest groups."[15] Sociology of knowledge, as Mannheim conceived it, is instead concerned with uncovering the facts the comprehension of which enables one to interpret what is said in such a way as to make it true, or at least to explain why it is taken as true. The fact that there are some who think that a statement like "Cuba is a more democractic society than the United States" is true, whereas there are others who consider it to be manifestly false, can be explained by showing how the two classes of speakers assign the meanings they do. What the sociology of knowledge does is to illuminate "the position behind a point of view."

The way to discover what is objective about a particular assertion, according to Mannheim, is to investigate the meaning-contexts that determine why people make the knowledge claims they do. Judgments that have social content do not wear their meanings on their sleeves; we need to know what the structures and circumstances are that give them their meanings if we are going to be able to assess their objective truth or falsity. Meanings of words are variables whose values are determined by the speaker's perspective, and nothing that is susceptible to such influence can be objective, in the sense that its validity can be ascertained without attending to the circumstances of its author.

The only kind of objectivity that can be attained, therefore, requires a relativization of social descriptions to the point of view of the respondent. When something is correctly but differently perceived from two perspectives, Mannheim suggests, an effort should be made to discover a "common denominator" whereby the results of the two approaches can be intertranslated. While there is no such thing as a nonperspectivist view, he maintains that it is possible, by critically comparing differing perspectivistic insights, to identify the extent to which a perspective is situationally determined. The knowledge of human affairs that is thus gained has what he calls "relational objectivity."[16]

Ernest Nagel has argued that the social sciences are really no worse off than physics for having to settle for relational objectivity.[17] For if the search for common denominators is "a phase in the search for invariant relations in a subject matter," the formulations of these relations will be valid irrespective of the particular perspective and hence will not differ in principle from similar formulations in natural science. If it is possible to relativize individual perceptions to identifiable points of view, then it should be possible to indicate what any observer should report, given that perspective. Physics is, after all, no less objective for having to specify observations in terms of frames of reference.

Nevertheless, I believe it can be shown that the fact that there is only relational objectivity has special and quite drastic implications for social science. The problem is that historical and social perspectives, unlike the conditions of measurement and observation in natural science, are not reducible to repeatable universal types. There are no "standard" conditions or observational standpoints to which all determinations can be referred. Social situations are in an important sense unique, and their efforts on judgments are not systematizable in the way that those of positioning are, say, on physical perception. If perspective determines what is seen and not merely the way it is seen—its nature, as it were, as well as its attributes—and if the significant variations in perspective can give rise to an indefinite number of kinds of percepts, then we cannot represent the object of a judgment simply as (objectively) a so-and-so, given certain conditions of observation. The mere identification of something like witchcraft or sport or preparation for war presupposes a cultural orientation that is neither separable from the characterization that the social scientist provides nor universalizable in the way that physical perspectives or frames of reference are. The situation is thereby clearly different from that of the phases of the moon, for example, or that of the moon's apparent size when seen near the horizon. The objects of social observation are not so much qualified by a point of view as they are constituted by it.

If all that can be investigated objectively is how social occurrences and states of affairs look from certain social and historical perspectives, then the prospects for an objective social science are much more limited than some of its proponents have claimed. There can be no cross-cultural science of politics, for example, save on a very abstract level. For if the categories that are derived from a society's own self-interpretation are extended to other societies in which the meanings of basic concepts are different, distortions cannot fail to occur: that is the principal implication of Mannheim's critique of social science's claim to objectivity. It may be possible to compare and explain differing conceptions of politics, but there can be no objective theory of political institutions and political change in general. Explanations of why particular events within a given society occur—the ones that are specified by "common denominators"—will necessarily be one-sided, if all we know is why they are regarded the way they are. We do not have an explanation of why a political system works the way it does if we know only that it is viewed from one perspective as a sort of market and from another as an organism or self-regulating machine. Apathy as a social phenomenon is not explained by showing how it may alternately be regarded as a source of inefficiency and as a requirement for stability. And how shall we explain a so-called terrorist act or an allegedly political execution? There can be no agreement as to what shall be accepted as an adequate explanation when there is not even agreement over how the act or practice is to be identified.

Social explanations, like naturalistic ones, presuppose a point of view and a set of preselected categories. There is always a potential multiplicity of theories that will account for a given set of phenomena. There is always more than one way to pick up a stick, more than one level of abstraction to employ, more than one typology that can be adopted. This feature of scientific theorizing is especially pronounced in social inquiry, because of the role that interpretation plays there. Every approach to social phenomena carries with it a perspective that determines the meaning of the statements it delivers. There is no single means of representing social affairs that does not reflect some orientation or other.

It has been argued, nevertheless, that there are criteria by which the best perspectivistic view may be selected, namely pragmatic ones.[18] The best theories, so it may be said, are those that fit more facts with less difficulty; the right way to pick up the stick is the way that permits one to wield it with maximum effectiveness. Theories can be selected for and tested and modified on the basis of the success with which they meet situations in which they are exposed to the risk of possible falsification. Wrong social theories, it is maintained, will be refuted both by facts and by social practice.

Whether or not potential theories in the natural sciences are always subject to such a procedure of winnowing through testing, social theories clearly are not. For in order for a social theory to be refuted, the people whose behavior it concerns must behave in ways that contradict the theory. But if the society is successful in maintaining and enforcing social norms and these norms have the effect of making behavior conform to the theory, then the theory, so far as it gives an account of the existing social order, will not be refuted by anything that anyone does. Societies can *make* theories true by the deployment of their own systems of punishments and rewards. Thus a society in which all organized activities are governed by positive and negative incentives and competition is mandated everywhere would be a society in which a competitive model of human behavior could not fail to gain confirmation, provided the sanctions are strong enough. Social order *depends* on people accommodating themselves to the roles they are assigned, and hence every society provides confirmation of whatever theory of human behavior or social organization is dominant in it. And since every society has its deviants, not even the existence of a sizable class of individuals who are locked up or otherwise disposed of will count as a refutation of a social theory. It is not a scientific refutation of a theory of human beings and society to show that adopting it will lead to an increase in the capacity of the few to dominate the many, or even that it implies that societies will lose their ability to select and train individuals competent to serve current and future social needs—unless, of course, the theory itself expressly denies that these consequences will occur. The only kind of theory of the social order that could be refuted by the ways people behave would be one that denied that there is a need for social sanctions. But since there are no societies that fail to exercise sanctions with respect to some activities or other, either all theories are refuted or no refutation by social practice is possible. In any case, it is clear that we lack effective

160

empirical criteria for nonevaluatively deciding among competing theories of "human nature" that could be used to justify one or another theory of the social order.

The reason why there cannot in general be objectivity in social science, then, is that the use of scientific method does not guarantee that acceptance of the results of social inquiry will not be influenced by considerations deriving from the social persective of the investigator. In other words, the criteria for deciding whether something has been objectively established in the social domain are suspect. Objectivity, Popper has suggested, is tied to the free competition of thought.[9] It follows that where thinking is constrained or distorted by perspective, objectivity is not possible. It must be only within restricted areas of social research that the outcome of a procedure governed by strict adherence to the pulse of inquiry will be determined by the evidence and by the canons of proper scientific method.

If there is value-free research in the social sciences, it can be found in the domain of piecemeal investigations. Social-science research can establish particular correlations, as between being a member of a certain group and tending to vote a certain way, and it can also assess the effectiveness of particular means of achieving particular goals. So long as one determines in advance which variables are to be examined and how they are to be identified and characterized, the results may be claimed to be value-neutral. It is the boast of behavioristic social science that, by properly restricting itself to examining the manifest features of what can actually be perceived as happening and by avoiding all subjective interpretation, it can provide objective information concerning the way individuals and societies behave. Detailed findings and behavioral characterizations no doubt offer the best prospects of objective renderings of social phenomena. By sticking to the "hard facts," the ones that would have to be acknowledged even by the most biased observer, social science, it would appear, can achieve at least modest results having a scientifically objective character.

There is, however, no such thing as an interpretation-free social fact. The behavior that social investigators record is both purposive and meaningful. Social behavior is specified not as squeezing a trigger or as moving a finger against a lever, but as committing homicide or voting Being a Protestant or a maternal uncle or owning a color television set is not like being six feet tall or living in the Arctic or having leprosy, but

161

more like being a football player or belonging to a club: it presupposes the subject's acceptance of a set of rules, roles, and relations. These must be grasped by the investigator if he is to identify and understand the behavior in question. There are no descriptions on the observational level at which social science operates that do not either contain or presuppose an intentional component. Some sort of interpretive understanding (*Verstehen*) is required to identify the data used by even the most behavioristic social science.

Therefore, a social science that aims to be objective cannot eschew interpretation, but must try to come up with "objective" or correct interpretations. Certainly this can be achieved in a number of instances: we do correctly identify activities such as cooking or bidding farewell or chastising someone. So long as the participants in a segment of social or institutional behavior know what they are doing and we as social-science investigators share their conceptions, there appears to be no problem in assigning interpretations in the process of gathering social facts. Most of the data that political scientists, sociologists, and social psychologists obtain is of this sort, where the interpretive element is not absent but is not in question.

Where a problem arises is in situations in which the "correct" interpretation is in doubt, where there seems to be more than one possible interpretation that is rich enough to be useful. We need to be able to specify whether someone is hunting or defending himself, reading or praying, playing or working. The job of assigning meanings or interpretations is not so difficult for behavior that is effectively controlled or circumscribed, especially when carried out in a familiar context, but it can be quite problematic when one is dealing with an alien society or subculture. There is very little that people do, apart from general biological activities and the performance of a few universal or nearly universal practices such as marriage and funeral rites, that an observer can grasp without internalizing the concepts of the social group within which the action occurs. Unless the investigator has come to share these ways of conceiving social acts and practices with the participants, his interpretations will be determined by his own cultural background. For a Western observer to describe Buddhism as a religion, for example, or Hopi Indian goods exchanges as buying and selling, may be a serious distortion. If being objective means getting the interpretation right, then to the extent that this requires getting inside the culture, there can be no objective social science across cultural lines.

The problem of objectivity in social science applies not only to descriptions but also to explanations. We have already seen that the assignment of causes to social phenomena and the construction and deployment of social theories involve the use of significance criteria and that these reveal a perspective. But what about explanations that limit themselves to the agent's own reasons for acting? Objectivity can be obtained, it might be supposed, by trying to show only that the act was rational for the agent, given his particular beliefs and attitudes. As long as the social scientist restricts himself to stating the reasons and not evaluating them, so it might be maintained, he should be able to avoid making any evaluative judgments of the actions he seeks to account for.

There are serious difficulties with this suggestion. In the first place, as we have already seen, explanations of actions in terms of reasons always involve judgments as to the appropriateness of the act relative to those reasons. A reason is explanatory of an action only if it is seen as good enough to make the act appear plausible under the circumstances. And that requires a judgment that depends on an appraisal based on social norms of rationality.

An even more troubling objection to the idea that objectivity in social science can be maintained by withholding value judgments from rational explanations of human actions is that adopting such a viewpoint itself amounts to making a value commitment. Showing how a person's reasons explain his actions, if it does not mean taking his point of view, does imply a detached or clinical stance. In removing oneself from the world in which these actions occur, one in effect *refuses* to judge. To withhold value judgments in rendering an account of another person's behavior is to regard him in a very special sort of way. One cannot ignore the ethical dimension of human action without making at least an implicit evaluative supposition.

There are a number of different ways of looking at a given action or practice, of which "objective" detachment is only one. While there may be instances in which this attitude is an appropriate one, there clearly are cases in which adhering to it will entail missing the point or significance of what is going on. There is more than descriptive content to the point that one sees more when one watches an event as a partisan observer. Football games and armed robberies are only two examples in which one's evaluative attitude is constitutive of one's observations and understanding. And when it comes to the study of alien cultures, or even slightly unfamiliar subcultures, it is not clear *what* attitude is conducive to proper understanding. Whether the practice of witchcraft or astrology or of a religion in which human sacrifice is practiced is most suitably viewed from the standpoint of participants, critics, or disinterested reporters is not something that can be decided without making value assumptions.

If being objective means withholding all evaluative characterizations, then there are certain things an objective social science cannot do. One thing it will not be permitted to do is to state or imply that anything is good or bad. It will not be able to deal with matters such as murder or acts of cruelty, for example, since to use such terms implies an evaluation. There can be no heroes or villains in that kind of objective social science.

Another implication of adhering to a nonevaluative procedure is that no action will be considered irrational. We have seen that making sense of human action requires being able to present it as resulting from and appropriate to one's beliefs and desires. But if objectivity is thought to require us to withhold moral judgment of any action, however horrendous, it may also be supposed to prohibit us from representing anyone's actions as neurotic, irrational, or the work of an inscrutable genius or moronic incompetent. Being objective, it would appear, precludes our ever saying that someone has completely bungled an action or taken leave of his senses.[20]

Any imputation of irrationality reflects the standpoint of a judge who neither shares nor accredits all of the aims and beliefs of the person whose behavior is being considered. One will judge an activity such as cigarette smoking or driving a car without fastening one's seatbelt as irrational only if one considers the gains of persisting and the costs of desisting insignificant in comparison with the risks involved. The labeling of an action as rational or irrational is dependent on context and is determined by whether it is rationalized by beliefs that are warranted and wants that are normal. The assessment of rationality is always relative to standards and hence is subject to a charge of bias arising from the acceptance of certain social norms of rational action.

And yet, just as we may want to say that there are criminals and not merely people who are called criminals, we would like to be able to acknowledge that there are blunders, and that there are neurotic and psychotic and abjectly stupid acts, and not merely acts that are so regarded. Even if it means giving up the whole idea of pursuing objectivity in the social domain, we would like to be able to characterize people as making mistakes, as having deviant aims, as holding unfounded beliefs, and as doing or failing to do things on account of stubbornness, perseverance, laziness, weakness of the will, or diligence. If it is ever a fact, albeit a socially constituted one, that people are sometimes irrational in the sense that their behavior fails to conform to the goals and expectations that a reasonable person can be expected to hold in that situation, it is a fact that a social investigator committed to "objectivity" is barred from expressing.

Any procedure for deciding when people are irrational has a built-in uncertainty, one that is connected with the problem of ascribing beliefs and attitudes. Since beliefs can be discovered only by attending to behavior (including verbal expression), and behavior can be properly characterized only if it is interpreted as expressive of beliefs, the elaboration of the belief structure of any individual or society whose behavior is being investigated depends on our making certain hypotheses that cannot themselves be directly tested. We have to assign meaning to behavior and content to beliefs, and we are able to test these assignments only by seeing how effective they are in enabling us to make sense of whole patterns of behavior.

Beliefs are identifiable only on the basis of a general presumption of rationality. We have to assume that the behavior we observe is in general appropriate to the beliefs and that the beliefs are appropriate to the circumstances. Just as in making a radical translation of the sentences of a completely alien language we try to make as large a number of utterances as possible come out true,[21] so also do we maximize the degree of rationality that we attribute to the members of another social group. Nevertheless we must expect, just as we do in our own culture, that some of the things some people do will be stupid, inept, or silly. However we characterize the behavior we observe, we must make judgments as to how we are to view and appraise the world. Since there is more than one way of ordering and judging the objects of our experience, we are forced to choose, to adopt a standpoint. So far as the enterprise of characterizing human social behavior is essentially tied up with values and valuation, the choice is not whether an account should or should not imply an evaluation, but rather which values ought to be assumed within the framework of discussion. Judgments are both pervasive and inevitable.

If the pursuit of objectivity in social science requires withholding evaluative characterization, and a refusal to apply evaluative categories implies an evaluational stance, then the notion of objectivity with respect to social inquiry must be self-contradictory and incoherent. Being objective cannot entail both bias and the absence of bias. Nor can it imply both that we can and that we cannot identify particular actions as irrational. Objectivity is a concept that lacks meaningful application in certain parts of the domain of social inquiry. It does not make sense to ask for an objective account of behavior the understanding of which presupposes one interpretive bias or another.

It is sometimes said that the value of objectivity, so far as methodology is concerned, is that it is the best guarantee that truth will be discovered. Findings we trust are those we think were objectively arrived at. Conclusions whose support comes from biased or otherwise unreliable sources may still be true, but they are suspect. Within social science there are indeed objectively acquired results, and there are studies that have been objectively designed and carried out. But objectivity is not a possible goal for social inquiry in general, because the use of objective procedures is something that can occur only within limits that are themselves imposed by values. These are values that are presupposed not only by the selection of questions to be asked and categories to be deployed, but also by the decision to withhold judgment on matters of human concern. A social science cannot possibly be objective if it issues statements that reveal bias, or if it fails to deal with social phenomena on the level at which people confront them.

# 10. Social Inquiry and Scientific Understanding

Science is knowledge of what there is. It describes the world and reveals how its components are connected. Explanation and prediction are accordingly secondary functions; they are *uses* to which scientific knowledge is put. The scientific corpus consists not of explanations, which are statements of why something is the case, but rather of statements of what is the case. Explaining is not part of science; it is something one does with science.

When successful, explanations bring about understanding; they make facts about the world intelligible. Scientific understanding, which is a form of knowing-why, is thus knowledge of explanations. If I understand why a piece of fruit turned sour or why people who consume large quantities of alcohol tend to have strong hearts and unhealthy livers, I must know some principles of science and also how these principles can be applied to explaining particular matters of fact. Scientific understanding is therefore broader than scientific knowledge because it embraces knowledge that is not part of science itself. Science is not the same as scientific understanding, though both are cognitive achievements.

Scientific understanding, since it is both cognitive and general, is necessarily predictive. Anyone who understands why bronze statues turn green or why the contamination of a bacterial culture by a certain bread mold causes it to die will know when to expect this effect and also what will prevent it from occurring. The notion of scientific understanding is broader than that of predictive power, but there is nothing that could be called scientific understanding that does not offer some predictive possibilities. The fact that we can apply the word "understanding" to cases wherein we lack the knowledge to predict what we can explain—the evolution of a species or species characteristic, for example, or the occurrence of a flood or volcanic eruption[1]—is fully compatible with recognizing that we have better understanding when our explanations have greater predictive potential. We may not have been able to predict that the only surviving flying vertebrates would be birds and bats, but with the knowledge that is embodied in an explanation of that fact we can make at least hypothetical predictions of what might happen in future instances. Predictiveness is guaranteed simply by the cognitive nature of scientific understanding: if understanding X means knowing why X happened, then it must imply knowing when X could happen again.

In scientific knowledge, as in all cognition, there is a separation between the knower and the known. In Hegel's terminology, what is known "stands opposed to us"; the objective world, whose independent existence science takes for granted, has a kind of "strangeness" in virtue of the scientist's detachment from it. This strangeness may be either welcomed or regretted, depending on whether one wishes to celebrate or denigrate the cognitive relation, but it is something that must be accepted if any possibility of science is acknowledged. Observation, classification, and description all require that there be something that is set apart from oneself: an object. Without a subject-object distinction there can be no science.

We have here a defining feature of the cognitive attitude. What can be understood scientifically is necessarily limited to what we can place in a sort of opposition, whether the subject matter is a family, a neurosis, or a bolt of lightning. The restriction pertains not to what can be studied but to how it can be studied, and how it is to be understood. Studying a human hand is obviously not the same as using it, and studying a love affair is not the same as living through it. Science comprehends only what can be objectified.

One of the things that the possibility of a social science depends on, therefore, is whether people and societies are understandable as objects. The crucial word here is "understandable": since anything may be understood as an object in the sense that it may be *regarded* as an object, the question is whether that sort of understanding is appropriate to the situation in which the things to be understood are social phenomena. The issue is whether social understanding is a species of scientific

168

understanding. Social inquiry, so far as it is committed to providing scientific understanding, must enable us to understand why human beings and societies are what they are and do what they do by showing that what is to be understood is inferable from knowledge of what is the case. It must, furthermore, yield understanding that is ultimately predictive, capable of allowing us to know what to expect of these objects in future situations. Social science deserves recognition as a cognitive discipline, or set of cognitive disciplines, only if it is able to represent the elements of human social life as objects, as predictable, and as susceptible to arrangement in systematic order.

A major thesis of this book is that a social science that meets these conditions is an impossibility. The aim of the present chapter is to consider some of the reasons why this should be the case and what the implications would be if there were such a science. The first point is concerned with the very idea of understanding humans and human groups as objects. Certainly we often do view people and societies as things outside of us, both in science and in ordinary life: it is part of living to take cognizance of others and to see them as things to be contemplated, admired, and found useful in various ways. On the other hand, as Kant has made us aware, a person qua knowing object—the "'I' that thinks"—necessarily eludes being constituted as an empirical object. That which is the subject of all judgments cannot be the object of any. The human is unique among things to be understood in that as knower he falls outside the world as known. *How* he experiences or thinks about things, as opposed to *what* is experienced or thought about, can be no object of cognition.

Anything we pick out as a feature or aspect of a person or society can, of course, *become* an object simply by being treated as something to be inquired about. Whatever can be said to have an "inner" or subjective aspect (except perhaps a disembodied spirit) can be represented as having an "outer" or objective aspect as well. Furthermore, it is impossible to prove that there are any objective features of the human condition that cognitive methods will inevitably fail to capture: anything you know to have been left out must thereby be conceived as an object of possible cognition. To assume that nothing vital to understanding eludes the cognitive attitude, on the other hand, is either to affirm a tautology that trades on equating "understanding" with "cognitive understanding" or else to adopt a constitutive principle that legislates what is to be regarded

169

as vital. Conceiving of human beings exclusively as objects of possible cognition amounts to endorsing the view that they are objects for all intents and purposes. It is only from a certain philosophical perspective that science can be seen as capable of telling us all we need to know about people and human societies.

Let us grant, nevertheless, the propriety of conceiving of people and societies as objects. In Chapter 8 we considered a number of reasons for believing that, even if treating social phenomena as objects is allowable, the objects of social inquiry may not exhibit the sort of regularity that permits the identification of particulars that can be arranged in systematic order. We saw that it is possible that the items we identify when examining social phenomena are not governed by laws; and that it is also possible that they are law-governed but that the laws are not discoverable, because we are unable to isolate particulars under descriptions that will yield true empirical generalizations having sufficient scope to yield predictive knowledge with any significant degree of generality. In this chapter I want to urge a much stronger conclusion, that the subject matter of the human sciences is such that a properly explanatory science of that domain is impossible in principle. I shall argue that a completely deterministic science of human social life would be self-defeating, and that the statistical-probabilistic variant of scientific explanation is equally unsatisfactory because it fails to explain the phenomena that fall within the range of its generalizations.

If human beings are a proper subject matter for deterministic science, their behavior must in principle be totally predictable. It is, of course, a familiar fact that human social behavior is predictable in at least some degree: human sociality clearly depends on our being able to anticipate each other's needs, decisions, and actions. Like laboratory animals, hurricanes, and African violets, humans often behave as they are expected to, even though not always. What is needed to demonstrate complete predictability-in-principle is not merely an extrapolation from partial to total predictability, however, but also the assumption that all failures of foreknowledge, all deviations from perfect prediction, are accountable by lack of knowledge of relevant causal laws and antecedent circumstances. It is this assumption that prevents the repeated failures of meteorologists, physicians, and diviners from being seen as undermining the deterministic character of their respective sciences. If humans are unpredictable only in the sense that the weather and earthquakes are, then there must always be some deterministic account that can be discovered that will explain why, on any particular occasion, a person did not behave as predicted.

The idea that humans will behave as predicted if the predictions are sufficiently well informed and are made in accordance with deterministic causal laws is, of course, in conflict with certain notions of free will. If that kind of predictability is possible, then there can be no such things as free agents who initiate the events that get ascribed to them as their actions. Without attempting to resolve the question of freedom and determinism, I would make two points. One is that agenthood is precluded only by the sort of predictability that requires that actions be deducible with logical necessity from causal laws. It is not antithetical to the idea of person qua agent that his actions be inferable from antecedents. The second point is that, in order for determinism to be true, it does not have to be the case that humans will always behave as predicted; the predictions may frequently turn out to be false, owing to lack of knowledge. All that the claim that there are free agents need imply is that there are actions whose occurrences, even when predictable, would not be explained merely by showing that they are in conformity with causal law.

A number of peculiarities exist with respect to actions and predictions. One of these is that it is in general odd to speak of predicting one's own actions.[2] I may be able to predict the way I will feel, and I sometimes can predict the way someone else will act, but to the extent that I am already cognizant of all the reasons I will have for acting one way rather than another in a particular instance, what *I* do is not something that I can be said to predict, in any straightforward sense. Hampshire and Hart have made the point that, when a person claims to be able to predict his own future actions on inductive grounds, he is implying that the actions will be in some degree involuntary, the effect of causes outside his control.[3] Predictions concern what is to happen, not what a person makes happen. There is, therefore, at least one case—one's own—for which prediction of action is impossible. It follows, furthermore, that there must also be cases of others' actions which one similarly cannot predict, namely, those that may be influenced by one's own future actions.

One of the reasons for saying that an agent cannot predict his own actions consists in the fact that, so far as they *are* his own actions, he can confound any prediction that he has made. Moreover, the same point applies equally to actions predicted by others, at least in those cases where the agent is aware of the prediction. If I have been told of the prediction, either I literally cannot help doing what has been predicted, in which case it is not a free action, or else I do not have to do as I was predicted and can in fact do otherwise. A communicated prediction is a kind of input that has an effect on the agent's performance only if he lets it, as it were; where the effect is determined, we are dealing not with an action but with ˎa movement.

Predictions affect people's behavior in curious ways. A person may either believe or disbelieve a prediction, or he may try to ignore it, but whatever he does his total state is altered as a result of learning of the prediction. MacKay has argued that this fact makes it impossible for there to be a complete specification of a person's state that has any logical claim to his assent, and that therefore a complete science of persons that satisfies the standard requirements of public and universal validity is impossible as well.[4] One can never be constrained to assent to a prediction of one's future action: for, in order for such a prediction to be scientifically compelling, it must be based on a specification of the person's state prior to performance of the act, but since this does not include his assent to the prediction, the specification will become out-of-date and no longer enjoy the same claim to assent once he assents to the prediction. If, on the other hand, the specification of the person's present state is so contrived as to be inaccurate, but only in such a way as to become correct if he believes the prediction, then it would not be a mistake for him to *disbelieve* the prediction at the time it is offered to him. "Any imaginable specification of my own current state," MacKay concludes, "must be *incomplete* in at least one key particular; namely the one that specifies whether I accept it or not."[5]

The preceding argument does not show that complete predictive knowledge of a person's behavior is impossible, but only that *if* such knowledge is possible, it will have to be kept from the person concerned. The exclusion is an important one, however, because it implies that knowledge of persons differs from all other scientific knowledge in that it fails to satisfy the criterion of being completely public and expressible in propositions that can demand the assent of everyone. Furthermore, the qualified-predictability thesis is applicable to human beings only so far as they are conceived apart from their relationships to others. For, as I have already pointed out, not only are one's own decisions and hence one's actions in general unpredictable, but so are the actions of others with whom one interacts. MacIntyre has presented an argument to show that the unpredictability runs still further, to the conclusion that the inability of agents to predict each other's behavior results in a corresponding inability of the observer whenever the behavior involves the interaction of two or more individuals.[6] Since the participants in a situation are unable to predict each other's behavior completely, owing to the dependence of that behavior on their own unpredictable decisions, an outside observer can fare no better, for to assume that he can would imply that he would also be able to make accurate predictions were he one of the participants. If complete predictive knowledge of human behavior is possible, it must be restricted to behavior that falls outside the large and important class of social interactions.

A person is a moral entity as well as an organism. In order for something to be a person, it must be a person for someone, potentially if not actually. A person is a creature whose every move I cannot anticipate. To the extent that I recognize him as a person, I must assume that he is capable in principle of confounding any prediction I might make regarding his behavior, whether I tell him of my prediction or not. You could never fall in love with someone whose reactions you could completely predict; neither could you even converse with such a being. Conversation presupposes a kind of openness with respect to the other's responses; merely to listen to someone involves acknowledging him as capable of responding contrary to one's expectations.[7] It does not follow, of course, that the behavior must be in itself unpredictable, considered from certain external points of view. The question is not whether the behavior of individual human beings is predictable or not, but rather whether anything whose behavior we could completely predict in that way is something that we would regard as like ourselves in respect of being a person. It is a defining or conceptual fact of human social life, and not just an empirical condition, that the sphere of human action is dominated by events that cannot be controlled or determined in any completely effective way. If there were a social science that had the power to predict completely the total course of human affairs, that sphere could not exist. A completely deterministic science of human action is therefore a philosophical impossibility; it could not be a science of human beings as we conceive them.

Scientific prediction is prediction according to law. To be able to make a scientific prediction is to be able to infer an occurrence on the basis of knowledge of laws plus antecedent circumstances. These laws may be either universal or statistical in form, and the predictions will have either deductive certainty or a high degree of probability, depending on the kind of law that is being deployed. Where predictions of phenomena in a given domain are found not to be completely reliable, it may be suggested that prediction is possible only on a statistical or probabilistic basis.

Corresponding to these two types of scientific prediction are two types of scientific explanation, deductive-nomological and statistical-probabilistic. A deductive-nomological explanation allows us to deduce the phenomenon to be explained from universal causal laws, whereas a statistical-probabilistic explanation allows us to infer that an occurrence is probable by subsuming it under statistical laws. Since the social sciences do not seem to be able to come up with explanations of the former sort, it has sometimes been thought reasonable to suppose that these disciplines can employ covering-law explanations of the latter kind. Actions and practices would be explained by exhibiting them as instances of psychological, sociological, or economic generalizations. Failure to discover nontrivial exceptionless generalizations, it is argued, should not necessarily prevent social scientists from using statements that express statistical regularities to explain and predict the phenomena that they are able to place under them.

Statistical-probabilistic explanations are weaker than deductive-nomological ones, but they do have a use in explaining certain kinds of phenomena. The generalizations we appeal to in explaining the contraction of an infectious disease or the efficacy of a cure, for example, are known to have only statistical validity. Such principles lack explanatory power with respect to individual actions, however, even though they often offer a basis for predicting what someone is likely to do or how an institution will develop. Demographic principles and political generalizations may serve to illuminate the actions of individuals or groups by placing them in a broader context, but they do not explain *why* these actions are performed. The fact that a person lives in a place where almost everyone pursues gardening does not by itself explain why *he* does it.

When a statistical generalization sheds light on an action, it does so by providing a clue as to where an appropriate rational explanation is to be

174

sought. An example of such a generalization might be one that connects types of upbringing with the likelihood of committing certain types of crime. To the extent that upbringing is relevant at all, it is so because it provides a set of circumstances that contribute to a particular configuration of attitudes and beliefs that are what rationalize certain courses of action. When we say that knowing about a person's upbringing helps us to understand a particular crime, we mean that we understand why it was more likely that the crime should have been committed by that person than by someone else. But a person does not commit a crime *because* of his upbringing.

It is important to note that the use of statistical generalizations to illuminate human actions is significantly different from the use of such propositions to explain other kinds of occurrences. When we explain a particular birth defect by citing the mother's prior exposure to radiation, for example, we are pointing to a determinate effect that has been brought about by a prior event through which a process that itself has only a certain probability of occurring. As in Russian roulette, once the improbable event has occurred, the result is determined. That is not the way statistical facts are understood to operate when the occurrence to be explained is an individual action. The fact that a delinquent youth has grown up in grinding poverty in a broken home does not constitute a determining cause of his action; it rather indicates the nature of the situation that has determined his perceptions and structured his options.

Generalizations that can be used to predict human behavior cannot ordinarily be used to explain it. Knowing that the demand for a commodity falls as a function of increasing price, for example, may enable us to predict certain consumer behavior, but we are not thereby able to *explain* any individual's economic behavior. The fact that someone can almost always be induced to move out of his apartment if the rent is drastically increased and a reasonable alternative is available does not need the support of a statistical generalization in order for it to be able to explain why he did move when he did. The explanatory power of the generalization is derivative from that of the particular instance.

A way of seeing why statistical generalizations do not explain the individual actions that fall under them is to consider the way exceptions tend to be regarded. When a person fails to behave as people generally do in a given type of situation, there is no intellectual compulsion to explain *why* the exception occurred as there is in the case where someone fails to

175

develop a certain expected somatic condition. A human action that does not conform to the generality is not something that must be causally explained in order to preserve the integrity of the original generalization. Nor need it be regarded as a statistical anomaly, as something that fails to make sense. We do not have to show why an action is not captured by the generalization in order to find the action intelligible.

When a generalization serves an explanatory function, it does so by calling attention to some sort of connection between events or states of affairs. In the case of events other than actions, the connections are assumed to be no more than constant or nearly constant conjunctions between members of two classes of events. The predictive power of knowing the generalization flows from the fact that it supports a counterfactual conditional, or at least a probabilistic variant of it: if the fact that all A's and B'c can be used to explain why $a$, a particular member of A, is a B, then we also know that if $x$ were an A, it too would be a B. If the general statement were "Almost all A's and B's," then the counterfactual would be, "If $x$ were an A, it would probably be a B." In the case of actions that are so explained, the kind of connection that must be grasped is a particular rational one. The relevant counterfactual (e.g., "If he had been subjected to continual harassment, he would have quit his job"), which will also allow us to make predictions of subsequent behavior, owes its plausibility not to an empirical generalization but rather to the rational connection that implies it. Generalizations in social science—for example, those that concern the voting behavior of various ethnic groups or the consumer preferences of members of certain occupations—do not explain the behavior they cover; they are themselves items that need to be explained. What we need to do in order to explain why such generalizations are true is to explain the behavior they describe. This can be done only on the basis of knowing how these people perceive and evaluate their situation. A person who is able to explain other people's behavior does not have to know any empirical generalizations; he need only be good at identifying their reasons and motivations—at penetrating the rational structure of their thought.

If there are such things as human actions as we have been conceiving them, then there can be no strict laws that govern all of human behavior. This is not to say that there are no laws of behavior, or even that there is no possibility of subsuming at least part of human behavior under general behavioral principles. The point is rather that behavior that is

176

picked out under action descriptions is necessarily conceived as free, in the sense that there is always room for distinguishing what one does from what one ought to do. So far as a person is presumed to have been free to do otherwise, there can be no covering law that explains why he acted as he did. A generalization often provides a backdrop that enables one to see an action in a certain light—for example, as typical of a class of common responses to a particular kind of situation—but it does not explain why it occurred.

Explanations of action, I have been arguing, have a different logic from explanations of other kinds of events. In order to grasp the meaning of an action we need to know the rules that define it; knowing that someone is applying for a job or packing a suitcase consists in knowing what rules or criteria govern the performance of actions of that kind. Understanding an action requires being able to see it as rational, which entails recognizing the rules and norms in the light of which it may be seen as appropriate. These rules are not the same as laws, since they do not describe what is the case but rather prescribe what should be done. Explanations in terms of rules do not tell why X occurred; rather they tell why the person who did X might have found it right or rational so to act.

Failure to notice the distinction betweeen rules and laws can lead one to mistake a rational account, or an explanation, in terms of rules, for an explanation of the covering-law type. Thus Danto offers the following as an explanation of why, in Monaco during the national holidays, American flags are seen to have been put out along with the Monegasque flags: the American flags are displayed in honor of one of the present sovereigns, Princess Grace Kelly, who is an American.[8] According to Danto, the explanation is an elliptical formulation of a deductive argument whose nomological premise is, "Whenever a nation has a sovereign of a different national origin than its own citizens, those citizens will, on appropriate occasions, honor that sovereign in some acceptable fashion." What Danto has adduced, however, as Wellmer has pointed out, is not a law but a rule, a normative principle.[9] As such, it indicates why the observed behavior has been prescribed, not why the norm is actually obeyed. Danto's principle, if construed descriptively, is simply not to be believed unless it is supported by the additional assumption that people will, in such an instance, do as they are instructed. Since this proviso, whose truth may very well be in doubt, is not itself a covering law, no explanation that relies on it deserves to be counted as a covering-law explanation. Neither Danto's explanation nor any other explanation that tries to deduce what a person does from what people in that situation are expected to do will satisfy the covering-law model.

If the difference between understanding social phenomena and understanding natural phenomena is as radical as the difference between understanding actions and understanding other kinds of events, then it is reasonable to assume that social science requires a different methodology. That is precisely the claim that is made by antipositivists such as Dilthey and Collingwood who have insisted upon a fundamental distinction between the *Naturwissenschaften* and the *Geisteswissenschaften*, between the natural sciences and the human or cultural sciences. The alternative to natural-science methodology that has been put forward is *hermeneutics,* the science of interpretation. The central idea that characterizes this somewhat heterogeneous movement is that social phenomena are more fruitfully viewed as texts to be understood and interpreted than as objects or events to be described and explained in the manner of empirical science. The kind of understanding that befits this realm is held to consist of grasping the meaning of the parts of human social life as expressions to be deciphered. Proper interpretation depends on identifying the context of a given expression, a context that is not always recognizable on a manifest level but may be hidden within the intentions of the participants. The model for hermeneutic interpretation is dialogue or conversation, in which familiarity with a speaker, a sharing of values, norms, and ways of seeing the world, is a prerequisite for mutual understanding. We can make sense of the written word only in virtue of our ability to understand spoken dialogue; by the same token, it is argued, the comprehension of human speech provides the basis for our understanding the actions, institutions, and cultural artifacts that make up the domain of social phenomena. These are the "texts" in which human intentions come to be expressed.

If social phenomena can be understood only hermeneutically, then the social scientist will have to know a great deal more about the social context than would ordinarily be required for scientific understanding construed in empiricist terms. Like the *Verstehen* theorist (cf. Chapter 4, above), the hermeneuticist recognizes that the social scientist needs to know what the acts, institutions, and circumstances mean *for* the people they concern, as though he were a potential participant. Just as an interpreter or translator needs to know the whole of the language or text he is expected to render, so the interpreter of social action must be familiar with the entire context of norms and practices of the society he aims to understand.

It is a consequence of hermeneutic theory, at least as it was originally expounded by Dilthey, that no attempt to explain social behavior can be successful unless it reflects agreement between the investigator and the participants as to the intersubjective meaning of the acts and situations being represented. Even the so-called behavioral studies of voting patterns or of the relocation of populations require that the investigators and those being investigated share a common understanding of the meaning of those movements that count as the casting of a vote or the migration of a population. One means of helping to assure that this condition is satisfied is for the social scientist already to be a member of the society he is studying: this is what is ordinarily the case with respect to sociology. As Apel has pointed out, the use of statistical methods and other "objective" procedures of social research already presupposes an understanding of meaning.[10] It is only because the indigenous social investigator is a member of the same community of interpretations as those whose behavior he seeks to comprehend that he is able to talk about and discover correlations concerning their suicide rates, marriage and divorce frequencies, religious affiliations, and election results. Apart from whatever technical or abstract conceptions that he himself introduces to help order and classify their behavior, his understanding of it must be in the same terms as theirs.

How then does one go about investigating activities and practices with which one is not already familiar? The method is essentially that of forming hypotheses, which are then checked to see whether they succeed in allowing one to make sense of subsequent behavior. What these hypotheses express, however, are not descriptive propositions such as are adduced in natural science and from which one is supposed to be able to deduce statements of observable events or states of affairs, but rather rules or norms that allow us to infer only what people will do if they behave as prescribed. The investigator is in a situation not unlike that of someone trying to figure out the rules of chess merely by watching a number of matches being played. The task is not impossible, but it is likely to be extremely difficult—like deciphering a coded message—unless one is able to enter into dialogue with one of the participants or with someone else who knows the game. Dialogue itself presupposes mutual acquaintance with a set of rules; learning a language means learning what sounds one *ought* to make. So learning the rules of a game will (almost always) require knowledge of a much wider set of rules. The situation with respect to understanding social actions and practices takes us even farther: in order to know that something is a game, a ritual, a commercial transaction, or a professional meeting, one must have already formed a set of ideas about the society as a whole. Just as understanding a single sentence ordinarily requires knowing more of language than is directly revealed in those words alone, so understanding an item of social behavior is in general possible only when one has considerable background knowledge of the norms and practices that go to make up the social context in which the behavior occurs. Unless he actually "goes native," the anthropologist is very likely to miss the point or social significance of the actions and other social phenomena that he is attempting to understand.

A hermeneutical approach to social phenomena is more like what one would use to understand a puzzling conversation than it is like the approach of a natural science to objects in a domain. Like the listener to a conversation, and unlike the practitioner of natural science, the hermeneuticist has to assume that he is dealing with subjects and not merely objects. Hermeneutics implies grasping another consciousness, and it requires one to project one's own consciousness far enough into another person's world to make a conversation relation hypothetically possible. Social understanding demands that we constitute reality in the way that we constitute objects in a process of linguistic communication. The task of the hermeneutic interpreter is then to penetrate the logic of communication and to make explicit those conditions that must be implicitly recognized in order for communication to be possible. He must try to break into the system of concepts used by those he seeks to understand—not to become a participant in a social situation, but in order to discover what one needs to know if one is a participant.

The central difficulty of the art of interpretation, in Dilthey's words, is that "the entirety of a work is to be understood from the individual words and their connections, and yet the full understanding of the individual already presupposes that of the whole."[11] This is the famous hermeneutic circle, and it is held to pertain to understanding the elements within a culture as well as the elements within a text. Applied to human social action, the difficulty amounts to the fact that understanding a social order or historical epoch depends on having an understanding of particular actions, and that understanding these actions depends on grasping the character of the context as a whole.

The circle is not an altogether vicious one, however, because of the possibility of entering it through the method of successive hypothesis and reinterpretation in the light of further experience. Interpretation of action is difficult, like learning a new language without the help of a lexicon or translator, but not impossible. In both instances, the process is one of continual self-correction facilitated by the existence of semantic points of contact that serve to confirm or disconfirm the way we have chosen to render something. Even if we cannot be certain that the interpretation we assign to particular items within a social whole is correct, we can expect to come up with one that can be defended against those who would contest it.

Later writers in the hermeneutic tradition have been exercised by a rather different problem, one that is specifically associated with interpreting historical and social action. The worry is that one can be systematically misled in one's interpretations of acts and utterances and be prevented by one's web of mutually reinforcing beliefs and attitudes from ever discovering one's misinterpretation. The problem is not simply that one can misconstrue a whole cultural event—mistaking an election for a religious rite, for example—for one can also be completely mistaken about an author's intention in producing a particular text. Rather, the problem is that the actors in real-life situations, those to whom the social investigator is supposed to have a quasi-communicative relation, may not themselves understand the nature or the significance of their actions. The political leader who states his reasons for taking his country to war, or the governor who defends his veto of a piece of legislation, may be totally unaware of the ideological and structural factors that, had they been cited, might better explain the actions. People are quite commonly deceived as to their deeper motives for behaving as they do, whether the action is one of going to church, giving a gift, or signing a petition. Self-knowledge is anything but infallible, and the illusions we live under are not necessarily discoverable through

181

conversation or dialogue. If hermeneutics is made to rest on a model of pure communication and takes only the intentional structure of subjective consciousness as basic, then it is destined to run aground on the unreliability of self-interpretation.

A response to this problem has been to call for a "critique of ideology," a method that takes as its model what has been called partially suspended communication."[12] The key insight that is used to elucidate this process comes from the observation that there is often a shift in orientation that occurs during conversation from that of participant to observer: one may find oneself looking upon the other as though he were a natural object and consequently begin to treat his utterances as symptoms rather than expressions. What a person says may be ideological in the sense that it reveals the effects of objective influences, influences that may distort his perceptions and reflections. Only by assuming that people can be regarded as objects as well as subjects can we explain how they may be susceptible to systematic misunderstanding of the meanings of their activities, and why they are often mistaken as to the nature of their needs and motives.

An activity that has served as a model for this approach is the practice of psychoanalysis. What the analyst tries to do is both to diagnose the patient's self-deceptions and to bring about a heightened self-awareness by enabling him to work through his own reinterpretations of the world of his experience. The idea is to reconstruct what the patient has forgotten from his faulty "texts"—his dreams, associations, and patterns of repetition—while the patient "remembers" or establishes new recollections.[13] The process is supposed to correct the systematic distortions that have made the patient's previous interpretations of past events and current realities radically idiosyncratic or even fantastic.

Critique of ideology is a method for improving the reliability of testimony. Like psychoanalysis, it is supposed to enable the subject to free himself from the self-deceptions that permeate his perceptions of the meaning of his actions and utterances. Just as the neurotic is helped to recognize his repressed feelings and desires and thereby achieve a greater degree of self-understanding, the individual within society can be helped to understand his own behavior and the reasons for his actions in ways that go beyond merely consulting his immediately introspectible ideas. Both methods have as their goal the bringing of the individual's own interpretation of his behavior into consistency with a proper public or intersubjective interpretation.

182

Hermeneutics and the critique of ideology can be seen as responses to the refractory nature of social life. That they exist at all is a testimony to the fact that the domain of social phenomena is not adequately dealt with when it is treated as a field for natural science. Because the subject matter of social science requires other kinds of understanding than scientific understanding, alternative approaches such as these have been seen as called for. Social science is accordingly said to demand a synthesis, one that will allow us to attend to all aspects of social life and avoid one-sided knowledge of the human condition.[14]

In developing this point of view, Habermas categorizes the several approaches as distinct ways of gaining knowledge.[15] What we have, he says, are three methodological frameworks: that of the empirical-analytic sciences, that of the historical-hermeneutic sciences, and that of the critically oriented sciences. The attitude that he specifically objects to is one he calls "scientism," which holds that legitimate knowledge is possible only in the system of the empirical sciences.[16] Science, he insists, is only *one* category of possible knowledge.[17]

The implications of this program are clearly inimical to the idea of a naturalistic social science. For if empirical-analytic science is not the only type of legitimate knowledge, if social inquiry yields several different types of knowledge only one of which has the character of empirical science, then the social studies must not be science. Hermeneutics and critique of ideology do contribute knowledge, as Habermas and others have shown, but not the kind of propositional knowledge that assumes a world that has a structure that is independent of the knower. It is rather knowledge of how to find one's way about in the world of human interactions.[18]

Those who point up the importance of hermeneutic interpretation and the need to "critique" the self-misunderstandings of human action are quite right to suggest that understanding of the human scene grows out of a plurality of approaches. It is another matter to suppose that each of these amounts to a methodological framework for *science*. The results of investigators' efforts at achieving interpretive understanding and overcoming the distortions caused by misperceptions do not need to be hailed as science, and it would be pointless to extend the meaning of the term "science" merely to include them. Science does not have a monopoly on rational approaches to a domain.

If the social studies were to count as scientific disciplines, they would have to depend on the use of methods that we have already seen to be inadequate for their domain. Science requires a set of presuppositions and a mode of understanding that is neither suitable nor accessible to social inquiry. There is no objective science of human beings and human societies that can provide that kind of understanding to any significant degree. That is why the idea of a naturalistic social science, like that of a perpetual-motion machine, is no more than a pseudoscientific myth.

# 11. The Fruits of Social Research

The social studies, we have seen, have not been outstandingly successful as science. They have turned up a great deal of information, but the project of creating a systematic body of laws and theories has not borne out the hopes of Comte, Mill, and the latter-day empiricists. I have tried to show why this has been the case, and why it is reasonable to doubt that the aims of those who envision a science of human social life will ever be realized.

When something fails to live up to its promise despite extraordinary and extensive efforts made in its behalf, there is reason to examine the basic assumptions and presuppositions that determine the nature of the enterprise and its relation to the domain in which it is carried out. One possibility that we have not yet considered is that the advocates and practitioners of social-science research may have been deceiving themselves as to the nature of their enterprise and its products. It is this idea that I wish to explore in this final chapter. The direction in which I shall move is toward considering the so-called social sciences as something other than science.

What I propose to do is to make a brief and highly selective review of some representative results of social science with the idea of assessing their status as cognitive achievements. It is not possible, of course, to argue validly from the fact that some examples of social-science research have not amounted to significant scientific achievements to the conclusion that there is no worthwhile social science, nor is it acceptable to argue from what has not been done to what cannot be done. The purpose of the examination is not to establish that there is not or cannot be a naturalistic social science—that question has already been explored on a conceptual level at some length—but rather, by trying to see where some of these efforts may have gone awry, to prompt a reconsideration of the entire enterprise. The critique will take a number of different tacks, not only because the social sciences comprise a variety of disciplines, but also because there are many ways in which the conduct of social inquiry can depart from the naturalistic model of science. The problem of assessing the status of social science will also lead us to question whether there really is a sharp division that can be drawn between science and philosophy. The conclusion—that social science is not usefully seen as of a piece with natural science—will have to be tempered by the recognition that whether or not something is a science may be only a matter of its distance from a demarcation line between science and nonscience that is no more than mythical.

# I

According to most informed opinion, if there exists a branch of social inquiry that is worthy of being called science, it is economics. It is mathematical, it employs formal models, and it often makes successful predictions. There is a set of variables among which economics has found functional relationships, and there is a set of institutions and collectives whose behavior economics seems to be capable of representing systematically. So far as it renders accurate accounts of the objects of its domain, and so far as economic phenomena include such items as unemployment, inflation, interest rates, debt, and level of production, economics appears to be a bona-fide social science.

Economics is not a science of human behavior, however, even though the behavior of economic institutions and collectives is constituted by the acts of individual human beings. It deals not with actions as such, but only with certain of their consequences. Like demography, economics amounts at most to the working out of the implications of a number of basic facts and assumptions concerning the behavior of individuals. The models that have been constructed are not supposed to describe or explain what people do, but rather have been devised to indicate what will happen if people behave in certain ways. The accuracy of economic predictions depends entirely on the extent to which *Homo sapiens* is correctly identifiable with *Homo economicus*, rational economic man. And even when the predictions are correct, that does not show that economic principles *explain* human behavior. It only confirms the assumptions that were made at the outset.

Economic models, so far as they are based on projections of economic indicators rather than on observations of what people do, neither describe nor purport to describe actual human behavior. When an economic model fails to yield correct predictions—when, for example, there is both rising inflation and rising unemployment, which existing theory says cannot happen—this is no falsification of any theory of human behavior. Explanations in economics, like economic forecasting, only *presume* that people will act in certain ways and that they are motivated by certain kinds of considerations. A competing model will very likely rest on the same presumptions. And even if the failure of an economic theory to explain certain changes were to lead to a revision of our assumptions about the way humans behave, this would still not show that economics represents an attempt to understand human behavior. Economics is a science of the collective results of action, not a science of action itself.

In order for economics to be a specifically human science, rather than a science of the behavior of things that just happen to be run by humans, it would have to be capable of explaining economic phenomena in terms of, and on the level of, the behavior of human individuals and human groups. It would need to show what it is about humans that makes economic processes possible. At the same time, it would have to do something that economics as currently understood cannot do: namely, explain why economic principles and projections sometimes fail. Just as it is a mark of an adequate physical science that it can explain why certain physical laws—the Ideal Gas laws, for example—do not hold under certain conditions, so it may be demanded of a social science that it be capable of explaining departures from the laws of economics.

# II

If there is a science that can explain why economic principles have true application in some cases but not in others, that science, one might think, should be psychology. However, it is open to question whether psychology is a science of the required sort, or whether it is capable of providing a proper grounding for economics or any other social or institutional science. Psychology fails to   provide scientific understanding of human activity, I shall argue, because the kinds of phenomena it illuminates are not the ones it needs to in order to play this role. Where it succeeds as empirical science it fails to be relevant, and where it succeeds in being relevant it fails as science.

Psychology, understood as a science of behavior, can be seen as comprising two parts, one concerned with dispositions, the other with capacities. The distinction being made is between what people will do and what they *can* do. It is the psychology of the latter domain, which includes the areas of memory and perception as well as learning theory and developmental psychology, that has produced science that most closely adheres to the naturalistic model. There the focus is not on how the human creature comes to perform actions but rather on how it comes to have the capacity to perform them. That such science, which is essentially biological in character, should resemble natural science is not surprising.

A psychology that sets forth what an organism is capable of doing and how it acquires these capabilities will not provide explanations of why people perform the actions they do or why they select the particular social arrangements they adopt. Knowledge of general capacities is useful only so far as it tells us what falls within the range of the possible. If we are going to explain something like economic behavior, on the other hand, we need a science that reveals what people will do, *given* their biological or psychological capacities.

If psychological research can contribute to an understanding of why people act as they do, one of its most promising directions will be toward discovering what the influences are on various types of human behavior and why these influences work as they do. If there are explanations on the psychological level that tell what makes people act as they do, a science that tries to relate environmental causes and human psychological nature to overt behavior ought to be the one to provide them. Such a psychology, were it to succeed, would deserve to be counted as a science on the level of, say, plant biology.

Clearly not all of psychology as it is currently pursued qualifies as basic science on the naturalistic model. Much of what is contributed by studies of motivation or of decision making, for example, is more akin to technological know-how than to science as such. When psychologists investigate the susceptibility of behavior patterns to particular sorts of influences, they begin with socialized individuals and then proceed to try

188

to find out how the social characteristics of these individuals are affected by changes in the environment and things that are done to them. Like television sets, human individuals are cultural products whose behavior can to some extent be controlled or altered simply by knowing what conditions yield what effects. Such knowledge is not ordinarily assumed to be valid for humans in general, but only for those who have received a particular kind of socialization. One need not know very much about the human species in general, or about machines in general, in order to discover the principles or rules of thumb that govern the behavior of some of them.

A large portion of social inquiry concerns the effects of specific institutions and types of practices, such as capital punishment or formal education, where investigation is concerned not with the nature and properties of anything fundamental but with the interdependencies of limited sets of social variables. The value of such research lies in its providing clues to possible solutions of particular social problems. Unlike research in human biology, however, it cannot be represented as seeking to achieve practical results *by means of* studying the nature of a part of reality. There is no distinction to be drawn in these areas between pure and applied science, because the former has dropped out. So far as much empirical research in sociology and social psychology is concerned, there is little or no basis to distinguish between an Edison, on the one hand, and a Faraday or a Newton on the other.

Not all research in psychology is concerned with the specific, the restricted, or the culture-bound. There is a large amount of research that aims at establishing conclusions of a more general nature, conclusions whose universality may be no less than that of the human emotions and attitudes. Investigators have studied the relationship between anxiety and frustration, for example, and between fear of mockery or disappointment and reluctance to perform altruistic acts. Furthermore, social psychology has not been lacking in theories that are supposed to provide a general framework for conceiving large numbers of specific correlations. One such theory is the theory of cognitive dissonance. This theory was put forward to account for and, it was hoped, to predict attitude change in a wide variety of cases in which people who are made to engage in behavior that is inconsistent with their prior beliefs and attitudes are found to resolve the inconsistency by either reinterpreting their beliefs or changing them.[1] By offering explanations of why we form

189

many of the beliefs we have, dissonance theory was thought to tell us something about human social behavior in general.

There is reason, however, to question the scientific value of theories of this kind, and a number of psychologists have done just that. What is troubling about such conceptions is that they may be at best generalized intuitions; at worst, they may be inflated platitudes. One may ask whether a host of empirical studies is what is needed to establish that frustration leads to aggression or that insults engender hostility. A reply that has been suggested is that although these are indeed common-sense beliefs, it is nevertheless an important task of social science to check up on such beliefs. Only where the beliefs are confirmed, so it is said, does the research necessarily appear banal and unilluminating.[2] While the point may hold true for some areas of social science, it is very doubtful whether it does for statements as general as the ones just mentioned. For in cases such as these, it is not clear that anything could ever *disconfirm* them, since one of the ways we identify insults or frustration is by looking for signs of hostility or aggression. A statement of this kind *can't* be proved wrong if its being right is guaranteed by the way the concepts are applied.

A theory like the theory of cognitive dissonance is supposed to give abstract expression to findings of a less general character, such as that a person will come to believe his own lies if he tells them often enough. Generalizations of this kind do not deserve to be elevated to the status of theoretical principles if they leave too many unexplained exceptions that cannot be viewed merely as statistical irregularities. Let us suppose that it has been established that factory workers who are promoted to foreman tend to become more pro-management, whereas workers who are made shop stewards tend to become more pro-union. (This is the sort of fact that the theory of cognitive dissonance is supposed to explain.) If the generalization that is drawn from such examples is that attitudes follow rather than precede behavior, it is faced with a large number of counterexamples. There are clear cases of effective persuasion, where attitudes change *before* behavior does, as well as cases in which people never do adapt their beliefs to the behavior they have been obliged to perform.

Defenders of the theory of cognitive dissonance have gone to some lengths to explain these apparent exceptions, and sometimes they have been able to provide experimental support for their interpretations. The following case will serve as an illustration.³ Students holding a negative attitude toward a certain police action were induced by means of cash payment to write essays in defense of the police. Their attitudes were found to remain relatively unchanged, contrary to what the theory of cognitive dissonance would have predicted. The theory is saved from falsification by the suggestion that the cash reward provided a good enough reason for the students to write the essays they wrote. This interpretation was borne out by the discovery that students who were induced to do the same thing for much less money did in fact acquire a much more favorable attitude toward the police.

Nonetheless, the failure of the students in the initial experiment to change their original attitudes does constitute an exception, if not to the statement that attitudes will change to reduce cognitive dissonance, at least to the more general claim that they will change to keep step with behavior. And if we regard the failure of a situation to bring about a change in attitude as evidence for a lack of cognitive dissonance, then the theory verges on circularity. If the only way to prevent the theory of cognitive dissonance from being falsified is to refuse to acknowledge its occurrence in any case in which doing something inconsistent with one's attitudes fails to change them, then the theory has very little content.

Although the theory of cognitive dissonance was for a considerable period a dominant conception in social psychology, it is perhaps not the best example of a theory of attitude change that could have been chosen. Other approaches do not seem to have fared much better, however, for they too raise questions as to what, if anything, the empirical studies they involve establish. A case in point is the so-called Yale approach to persuasive communication, which has led to the identification and measurement of a number of factors that influence the effectiveness of attempts at persuasion.⁴ The principal achievement of this program has been to demonstrate that factors that we already know make a difference—factors such as source's credibility, type of appeal, and a subject's receptivity—do in fact play a part in determining the extent to which opinion changes. That, after all, is what is expressed by what has solemnly been proposed as a "formal two-factor model": $p(O) = p(R)p(Y)$.⁵ This formula, which states that the probability that opinion will change is a function of both the probability that the message will be received and the probability that the subject will yield to it, merely expresses what we know if we know what persuasion *means*. Nothing that could be discovered would show that persuasive communication is *not* affected by these factors.

Apparently oblivious to the fact that testing psychological models may amount to no more than instantiating conceptual truths, psychologists have continued to come up with alternative models that have the same logical deficiency.[6] When one model is superior to another, it is only because it embodies a more accurate or more complete conceptual analysis of the process being investigated. In the case of persuasion, the model will consist of an account of what one has to do—inform, appeal to the recipient's values, impart an intention, and so on—in order to change a person's attitudes or behavioral propensities. In all cases, the model is entirely dependent on what a logical analysis of persuasive communication reveals.

The empirical studies that psychologists carry out do not really establish that persuasion is affected by such things as whether or not the subject receives the message, any more than interviewing bachelors establishes that all bachelors are unmarried. It is only the relative importance of specific features of a process of persuasive communication, such as tone of voice, that requires empirical investigation. Elevating particular findings to the abstract level of a formal model is what renders these results obscure. It is as though psychologists are so interested in supporting conclusions of a general nature that they express their results in terms of propositions that, because they represent connections of concepts, cannot possibly be false.

An approach to theorizing in psychology that many have thought quite promising is one that involves a search for intervening variables between outside stimuli and behavior. Instead of introducing hypothetical constructs such as cognitive dissonance that have been criticized for lack of empirical content, an effort is made to identify whatever it is within a human subject that reacts to those features of the environment that affect his behavior. The hope is that by trying to find out how external influences on behavior are mediated it will be possible to discover what sorts of conditions have positive or negative effects on certain kinds of performance, why certain measures increase motivation, and why certain kinds of persuasion are more effective than others. What is envisioned is the experimental study of actual states of the human subject.

The approach makes a good deal of sense on an abstract level, and some specific findings have offered interesting predictive possibilities, but the actual theoretical output has been of doubtful value. An example will serve to illustrate. It was found that a more effective way of persuading alcoholics to sign up for an Alcoholic Treatment Unit than stressing the consequences of continued heavy drinking is to attempt to change the subject's beliefs about the consequences of not signing up, even though the consequences mentioned may be the same in both cases.[7] These results were interpreted as showing that *intentions* are the real dependent variable in such cases of persuasion, and that they, rather than attitudes, are the primary determinants of overt behavior.

However, it is a conceptual truth, not an empirical discovery, that you need to create an intention in order to get someone to perform a voluntary act such as signing up. And since actions follow necessarily from intentions—performance being the main criterion of having an intention—it is at least a little bit odd to speak of *discovering* that intentions are determinants of behavior. The only relevant empirical question here is how to bring about the intention. The value of the research lies in its demonstration of what methods work. The "theory" that has been called forth to explain *why* they work is not a theory of human psychology; it merely helps to explicate the logic of mental concepts.

Despite the existence of a number of interesting findings concerning the ways in which behavior can be influenced, it is somewhat disappointing to observe that much of what psychology has presented is not very informative. A good deal of what we know about human behavior, furthermore, has not been the result of any program of research. One does not ordinarily do experiments to learn how to win friends and influence people. It is not psychology that teaches us that a major determinant of a person's choice of activities, how hard he strives, and how long he persists is his belief in the extent to which he is able to control outcomes—despite the number of studies that have been performed to establish just that proposition.[8] Empirical studies do not validate such insights; they only instantiate them. Nor do we need psychology to explain why housewives are more willing to purchase cake mixes that require them to break an egg and add it to the mixture (they like to retain the feeling that they are making their own contribution); or why students prefer teachers who praise their best efforts (people tend to be well disposed toward those who enhance their self-esteem). In cases like these, our ordinary common-sense explanations are the best we have, and they are not improved by being expressed in the abstract terminology of a psychological theory.

That psychology tells us so much of what is already familiar or truistic would not be so disturbing were it not for the fact that it *has* to be that way, given the kinds of explanation that are frequently sought. When psychologists try to explain an empirical correlation that has been discovered—and this is especially true in social psychology—the explanation often has the form of rational explanation. The concepts that are appealed to, so far as they are constrained to reflect the structure of ordinary reasoning, are either borrowed or derived from our everyday ways of talking about mental phenomena. To the extent that psychological explanations use concepts that belong to the set of ordinary mentalistic concepts—intention, desire, feeling, distress, or self-esteem—they simply follow our customary ways of talking about human behavior. Many of the so-called theories we have in experimental psychology are simply common-sense theories in disguise. That is not something we can say about theories in the natural sciences.

# III

Although they are not always the most admired by social scientists, the most impressive results of social inquiry, in many important respects, are the very broad theories. What a theory like Marx's historical materialism or Freud's psychoanalytic theory contributes is an explanatory framework whereby a wide range of diverse phenomena are organized and placed in a perspective. A conceptualization like Weber's theory of corporate groups or Durkheim's theory of the relation of the individual to social authority provides a way of looking at structures and relationships that enables us to discover coherence and generality where previously only particularity was seen. Such theories, I have pointed out, are empirical in the sense that they are inspired by and draw support from empirical facts, but they are extremely "loose" in that they lack close connections with the facts they are supposed to explain and are compatible with many other possible sets of facts. However, it is not true that they can accommodate *all* possible facts; any of these theories would simply be false if the world were radically different from the way it is.

The problem is that such theories are notoriously unconvincing. When a theory has only a loose fit to social reality, confirmation, as Popper pointed out, is cheap, especially when it turns out that the theory is confirmed by almost anything that happens.[9] Such a theory would be easily replaceable by a rival interpretation that offers a different perspective or by a theory that picks out different aspects or features of human social life. There is no scientific compulsion to believe a theory for which an alternative can be found that appears to be equally well supported by the same evidence.

In principle there is no reason why theories in natural science should not be afflicted with the same problem. Since there are an infinite number of logically possible sets of hypotheses that can be devised to explain any given set of data, no theory can claim to have a legitimate title to exclusive jurisdiction in its domain; its authority is de facto rather than de jure as it were. In practice, however, we are rarely if ever faced in natural science with a multiplicity of theories all equally compatible with the facts. The reason this is true appears to be that in the natural sciences it is extremely difficult to come up with even a single theory that will accommodate all the facts in the domain. On the other hand, social phenomena, for which there typically exists no theory that has even a moderately tight fit, tend to submit to a number of different conceptualizations. Natural phenomena are thus a special case in that we typically find that there is at most one empirically adequate conceptual scheme that will embrace them.

A number of people have suggested that the reason why broad social theories have not warranted universal endorsement is their failure to yield specific testable implications. Too many things can happen, it is argued, that are compatible with a given theory being true. A theory, if it is a scientific theory, must make *risky* predictions, as Popper has put it, and the only confirmations that deserve to be counted are those that result from such predictions. In order for a theory to be scientific, so it is maintained, it must have a degree of specificity that is sufficient for the prediction of particular events whose occurrence or nonoccurrence is capable of disconfirming it.[10]

Whatever the merits of this view as an account of what scientific theories should do, it does not seem to reflect or to have legislated acceptable scientific practice. As Kuhn and others have shown, refractory data can be and typically are accommodated in any number of ways that will keep them from torpedoing an existing theory.[11] It is not true that a conceptualization must provide specific predictions in order to be recognized as a scientific theory; the theory of evolution is a case in point. What a theory is primarily supposed to do is to help us *understand* a range of phenomena. Scientific understanding entails being able to explain the phenomena in terms of a set of true common principles in virtue of which they have been ordered. While it is true that all such understanding implies the possibility of predictions, such tests may be extremely rare, especially when the theory is highly abstract. No one would deny that the general theory of relativity has always been a genuine scientific theory, ever since Einstein first presented it, even though it was a long time before anyone was able to test it.

What makes a general explanatory theory compelling is not its predictive capacity but rather its lack of competitors. Predictive tests may be seen as a rational means of weeding out competitors only when there is more than one theory that will explain the known facts. The practice of making and testing predictions in the natural sciences has usually led to situations in which there is only one theory that can account for all the data. When not even the only existing theory can do that, it is still likely to be generally accepted until there is a rival theory to displace it; degree of falsifiability alone is not the basis for acceptance when there is only one general theory on the horizon. A theory that explains but fails to predict, or even one that often yields false predictions, is almost always better than no theory at all.

With general social theories, the situation is one in which there are several competing theories that cannot be decided among on the basis of the data or by testing specific predictions. It is not a matter of what evidence there is that determines whether, for example, the theory of alienation or the theory of anomie provides a better rendering of the situation of human beings in modern industrial society. So far as the empirical evidence is concerned, there is as much support for viewing the symptoms of modern society—greed, competitiveness, the sense of playing a role in an impersonal system, and the lack of community—as results of a breakdown in social integration as there is for interpreting these phenomena as reflections of the growth of capitalism.[12] Similarly, the data alone will not enable us to decide whether the growth of civilization has served to help human beings realize their individual happiness, or whether civilization has worked to repress it, as the neo-

Freudians argue.[13] It is in the nature of phenomena such as wars, religious movements, and the careers of institutions of power and authority to submit to multiple conceptualizations that are capable of representing all of the facts adduced in a consistent and coherent order.

It would nonetheless be a mistake to call general social theories nonscientific solely because they do not yield specific predictions that provide a basis for rational decision among competing theories. To do so would be to imply that many acknowledged scientific theories, as well as these questionable social theories, are nonscientific. Accepting this criterion would mean denying that theories of cosmogony, theories of light, and theories of matter belonged to science during the times when more than one theory would explain all the available data. The fact that a theory has a competitor from which it cannot be distinguished by empirical means does not by itself disqualify it as a scientific theory.

What is it, if not lack of empirical content, that warrants the judgment that general social theories are nonscientific? The answer, I submit, is that the debates among their defenders are ultimately and inescapably philosophical in character. Inspection of scientific theories reveals that it is not possible to demarcate science from nonscience on the basis of testability or possession of empirical content, but it is possible to make at least a rough distinction based on the grounds on which the defense of a theory must finally rest. When the facts alone cannot convince someone to accept a theory, when the tribunal of experience cannot offer a decision judgment, other grounds—the metaphysical, epistemological, ethical, and political implications of a conceptualization—will decide, if anything does. Temperament, ideology, and philosophical argument are what determine how one thinks when the data do not favor any one theory of the domain.

There is no sharp distinction that can be drawn between science and philosophy, but that does not imply that there is no difference between a philosophical thesis and a scientific thesis. What makes a debate primarily scientific is the degree to which empirical argument dominates, and whether there is a realistic expectation that the dispute will ultimately be resolved by empirical means. The claim that social theories are basically philosophical amounts to the claim that no such expectation is warranted.

The aim of a social theory is to make sense of social phenomena by showing that they reflect or result from processes of a more fundamental nature, that they are manifestations of an underlying order. Such theories, although they clearly have empirical impact, are philosophical in the sense that they contain implicit or explicit recommendations as to how we should conceive of human sociality. Thus Durkheim's work on suicide was significant not merely because it showed that suicide is more common among the wealthy than among the poor, or that it is more common among Protestants than among Catholics, but because it was able to exhibit such findings as measures of social integration. Durkheim's idea was that social integration is the central feature of human social life, and it was this idea that determined what sorts of things he thought should be looked at in order to better understand the phenomenon of suicide. In selecting a class of actions that are as individual and personal as any meaningful action we are likely to imagine, and by using them as a basis for identifying currents of altruism, egoism, and anomie running through a society, Durkheim took a stand on a philosophical issue, not an empirical one. He was in favor of holism and against individualism, and in favor of directing attention to the social meaning of individual actions. His was not merely a theory with philosophical implications, but a philosophical theory itself, one whose thrust was to tell us which of several normative conceptions of the relation betwen society and the individual we ought to endorse. There are other ways of interpreting the same suicide data, and other ways of conceiving the relation between human beings and the social order—for example, the one supported by philosophical individualism. The difference between Durkheim's view of social life and the view of a Freud or that of the thinkers of the Enlightenment is a philosophical difference. It is not one that is going to be settled by an appeal to "the facts."

Theories of society have a closer affinity to philosophical theories than they do to theories of natural science. They are not the sort of theories whose truth or falsity can, in principle, be established independently of values and metaphysical commitments. The point is not simply that social theories have philosophical import, for the same can be said of Copernican astronomy, the theory of relativity, or the theory of evolution. Rather what is at stake is a matter of taking certain kinds of evidence seriously. What often separates the supporter of one kind of theory from that of another kind is the use of different criteria for determining what data are relevant. That is why someone who insists on explanations of social behavior in terms of psychological facts will never convince anyone who believes that explanations of the same phenomena must appeal to facts of a sociological nature.

Social theories, like theories of natural science, deliver an interpretation of events in the world. But a social theory also establishes an interpretive relationship between subject and object that is in general quite different from the one that is characteristic of natural science. Deployment of a social theory carries an implicit recommendation as to how one *ought* to regard certain phenomena. More is at stake in the debate over the relative merits of a functionalist and a historical or dialectical account of such an institution as the Royal Family, or the explanatory value of a Hobbesian versus a Marxian account of an event such as the American Civil War, than merely establishing what took place or what caused what. When different accounts reveal radically different approaches and orientations, the choice between them must ultimately be made at the level of fundamental values and philosophical beliefs.

The relationship between competing social theories exhibits many of the features that occur when there is dispute between what Kuhn has called incommensurable paradigms.[14] Unlike the situation in natural science, however, wherein anomalies accumulate and impose considerable strain on older theories while being readily accommodated by newer ones, there are no crises in social theory. There is no single finding or set of findings that will decide the case between a Weber and a Tawney, for example, on whether capitalism is what gave rise to Calvinism or whether Calvinism is rather one of the things that led to capitalism.[15] Because one is dealing not with causal laws but with patterns of action, and because the data that are presented are themselves so disparate, debates among social historians do not ordinarily have specific points of conflict. There are so *many* things to be explained by a social theory, and so many aspects of social phenomena to be selected from, that direct confrontation between competing conceptualizations rarely if ever occurs.

The problem with trying to think of social theories as scientific theories is not just that there is an irreducible multiplicity of incommensurable theories, for, as Feyerabend has argued, science is not necessarily unable to tolerate such a state of affairs.[16] The real difficulty is that there are no hard data that are explained by one theory that are not equally well accommodated by the other. The situation is not unlike the one that surrounded atomism when it was more a metaphysical than a scientific theory: because there were few if any empirical considerations prior to the nineteenth century that would support atomism in opposition to the competing Aristotelian view, the debate turned largely on such questions as whether the notion of a void could be made philosophically acceptable.[17] Atomism was eventually able to deliver the goods and to gain accreditation as a scientific theory. Social theory, I have argued, is unlikely ever to do so.

# IV

Like most working natural scientists, many social scientists have ignored the pursuit of theories of an abstract and highly general character and have devoted their attention to research of a much narrower scope. We have already seen that much of social science's output has been concerned with phenomena of a rather restricted and culture-specific sort. But there is other research whose conclusions appear to be less restricted in their application, research that seems to yield genuine insights. I would like to consider briefly two kinds of research programs that appear to offer contributions of this sort.

Only one of these types of contributions involves experimentation or systematic observation. The Western Electric researches, in which the "Hawthorne effect" was first identified, may be taken as representative.[18] One of the things that was found as a result of studying the effects of various items on worker productivity was that the performance of workers (measured in terms of output) is improved not only by the introduction of certain changes, such as an increase in illumination, but also by the opposite change, a decrease in illumination. It appears that it was not the nature of the change that caused people to work faster, but merely the fact that a change was made at all.

It is important to ask just what this discovery amounts to. For while it may be true that a change in routine will cause people to perk up a bit (especially when they are not able to choose their activity), it is not true that *all* changes in working conditions will enhance performance. The Western Electric researches do not support any broad generalizations other than the truism that people work harder when they think someone is taking an interest in their work. That dimming the lights is one of the things that stimulates productivity is not the sort of fact that yields significant generalizations. Empirical studies of this kind will neither generate nor validate general insights; they can only establish or refute particular instances.

The other kind of social-science contribution still to be looked at consists of some results that derive from studies of particular forms of social life in their proper institutional settings—*in vivo*, as it were, as opposed to the *in-vitro* studies of the experimentalist. There is Tocqueville, who was able to see that democracy, because it is a system of power with roots in public opinion rather than in traditional authority, can be expected to lead to a greater degree of uniformity and a decline of the very same individuality that the system was supposed to allow.[19] There is Simmel, who saw the connection between the characteristics of life in cities and the acquiring of blasé attitudes.[20] And there is Goffman, whose investigations of "total institutions" led him to recognize that individuals are capable of playing any of a number of quite different roles in accordance with existing conditions and whatever response patterns are demanded by the particular social contexts in which they find themselves.[21]

These are not the sort of findings that depend on a program of controlled scientific research, either for inspiration or for validation. the stuff of which "discoveries" like these are made is accessible to anyone who looks, although it typically requires a creative intellect to make observations as significant as those that social thinkers like these have made. The conclusions drawn, while they are often based on very detailed examinations of the phenomena being considered, are not subject to independent or determinate testing. They are not expected to explain phenomena other than those that gave rise to them, and their extension to other contexts is a matter of unsupported speculation. Their value, like that of the experimental studies just considered, lies in the insights they provide into specific segments of social life.

The fact that so many of the insights attributed to social scientists come not from controlled investigation but rather from informal observation and reflection suggests a comparison with what is found in first-rate literature and also in proverbs and aphorisms. Just as it does not require an empirical study to establish the psychological truth revealed in Shakespeare's "The lady doth protest too much, methinks," neither does it to recognize the aptness of Weber's remark that every system of authority attempts to establish and cultivate the belief in its "legitimacy." Insights such as these may tell us or remind us of what we already know, or they may point out things we have not adequately noticed. Being already well confirmed by common-sense experience, they are not the sort of things that a scientific study could show to be false. Where common sense and ordinary observation form the standard, there is no need for experiment or controlled observation to prove that an insight is a contribution to knowledge.

# V

Whether one stresses the failure of social-science research to give rise to a cumulative and systematic body of scientific knowledge, the paucity of its important results, or the fact that the most interesting discoveries about human life seem not to have required any of the apparatus of scientific inquiry, some reevaluation or reinterpretation of the social-science enterprise is called for. One response has been to declare social science and social-science discourse to be fraudulent in the way sorcery is. That is the view of at least one sociologist, Andreski, who charges that what publications in social science reveal is primarily an "abundance of pompous bluff," "a torrent of meaningless verbiage and useless technicalities," and an "interminable repetition of platitudes and disguised propaganda."[22] The allegedly scientific study of human affairs, in Andreski's judgment, is marked by sterility and deception.

An interpretation of sociology that is less vituperative but equally critical of its scientific pretensions is revealed in Cioffi's suggestion that sociologists often deserve to be characterized not as theorists but as "story-tellers posing as theorists."[23] Cioffi asks what is accomplished by a work such as Veblen's analysis of conspicuous consumption in *The Theory of the Leisure Class,* or Goffman's account of impression management in *The Presentation of Self in Everyday Life.* The answer, he argues, is not the communication of a discovery of something that no one knew existed, but rather the manipulation of our sentiments toward certain facts. Veblen did not introduce the idea that conspicuous consumption is a means of status affirmation as a novel thesis, Cioffi maintains, but rather as a device for calling attention to a similarity he perceived between members of the modern leisure class and ancient predatory "barbarians" who were also engaged in acquiring wealth by force rather than work. Cioffi makes a similar point with respect to Goffman's juxtaposing of instances of impression fostering, such as the practice of adopting a more cultured accent when speaking over the telephone, the use of better-quality curtain material on the front windows of one's house than on the back ones, unscrupulous practices employed by some used-car salesmen, and techniques adopted by civil servants and foreign diplomats: Goffman is not merely showing how widespread are the instances of the truism that people often deceive others in order to enhance their own status or position; he is urging us to see social encounters in a particular light. A sociology that is committed to producing accounts of this sort cannot have as its primary concern the imparting of scientific knowledge.

We can accept this sort of characterization of the products of social inquiry without impugning the motives of social scientists or supposing that they consciously misrepresent the nature of their enterprise. Research can serve a variety of interests that are not immediately recognized by those who pursue it. "Knowledge for knowledge's sake" is not and cannot be all that social science is concerned with. I have already mentioned the interests in prediction and control and in communicative understanding. A further interest, one that can be seen to permeate a great deal of social inquiry, is revealed by the "truth-is-stranger-than-fiction" attraction that many findings appear to have. There is a widespread fascination with the bizarre in human experience, and a common titillation that comes from seeing familiar social and psychological facts presented in a new light. More than just scientific curiosity is satisfied by anthropological descriptions of sexual practices in alien cultures, by comparison of ancient and modern burial rites, and by analysis of methods of social control. Furthermore, it is not merely the subject matter that is found interesting but the way in which it is retailed. Reports of the results of social investigation are in this way like essays or poems. Their role may be not so much to inform as to entertain, to enlighten, to shock, or to create an attitude or mood. The interest in much of social science, in short, is more akin to a literary interest than to a scientific one.

So far as social science is a quasi-literary or philosophical pursuit, it can

203

hardly be expected to provide empirical solutions to the great social problems of our time. There are many people, of course, who believe that a properly executed (and funded) program of social research can ultimately do just that. The record is not very encouraging, however. There is virtually no evidence to support the supposition that applying the results of social-science inquiry will ever be necessary *or* sufficient for the prevention of war, the prevention of crime, or the elimination of prejudice. In place of achievements, we have frequent rehearsals of a myth, the myth that the solution of these problems awaits the accumulation of greater knowledge of psychology or social anthropology or political sociology. Even as harsh a critic of the pretensions of contemporary sociology as C. Wright Mills speaks of the goals of social science as "the avoidance of war and the rearrangement of human affairs in accordance with the ideals of human freedom and reason."[24] His faith—and that is what it truly is—is the battered faith of the Enlightenment, but it is the faith in a philosophical ideal, not a realizable goal. There is no research program that offers the chance of revealing how it might be attained.

The usefulness of social research in the gathering, discovering, and presenting of facts cannot be denied, of course. The backing that such contributions give to specific policy recommendations, however, is no more "scientific" or theoretical than is the support that past experiences give in, say, selecting a product for a particular paint job. One rather curious characteristic of social science is that its successes tend to be identified almost exclusively with the data it collects—despite the fact that the data themselves neither explain anything nor do they solve any problems. Modern social science appears to have virtually nothing to teach historians, for example, even those who have been most influenced by it, aside from the use of certain techniques for corroborating hypotheses. What we have learned about the world from social scientists does not differ in kind from what has been recounted to us by historians and journalists.

What is supposed to set social science apart from more speculative activities is that it uses facts, and that it accepts the requirement that whatever is stated must square with these facts. That it does so, however, does not adequately distinguish social science from philosophy or theology. In the first place, as we have seen, being faithful to empirical considerations will not by itself guarantee that one's interpretation can be relied on to reveal the way the world is. There are any number of ways of construing social reality and accommodating a given set of observations, each with its own bias or evaluative force. Second, unless one adopts a very narrow and not uncontroversial view of the nature of philosophy, it must be acknowledged that philosophical arguments employ empirical facts in much the same way that scientific arguments do. Facts occupy an important place in any kind of rational discourse about the world, and also in any rational discourse about how we ought to look upon it.

Social science, like natural science, occupies a large place in contemporary Western culture. Unlike natural science, it offers no unified account of a world that everyone, regardless of his values or cultural orientation, will agree is given to all in experience. Social science has given us much to say about human beings and human society, but mostly what it has contributed is a compendium of facts, stories, insights, and world views. Once its scientific aspirations are set aside and its pretensions stripped away, it is, at its best, a set of humanistic disciplines.

# Afterword

Once upon a time there was a gardener who set to work in a field to grow vegetables. After lengthy and repeated efforts, he discovered that the soil on which he was laboring simply would not produce anything that deserved to be called a vegetable. It did yield a number of pretty flowers, however, along with a lot of weeds, and it also gave rise to several plants that could be used as weapons or as drugs. Even though most of the plants that were grown were quite useless, it turned out that working in the garden was good for the gardener's soul, so long as he had no illusions that he was ever going to produce vegetables. Furthermore, the activities of turning over the earth and cultivating these plants introduced new patterns in the face of the land. New landscapes were created where previously there had only been barren land or random vegetation.

The would-be social scientist is like that gardener, having started out in pursuit of the sort of knowledge that natural science contributes, but finding himself instead engaged in a quite different sort of activity. Like the gardener's soil, the social investigator's domain turns out to reveal peculiarities whose presence results in the perversion of the original goals. But perhaps that is all right, because there are other things of value that the social studies may produce. The student of society works on a terrain that is interesting in many more ways than is any field whose promised yield is scientific knowledge.

This inquiry began with an attempt to understand human action. I tried to show why action cannot be understood in the same manner as corrosion of metals or reproduction, and that what can be understood in that way cannot be action. I then went on to argue that, because social phenomena are all inextricably bound up with action and because what is peculiar to human action is not capturable by the kind of net employed by natural science, there can be no significant social science modeled on that kind of science. The only science that could tell us why people do as they do would have to be a most unnatural science.

If the social studies must be called sciences, they must be moral sciences. Their normative character is vested, not only in their assumptions and presuppositions, but also in the categories employed and in the selection of facts exhibited. A social theory may tell us how we should view the social world, but it cannot tell us what the nature of that world is. Social inquiry cannot reveal what human nature is, but can suggest only what it ought to be. Because a human being, so far as it is an agent, is capable of doing other than it does, it can always display a different "nature" from the one that is expected of it. Such a creature, whose freedom entails that it cannot be counted on not to defy law-based predictions, cannot be an object of empirical science. Something whose behavior is neither random nor causally necessitated is nothing for science to get mixed up with.

# Notes

## Introduction

1. See, e.g., *Beyond Freedom and Dignity* (New York: Knopf, 1971).

2. The most important of these include N.R. Hanson, *Patterns of Discovery* (Cambridge: Cambridge University Press, 1958); Stephen Toulmin, *Foresight and Understanding* (New York: Harper & Row, 1961); T.S. Kuhn, *The Structure of Scientific Revolutions* (Chicago: University of Chicago Press, 1962); and P.K. Feyerabend, *Against Method* (London: NLB, 1975).

## 1. The Primacy of Action

1. D.G. Brown, *Action* (Toronto: University of Toronto Press, 1968), p. 35.

2. Even Brown (ibid.), who insists on the primacy of inanimate action, considers human and inanimate action to be two *kinds* of action.

3. Roderick Chisholm has reintroduced the medieval distinction between *transeunt* and *immanent* causation as a means of distinguishing the causation of events by events from the causation of events by actions; see his "Freedom and action," in Keith Lehrer, ed., *Freedom and Determinism* (New York: Random House, 1966), p. 17. G.H. von Wright makes the same distinction, but what Chisholm calls "immanent causation," he calls "action," preferring to opt for a single kind of causation. See his *Explanation and Understanding* (Ithaca, N.Y.: Cornell University Press, 1971), pp. 64-69, 191-192. Though I tend to agree with von Wright that agency is less confusingly conceived as not requiring a special notion of causation, it does not matter for my

purposes which of these positions is adopted, so long as the distinction between actions and other kinds of events is maintained.

4. *Nicomachean Ethics,* 1111a22.

5. Ibid., 1110b15-16.

6. Ibid., 1113b17-18.

7. Ibid., 1110a16-17.

8. See, e.g., Carl G. Hempel, *Philosophy of Natural Science* (Englewood Cliffs, N.J.: Prentice-Hall, 1966), Ch. 5.

9. Whether or not the explanation of human action, even thus construed, can be accommodated by the standard or causal view of scientific explanation has been a topic of considerable debate. See the discussion in Chapters 4 and 5.

10. See, e.g., D.M. Armstrong, *A Materialist Theory of Mind* (New York: Humanities Press, 1968).

11. Ludwig Wittgenstein, *Philosophical Investigations,* trans. G.E.M. Anscombe (London: Macmillan, 1953), Part 1, §621.

12. See Robert A. Jaeger, "Action and Subtraction," *Philosophical Review* 82 (1973): 320-329.

13. *Analytical Philosophy of Action* (Cambridge: Cambridge University Press, 1973), Ch. 3.

14. For a clear statement and defense of this view, see Jerome A. Shaffer, *Philosophy of Mind* (Englewood Cliffs, N.J.: Prentice-Hall, 1968), Ch. 5.

15. Gilbert Ryle, *The Concept of Mind* (London: Hutchinson, 1949), pp. 67-69.

16. This argument has been put forward by a number of writers, most notably A.I. Melden. See his *Free Action* (London: Routledge & Kegan Paul, 1961), esp. pp. 53, 114.

17. Or, as Austin has put it, "could have if I had chosen" is not a causal conditional; see J.L. Austin, "'Ifs' and 'Cans,'" in *Philosophical Papers* (London: Oxford University Press, 1961), pp. 153-180.

18. Such a situation is described by Harry G. Frankfurt in "Alternative Possibilities and Moral Responsibility," *Journal of Philosophy* 68 (1971): 829-839.

## 2. The Social Nature of Action

1. The notion of a basic action was introduced by Arthur Danto in "Basic Actions," *American Philosophical Quarterly* 2 (1965): 141-148.

2. See Arthur Danto, *Analytical Philosophy of Action* (Cambridge: Cambridge University Press, 1973), pp. ix-x.

3. A similar view of basic actions has been presented by Rudiger Bubner in *Handlung, Sprache and Vernunft* (Frankfurt: Suhrkamp, 1976), pp. 91-100.

4. *Nicomachean Ethics,* 1111b9.

5. Max Weber, *The Theory of Social and Economic Organization* (New York: The Free Press, 1964), p. 88.

6. *The Open Society and Its Enemies* vol 2 (Princeton: Princeton University Press, 1971), p. 93.

7. Danto, *Analytical Philosophy of Action,* pp. 20-21.

8. Alvin I. Goldman, *A Theory of Human Action* (Englewood Cliffs, N.J.: Prentice-Hall, 1970), p. 10.

9. This and other distinctions between actions and relations are discussed by Anthony Kenny in *Action, Emotion and Will* (London: Routledge & Kegan Paul, 1963), Ch. 7. See also Donald Davidson, "The Logical Form of Action Sentences," in Nicholas Rescher, ed., *The Logic of Decision and Action* (Pittsburgh: University of Pittsburgh Press, 1967), pp. 81-95.

10. See W.V. Quine, *Word and Object* (New York: Wiley, 1960), p. 144.

11. Suggested by John Troyer, "though not without trepidation."

12. I owe this formulation to Sam Wheeler, who attributes it to Donald Davidson. I also follow Davidson in denying that sentences name meanings, that these are abstract entities. See his "Truth and Meaning," *Synthese* 17 (1967); 304-323.

13. Weber, p. 88.

## 3. What Social Science is About

1. Principal expositions of the position are to be found in Karl Popper, *The Open Society and Its Enemies* (Princeton, N.J.: Princeton University Press, 1971) Ch. 14, and *The Poverty of Historicism* (London: Routledge & Kegan Paul, 1957), Chs. 7, 23, 24, 31; F.A. Hayek, *The Counter-Revolution of Science* (Glencoe, Ill.: The Free Press, 1955); J.W.N. Watkins, "Ideal Types and Historical Explanation, *British Journal for the Philosophy of Science* 3 (1952); 22-43, and "Historical Explanation in the Social Sciences," Ibid., 8 (1957); 104-117.

2. Maurice Mandelbaum, "Social Facts," *British Journal of Sociology* 6 (1955); 305-317.

3. Edna Ullmann-Margalit has suggested that Mandelbaum's argument fails to show that social-scientific language is irreducible to language comprising terms relating to the actions and beliefs of individuals only, because it does not distinguish between the use and mention of societal terms; that translations that mention terms like "bank" and "marriage," or the use of such words in reporting the actual speech and thought of people, no more commit us to the existence of irreducible social wholes than do mentions of the term "witch" in describing people's beliefs commit us to belief in witches. See *The Emergence of Norms* (Oxford: Clarendon Press, 1977), p. 16n. If her point is that all of these expressions can be used predicatively or buried in intentional contexts, I would agree. But then it is hard to see what is gained by trying to support methodological individualism in this way, given that *any* singular term can be eliminated from referential position (See W.V. Quine, *Word and Object* [New York: Wiley, 1960], pp. 181-186). And nations, courts, and legislatures are not like witches, in that there is nothing either fictional or metaphorical in the way these concepts are used to describe the social behavior of human individuals. We cannot know what it is to be a soldier if we cannot *use* such terms as "army" and "country."

4. *The Open Society* vol. 2, p. 324 (italics added).

5. "Ideal Types," p. 464.

6. These points have been made by Steven Lukes in "Methodological Individualism Reconsidered," *"The British Journal of Sociology* 9 (1968); 119-129; and by Alan Ryan in *The Philosophy of the Social Sciences* (London: Macmillan, 1970), pp. 178-179.

7. Ernest Gellner, "Explanations in History," *Proceedings of the Aristotelian Society,* suppl. vol. 30 (1956); 157-176.

8. I am indebted for this exposition of Popper's view to J.O. Wisdom; see his "Situational Individualism and the Emergent Group-Properties," in R. Borger and F. Cioffi, eds., *Explanation in the Behavioral Sciences* (Cambridge: Cambridge University Press, 1970), pp. 271-278.

9. Emile Durkheim, *The Rules of Sociological Method* (New York: The Free Press, 1964), pp. 103-104.

10. Hayek, pp. 56, 57.

11. *The Poverty of Historicism,* p. 135.

12. Ibid., p. 136.

13. Hayek, p. 55.

14. *The Poverty of Historicism,* p. 135.

15. Ibid., p. 138.

16. Peter Winch, *The Idea of a Social Science* (London: Routledge & Kegan Paul, 1958), pp. 127-128.


*4. Reasons and Social Inquiry*

1. See N.R. Hanson, *Patterns of Discovery* (Cambridge: Cambridge University Press, 1958), p.22

2. See Donald Davidson, "Actions, Reasons, and Causes," *Journal of Philosophy* (1963); 658-700.

3. "Freedom to Act," in Ted Honderich, ed., *Essays on Freeedom of Action* (London: Routledge & Kegan Paul, 1973), p. 147.

4. Richard Norman, *Reasons for Actions* (New York: Barnes & Noble, 1971) Chs. 1,3.

5. G.E.M. Anscombe, *Intention* (Oxford: Basil Blackwell, 1958 § 37.

6. Norman, p. 55.

7. This is the position that Norman argues.

8. William Dray, *Laws and Explanation in History* (Oxford: Clarendon Press, 1957), p. 132.

9. Carl G. Hempel, *Aspects of Scientific Explanation* (New York: The Free Press, 1965), pp. 469-472.

10. Ibid., p. 464.

11. "Actions."

12. Dray, p. 124.

13. Richard Miller has identified this distinction between an agent's professed reasons and his real reasons as the distinction between the agent's reasons for acting and the reasons why he acted as he did, and points out that it is a significant failing of methodological individualists that they restrict explanation to the former, thereby excluding the influence of what Miller calls "objective interests" on social phenomena; see his "Methodological Individualism," *Philosophy of Science* 45 (1978); 387-414. It is my position that both kinds of reasons merit consideration, and that they explain behavior in the same way.

14. Rational Behaviour and Psychoanalytic Explanation," *Mind* 71 (1962); 326-341.

15. At least since Wittgenstein, philosophers have generally recognized that the attribution of mental states such as beliefs and desires does not depend on identifying or characterizing states of awareness. See, e.g., Gilbert Ryle, *The Concept of Mind* (London: Hutchinson, 1949); D.C. Dennett, *Content and Consciousness* (London: Routledge & Kegan Paul, 1969).

16. The argument of this paragraph is based on that of Peter Winch in *The Idea of a Social Science* (London: Routledge & Kegan Paul, 1958). The sorts of consideration being mentioned here are also characteristic of a *hermeneutical* approach to social phenomena—a topic that will be given some attention in Chapter 10.

17. *The Theory of Social and Economic Organization* (New York: The Free Press, 1964), pp. 94-96.

18. See, e.g., Ernest Nagel, *The Structure of Scientific Explanation* (London: Routledge & Kegan Paul, 1961), pp. 480-485.

19. Hilary Putnam has suggested that *Verstehen* be seen as a source of plausibility or prior probability of interpretive hypotheses, presumably because he likewise regards empathetic understanding as a requirement for explaining social action; see *Meaning and the Moral Sciences* (London: Routledge & Kegan Paul, 1978), pp. 74-75. Putnam, recognizing that an interpretation may be mistaken, insists that these hypotheses still need to be checked by something like ordinary scientific method. It is worth pointing out, however, that whereas empirical testing can in principle produce results that will falsely disconfirm a true hypothesis, owing to undetected auxiliary factors and deformations, the plausibility test *must* be passed. An implausible reason is no explanation at all.

20. See, eg., Jane R. Martin, "Another Look at the Doctrine of *Verstehen*," *British Journal for the Philosophy of Science* 20 (1969): 67.

21. Winch, p. 89.

22. Winch (pp. 111-113) makes this point in criticizing Weber for suggesting that empirical data provide the ultimate tribunal for judging the correctness of an interpretation.


## 5. *Rationality and the Methods of Social Inquiry*

1. *The Divided Self* (Harmondsworth, England: Penguin Books, 1965).

2. *Suicide: A Study in Sociology.*

3. Bronislaw Malinowski, "Anthropology," *Encyclopedia Britannica,* suppl. vol. 1 (London and New York, 1926), pp. 132-133.

4. A.R. Radcliffe-Brown, *Structure and Function in Primitive Society* (New York: The Free Press, 1965), Ch. 9.

5. Robert K. Merton, *Social Theory and Social Structure,* enlarged ed., (New York: The Free Press, 1968), ch. 3. See also Dorothy M.

Emmet, "Functionalism in Sociology," in *The Encyclopedia of Philosophy*, vol. 3 (New York: Macmillan, 1967), pp. 256-259.

6. Alan Ryan, *The Philosophy of the Social Sciences* (London: Macmillan, 1970), pp. 190-191.

7. Merton, pp. 126-136.

8. Peter L. Berger, *Invitation to Sociology: A Humanistic Perspective* (Garden City, N.Y.: Anchor Books, 1963), pp. 40-41.

9. G.A. Cohen has pointed out that many assignments of function in sociology are not intended to be explanatory; they refer only to (possibly hidden) beneficial effects; see *Karl Marx's Theory of History: A Defence* (Princeton, N.J.: Princeton University Press, 1978), pp. 257-258. These nonexplanatory uses of "function" include many instances of what Merton has called "latent" functions, such as the effect on community solidarity of punishing a criminal, or the effects on the cost of labor and the price of commodities of a large cadre of unemployed workers (Marx's "industrial reserve army"). Even though these uses of "function" are not explanatory—we would not say that these items exist *because* of their unexpected effects—they too can be seen as having a basis in the rational model of order. For in order for an item to be represented as providing a benefit, it must be made to look as if it was intended to produce that benefit. Any sort of functional analysis that tries to reveal benefits may be said to indicate what would have been a reason for bringing something about.

10. Claude Levi-Strauss, *The Savage Mind* (Chicago: University of Chicago Press, 1966), pp. 237-244.

11. *Structural Anthropology* (Garden City, N.Y.: Anchor Books, 1967), pp. 173-200.

12. Ibid., p. 13.

13. Ibid., p. 288.

6. *Biology and Social Inquiry*

1. See Konrad Lorenz, *On Aggression* (New York: Bantam Books, 1967).

2. See Edward O. Wilson, *Sociobiology: The New Synthesis* (Cambridge: Harvard University Press, 1975), Ch. 27.

3. Ibid., p. 4.

4. Wilson.

5. G.B. Schaller, "The Behavior of the Mountain Gorilla," in I.

DeVore, ed., *Primate Behavior: Field Studies of Monkeys and Apes* (New York: Holt, Rinehart & Winston, 1965), pp. 324-367.

6. Jane Goodall, "Chimpanzees of the Gombe Stream Preserve," in DeVore, ed., *Primate Behavior,* pp. 425-473.

7. Wilson, p. 551.

8. "Human Decency Is Animal," *New York Times Magazine,* October 12, 1975, p. 48.

9. For elaboration of these points, see e.g., Anthony Leeds, "Sociobiology, Anti-Sociobiology, and Human Nature," *The Wilson Quarterly* 1 (1977): 127-139.

10. Wilson, pp. 564-565.

11. Ibid., pp. 550-551.

12. Ibid., p. 117.

13. *On Human Nature* (Cambridge: Harvard University Press, 1978), p. 152.

14. Ibid., p. 153.

15. Wilson, pp. 564-565.

16. Ibid., p. 553.

17. See N. Tinbergen, "On War and Peace in Animals and Men," in Heinz Friedrich, ed., *Man and Animal* (London: Paladin, 1972), pp. 118-142.

18. J. D. Carthy and F. J. Ebling, eds., *The Natural History of Aggression,* Institute of Biology Symposia No. 13 (New York: Academic Press, 1964), p. 5.

19. Lorenz, p. 229.

20. Robert Ardrey, *African Genesis* (London: Collins, 1961), p. 316.

21. *Sociobiology,* p. 564.

22. Ibid., p. 255.

23. "Pair-Formation in Ravens," in Friedrich, ed., *Man and Animal,* pp. 17-36.

7. *The Place of Causation in Social Science*

1. F.H. Bradley, *The Principles of Logic,* vol. 2 (London: Oxford University Press, 1962), p. 545.

2. Ibid., vol. 2, pp. 538-544.

3. Michael Scriven, "Causation as Explanation," *Nous* 9 (1975): 3-16.

4. See Donald Davidson, "Actions, Reasons, and Causes," *Journal of Philosophy* 60, (1963): 685-700.

5. G.E.M. Anscombe, "Causality and Determination: An Inaugural Lecture" (Cambridge: Cambridge University Press, 1971), p. 29.

6. Davidson.

7. This view has been given effective expression by Richard Taylor in *Action and Purpose* (Englewood Cliffs, N.J.: Prentice-Hall, 1966), Ch. 3; Anscombe; and Scriven. See also Alasdair MacIntyre, "Causality and History," in J. Manninen and R. Tuomela, eds., *Essays on Explanation and Understanding*, (Dordrecht The Netherlands: D. Reidel, 1976), and H.L.AS. [Hart and A.M. Honore, *Causation in the Law (London:* Oxford University Press, 1959).]

8. The formulation is due to Hilliard Aronovitch, "Social Explanation and Rational Motivation," *American Philosophical Quarterly* 15 (1978): 202.

9. Anscombe, pp. 9-10.

10. Ibid., p. 11.

11. Davidson, p. 685.

12. Roderick Chisholm, "Freedom and Action," in K. Lehrer, ed., *Freedom and Determinism* (New York: Random House, 1966), p. 30.

13. "Freedom to Act," in T. Honderich. ed., *Essays on Freedom of Action* (London: Routledge & Kegan Paul, 1973).

14. G.H. von Wright, *Explanation and Understanding* (Ithaca, N.Y.: Cornell University Press, 1971), Ch. 3.

15. Alvin I. Goldman, *A Theory of Human Action* (Englewood Cliffs, N. J.: Prentice-Hall, 1970), pp. 99-105.

16. von Wright, pp. 140-141.

17. Karl Marx, *The Eighteenth Brumaire of Louis Bonaparte,* in Robert C. Tucker, ed., *The Marx-Engels Reader* (New York: Norton, 1972), p. 437.

## 8. *Theory in Social Science*

1. Michael Scriven, "A Possible Distinction between Traditional Scientific Disciplines and the Study of Human Behavior," in H. Feigl and M. Scriven, eds., *Minnesota Studies in the Philosophy of Science,* vol. 1 (Minneapolis: University of Minnesota Press, 1956), pp. 330-339.

2. C. Wright Mills has provided a penetrating critical discussion of this possibility; see *The Sociological Imagination* (Hardmondsworth, England: Penguin Books, 1970), pp. 76-80.

3. Sidney Morgenbesser, "Is It a Science?" *Social Research* 33 (1966): 255-271.

4. See, e.g., George C. Homans, "Bringing Men Back In," *American Sociological Review* 29 (1964): 809-818.

5. Steven Lukes, "Methodological Individualism Reconsidered," *British Journal of Sociology* 19 (1968); 119-129.

6. See, e.g., B.F. Skinner, "'Superstition' in the Pigeon," *Journal of Experimental Psychology* 38 (1948); 168-172.

7. See Berkeley Rice "Skinner Agrees He Is the Most Important Influence in Psychology," *New York Times Magazine,* 17 March 1968, pp. 87-88.

8. John Stuart Mill, *A System of Logic,* Book VI, Ch. 10, § 4 (London: Longmans, Green, 1959), pp. 597-598.

9. *The Open Society and Its Enemies*, vol. 2 (Princeton, N.J.: Princeton University Press, 1971), ch. 14.

10. *The Social System* (Glencoe, Ill.: The Free Press, 1951).

11. Ibid., pp. 41-42.

12. George V. Plekhanov, "The Materialist Conception of History," in *Fundamental Problems of Marxism* (New York: International Publishers, 1969), p. 116.

13. Ibid., pp. 126-134.

14. It may be acknowledged that more sophisticated presentations of historical materialism than Plekhanov's have been given. These can be seen to fall into two general types. One of these, exemplified by Jurgen Habermas in "Towards a Reconstruction of Historical Materialism," *Theory and Society* 2 (1975); 287-300, offers an elaborate working out of ways of accommodating a wide range of social variables. By introducing into a broad conceptual scheme such elements as "indigenous learning mechanism," "institutional core," and "evolutionary innovation," and by keeping the principles on an abstract level, Habermas is able to encompass any number of types of historical development. The effect is the same as with Plekhanov, however: whatever changes occur, whatever their particular antecedents, the theory is made to appear capable of handling them.

The second way of presenting historical materialism avoids the sort of extreme claims that Plekhanov made by not insisting that the theory has to explain everything. Thus G.A. Cohen, in a recent and compelling book, Karl Marx's *Theory of History: A Defence* (Princeton, N.J.: Princeton University Press, 1978), makes his case by showing how effectively Marxist theory explains some very important social facts, such as why certain relations of economic production are the way they are. The theory is not presumed to be capable of explaining every aspect of history or social structure.

15. *The Elementary Forms of Religious Life* (Glencoe, Ill.: The Free Press, 1954).

16. "The Role of the Individual in History," in *Fundamental Problems of Marxism,* pp. 167-169.

17. Jean-Paul Sartre, *Search for a Method* (New York: Vintage Books, 1968) pp. 131-132.

## 9. *Objectivity and Social Inquiry*

1. Max Weber, "'Objectivity,' in Social Science and Social Policy," in *The Methodology of the Social Sciences* (New York: The Free Press, 1949), pp. 50-113.

2. Ibid., p. 81.

3. Ernest Nagel, *The Structure of Science* (London: Routledge & Kegan Paul, 1961), p. 486.

4. May Brodbeck, ed., *Readings in the Philosophy of the Social Sciences* (New York: Macmillan, 1968), p. 83.

5. Weber, p. 75.

6. Karl Mannheim, *Ideology and Utopia* (London: Routledge & Kegan Paul, 1960).

7. *The Structure of Scientific Revolutions* (Chicago: University of Chicago Press, 1962).

8. Alan Ryan, "'Normal' Science of Political Ideology?" in Peter Laslett, W.G. Runciman, and Q. Skinner, eds., *Philosophy, Politics and Society,* 4th series (Oxford: Basil Blackwell, 1972), p. 92.

9. In addition to Kuhn, including his "Postcript" to the second edition of *The Structure of Scientific Revolutions* (Chicago: University of Chicago Press, 1970), see Paul K. Feyerabend, "Explanation, Reduction, and Empiricism," in H. Feigl and G. Maxwell, eds., *Minnesota Studies in the Philosophy of Science,* vol. 3 (Minneapolis: University of Minnesota Press, 1962), pp. 28-97; "Problems of Empiricism," in R.G. Colodny, ed., *Beyond the Edge of Certainty* (Englewood Cliffs, N.J.: Prentice-Hall, 1965), pp. 145-260; "Against Method," in M. Radner and S. Winokur, eds., *Minnesota Studies in the Philosophy of Science,* vol. 4 (Minneapolis: Universitiy of Minnesota Press, 1970), pp. 117-130 (this last essay is also published in a longer version as a book, *Against Method* [London: NLB, 1975]. See also Israel Scheffler, *Science and Subjectivity* (Indianapolis: Bobbs-Merrill, 1967),

and I. Lakatos and A. Musgrave, eds., *Criticism and the Growth of Knowledge* (Cambridge: Cambridge University Press, 1970).

10. Mannheim, p. 243.

11. Ibid., p. 245.

12. Alasdair MacIntyre, "Is a Science of Comparative Politics Possible?" in Laslett, Runciman, and Skinner, eds. *Philosophy, Politics and Society,* pp. 10-11.

13. Mannheim, p. 238.

14. See, e.g., Brodbeck, p. 81.

15. Mannheim, p. 238.

16. Ibid., p. 270.

17. Nagel, pp. 501-502.

18. See Alan Ryan, *The Philosophy of the Social Sciences* (London: Macmillan, 1970), p. 240.

19. *The Poverty of Historicism* (New York: Harper & Row, 1964), p. 155.

20. For an interesting illustration of the rational construction of a seemingly insane act, see J.W.N. Watkins' discussion of the case of a commanding officer's deliberate execution of a naval maneuver that resulted in the sinking of his own vessel, in "Imperfect Rationality," in R. Borger and R. Cioffi, eds., *Explanation in the Behavioural Sciences* (Cambridge: Cambridge University Press, 1970,) pp. 167-217.

21. Cf. W.V. Quine, *Word and Object,* (New York: Wiley, 1960) Ch. 2.

## 10. *Social Inquiry and Scientific Understanding*

1. See Michael Scriven, "Explanation and Prediction in Evolutionary Theory," *Science* 103 (1959): 477-482.

2. Although it is not unusual to speak of predicting one's decisions and hence the actions that folow from them. It is only when one is not certain as to whether the conditions that will influence one's decision will in fact obtain, however, that one can be said to predict one's own decision. The prediction of one's action in such a case is derivative from a prediction of the outcome of processes of which one is, in effect, a spectator.

3. Stuart Hampshire and H.L.A. Hart, "Decision, Intention and Certainty," *Mind* 67 (1958); 1-12.

4. Donald MacKay, "Scientific Beliefs about Oneself," in *The Proper Study,* Royal Institute of Philosophy Lectures, vol. 4 (London: Macmillan, 1971), pp. 48-63.

5. Ibid., p. 52.

6. "Predictability and Explanation in the Social Sciences," *Philosophical Exchange* 1 (1972); 5-13.

7. Cf. Hans-Georg Gadamer, *Truth and Method* (New York: Seabury Press, 1975), p. 320.

8. Arthur Danto, *Analytical Philosophy of History* (Cambridge: Cambridge University Press, 1965), pp. 220-221.

9. Albrecht Wellmer, "Some Remarks on the Logic of Explanation in the Social Sciences," in *The Proper Study,* pp. 59-60.

10. Karl-Otto Apel, "Scientifik, Hermeneutik, Ideologie-Kritik: Entwurf einer Wissenschaftlehre in erkenntnisanthropologischer Sicht," *Man and World* 1 (1968); 37-63.

11. Wilhelm Dilthey, *Gesammelte Schriften,* 5 : 330 (quoted in Jurgen Habermas, *Knowledge and Human Interests* [London: Heinemann, 1972], p. 173).

12. See, e.g., Apel.

13. See Habermas, *Knowledge and Human Interests,* p. 230.

14. See, e.g., Brian Fay and J. Donald Moon, "What Would an Adequate Philosophy of Social Science Look Like?" *Philosophy of Social Science,* 7 (1977); 209-227.

15. "Knowledge and Human Interests: A General Perspective," in *Knowledge and Human Interests,* pp. 301-317.

16. Ibid., p. 71.

17. Ibid., p. 4.

18. The idea that hermeneutics is not a method of achieving cognition is given effective expression by Richard Rorty, in *Philosophy and the Mirror of Nature* (Princeton, N.J.: Princeton University Press, 1979), Ch. 7. For Rorty, hermeneutics is not "another way of knowing"; it is rather "another way of coping"; it is what you do when you can't *get* knowledge. Rather than accepting a distinction among kinds of knowledge as I am doing here, Rorty recommends that we simply *give* the notion of cognition (and along with it the word "knowledge") to predictive science. There is agreement, however, that hermeneutics is not a way of gaining scientific knowledge.

## 11. *The Fruits of Social Research*

1. See Leon Festinger, *A Theory of Cognitive Dissonance* (Evanston, Ill.: Row-Peterson, 1957).

2. Anthony Giddens, *Central Problems in Social Theory* (Berkeley: University of California Press, 1979), p. 249.

3. See Daryl J. Bem, *Beliefs, Attitudes, and Human Affairs* (Belmont, Calif.: Brooks/Cole, 1970), pp. 57-58.

4. M. Fishbein and I. Ajzen, *Belief, Attitude, Intention, and Behavior* (Reading, Mass.: Addison-Wesley, 1975), pp. 451-457.

5. Ibid., p. 452 ff.

6. Ibid., pp. 457-474.

7. Ibid., pp. 503-509.

8. See, e.g., A. Bandura, "Toward a Unifying Theory of Behavioral Change," *Psychological Review* 84 (1977): 191-215.

9. *Conjectures and Refutations* (New York: Harper & Row, 1968), pp. 33-65.

10. Ibid..

11. T.S. Kuhn, *The Structure of Scientific Revolutions* (Chicago: University of Chicago Press, 1962). See also W.V. Quine, *From a Logical Point of View* (Cambridge: Harvard University Press, 1953), pp. 42-46.

12. See Steven Lukes, "Alienation and Anomie," in Peter Laslett and W.G. Runciman, eds., *Philosophy, Politics and Society,* 3rd series (Oxford: Basil Blackwell, 1969), pp. 134-156.

13. See, e.g., Herbert Marcuse, *Eros and Civilization* (Boston: Beacon Press, 1955).

14. Kuhn.

15. See Max Weber, *The Protestant Ethic and the Spirit of Capitalism* (New York: Scribner's, 1958), and R.H. Tawney, *Religion and the Rise of Capitalism* (New York: Harcourt Brace, 1952).

16. P. K. Feyerabend, *Against Methods* (London: NLB, 1975); see especially Ch. 4.

17. See A.G. van Melsen, *From Atomos to Atom* (New York: Harper Torchbooks, 1960).

18. For an account of these researchers, see Elton Mayo, *The Human Problems of an Industrial Civilization,* 2nd ed. (New York: Macmillan, 1946).

19. Alexis de Tocqueville, *Democracy in America* vol. 1 (Garden City, N.Y.: Anchor Books, 1969), Part II, Ch. 7.

20. *The Sociology of Georg Simmel,* trans. Kurt H. Wolff (New York: The Free Press of Glencoe, 1964), pp. 413-414.

21. Erving Goffman, *Asylums* (Garden City, N.Y.: Anchor Books, 1961), Ch. 1.

22. Stanislav Andreski, *Social Science as Sorcery* (New York: St. Martin's Press, 1972), pp. 134-136.

23. Frank Cioffi, "Information, Contemplation and Social Life," in *The Proper Study,* Royal Institute of Philosophy Lectures, vol. 4 (London: Macmillan, 1971), pp. 105-131.

24. *The Sociological Imagination* (Harmondsworth, England: Penguin Books, 1970), p. 213.

# Index